ESSENTIALS OF STRATEGIC MANAGEMENT

J. David Hunger

Iowa State University

Thomas L. Wheelen

Trinity College and
University of South Florida

PRENTICE HALL PUBLISHING COMPANY
UPPER SADDLE RIVER, NEW JERSEY

Library of Congress Cataloging-in-Publication Data

Hunger, J. David, 1941–
    Essentials of strategic management / J. David Hunger, Thomas L. Wheelen. —2nd ed.
      p. cm.
    Includes bibliographical references and index.
    ISBN 0-13-019600-2
    1. Strategic planning.   2. Case method.   I. Wheelen, Thomas L.   II. Title.

HD30.28.H867 2000
658.4′012 — dc21

00-034711

Senior Editor: David Shafer
Managing Editor (Editorial): Jennifer Glennon
Executive Marketing Manager: Michael D. Campbell
Production/Manufacturing Manager: Gail Steier de Acevedo
Manufacturing Buyer: Natacha St. Hill Moore
Senior Prepress/Manufacturing Manager: Vincent Scelta
Cover Design: Kewi Design
Cover Image: PhotoDisc
Full Service Composition: Impressions Book and Journal Services, Inc.

10 9 8 7 6 5 4 3 2
ISBN 0-13-019600-2

DEDICATED TO

Kathy, Richard, Tom

Betty, Merry, Lori, Suzi, Kari,
Jeff, Maddie, and Smokey

CONTENTS

PREFACE

We wrote this book to provide you with a short, concise explanation of the most important concepts and techniques in strategic management. There is no fluff in this book. *Essentials of Strategic Management* is significantly shorter than our other books, but we have not "dumbed it down" or made it "cutesy." It is a rigorous explanation of many topics and concerns in strategic management. We condensed the content of the field into 11 carefully crafted chapters. The key concepts and techniques are here. We cite only enough examples to help you understand the material. Although the content is based on rigorous research studies, we don't report every study and we don't provide endless footnotes. For those who want more research detail and illustrative examples, please see our other textbook, *Strategic Management,* 7th edition. For a combination of text and cases, please see *Strategic Management and Business Policy,* 7th edition. If you would like to use cases to accompany *Essentials of Strategic Management,* please consider our *Cases in Strategic Management,* 7th edition.

CONTINUING FEATURES FROM 1ST EDITION

Both 1st and 2nd editions of *Essentials of Strategic Management* contain the following features:

- A strategic decision-making model based on the underlying processes of environmental scanning, strategy formulation, strategy implementation, and evaluation and control is presented in chapter 1 and provides an integrating framework for the book.
- Michael Porter's approach to industry analysis and competitive strategy (plus competitive tactics) is highlighted in chapters 3 and 5.
- The resource-based view of the firm, in chapter 4, serves as a foundation for organizational analysis.
- Functional analysis and functional strategies receive major attention in chapters 4 and 7. Sections on R&D and R&D strategies emphasize the importance of technology to strategy and product-market decisions.
- Strategy implementation deals not only with organization design and structure, but also with executive leadership and succession, reengineering, total quality management, MBO, and action planning in chapters 8 and 9.
- Chapter 10 on evaluation and control explains the importance of measurement and incentives to organizational performance. Benchmarking and economic value-added measures are highlighted.

- International considerations are included in all chapters and are high-lighted in special sections in chapters 3, 8, 9, and 10.
- Environmental scanning and forecasting is given emphasis equal to industry analysis in chapter 3.
- Suggested EFAS, IFAS, and SFAS Tables in chapters 3, 4, and 5 enable the reader to better identify and evaluate strategic factors.
- Top management and the board of directors are examined in detail in their roles as strategic managers in chapter 2.
- Social responsibility is discussed in chapter 2 in terms of its importance to strategic decision making.
- Suggestions for in-depth case analysis provide a complete listing of financial ratios, recommendations for oral and written analysis, and ideas for further research in chapter 11. The strategic audit is proposed as an aid to case analysis. This chapter is most useful for those who wish to supplement this book with cases.
- Each chapter begins and ends with a brief situation vignette of an actual company that helps illustrate the material.
- Each chapter ends with a list of key terms (which are also *italicized* within the text) and a set of discussion questions.

FEATURES NEW TO THIS EDITION

This second edition of *Essentials of Strategic Management* contains the following new features:

- Introduces the concept of the learning organization as a way to involve everyone in strategic management.
- Discusses the impact of hypercompetition on industry analysis and competitive strategy.
- Proposes an industry matrix as a way to compare key competitors in an industry.
- Discusses how value-chain analysis can be used to assess a company's strengths and weaknesses.
- Expands business strategy to include both competitive and cooperative strategies.
- Expands corporate strategy to include corporate parenting of business units.
- Emphasizes core and distinctive competencies.
- Adds ISO 9000 and activity-based costing to chapter 10, Evaluation and Control.

INSTRUCTORS' MANUAL

An instructor's manual has been carefully constructed to accompany this book. It includes a series of multiple choice questions and answers to discussion questions plus a set of additional discussion and essay questions to use in exams.

ACKNOWLEDGMENTS

We are grateful to the people who reviewed this book: William E. Lindsey, Loyola Marymount University; Malika Richards, Drexel University; and Nicholas C. Georgantzas, Fordham University; for their constructive criticism and suggestions. Their thought and effort have resulted in a book that is superior to the first edition. Our thanks go to Jennifer Glennon, Managing Editor, Prentice Hall, who supervised this edition. Without her support and encouragement, this edition would never have been written. We are very grateful to Gail Steier de Acevedo of Prentice Hall and the staff of Impressions Book and Journal Services for their patience and expertise during the copyediting and production process. We also thank Lori and Betty Hunger for their help in preparing the index.

In addition, we express our appreciation to Ben Allen, Dean, and Brad Shrader, Management Department Chair, of Iowa State University for their moral support. No support of any type was provided by the University of South Florida in the development and publication of this book. Both of us thank Mary Clare McEwing and Michael Payne of Addison Wesley Publishing Company for their help in developing the first edition of this book. We wish you two the best, wherever you may be!

Finally, to the many strategy and policy instructors and students who have moaned to us about the increasing size and cost of textbooks: We have tried to respond to your concerns as best we could by providing a comprehensive yet usable text that is half the size and cost of other books on the market. Instead of the usual five-course meal (complete with heartburn), we are offering you "lean cuisine." This book should taste good with fewer empty calories. Enjoy!

J.D.H.
T.L.W

CHAPTER 1

BASIC CONCEPTS OF STRATEGIC MANAGEMENT

In 1997, Minoru Arakawa, President of Nintendo of America, was faced with a crucial strategic decision. His company had been very successful in the video game business, but its product line was becoming stale. In this trend-driven business, product lives tend to be fairly short. To maintain its lead in this fast-paced industry, Nintendo had to develop new games and concepts to keep the interest of its young customers.

This was not the first time that the company had faced a major challenge. In 1985, Nintendo of America had been struggling as the operator of fading arcade games like Donkey Kong. With the video game industry fading in popularity, game manufacturers Atari and Coleco were also struggling. To revive the company, Arakawa imported Nintendo's home-game console from Japan. The Nintendo system was such a huge success that many in the industry credited Arakawa with reviving the U.S. video game market.

By 1997, however, Nintendo needed to again revitalize its product line or it would lose customer interest. President Arakawa wondered if one of the new video game crazes in Japan would be worth importing into North America. The game featured 150 tiny, collectible monsters and was dearly loved by Japanese children. Arakawa knew, nevertheless, that Japanese styling was not always accepted in America. He remembered how Japanese automobiles had been ridiculed as strange and somewhat ugly when first imported into the United States. Only after the cars had been redesigned and renamed for the North American market were they finally accepted by the marketplace. Would the distinctively Japanese-style monsters be accepted in North America?

Market research revealed that American children hated the Japanese game. Arakawa's co-workers dismissed the game as being too confusing. The consensus was that the game had to be redesigned to suit American youth. Going against heavy objections from his management team, Arakawa went with his intuition. He decided to import the game with no adaptation to the American market whatsoever—a very risky undertaking. Nintendo became the sole distributor in America of Pokemon, a video game that soon took the continent by storm![1]

Nintendo of America's story suggests why the managers of today's business corporations must manage firms strategically. They cannot make decisions based on long-standing rules, historical policies, or simple extrapolations of current trends. Instead, they must look to the future as they plan organization-wide objectives, initiate strategy, and set policies. They must rise above their training and experience in such functional and operational areas as accounting, marketing, production, or finance, and grasp the overall picture. They must be willing to ask three key strategic questions:

1. Where is the organization now? (Not where does management hope it is!)
2. If no changes are made, where will the organization be in 1 year, 2 years, 5 years, or 10 years? Are the answers acceptable?
3. If the answers are not acceptable, what specific actions should management undertake? What risks and payoffs are involved?

1.1 THE STUDY OF STRATEGIC MANAGEMENT

Strategic management is that set of managerial decisions and actions that determines the long-run performance of a corporation. It includes environmental scanning (both external and internal), strategy formulation (strategic or long-range planning), strategy implementation, and evaluation and control. The study of strategic management therefore emphasizes the monitoring and evaluating of external opportunities and threats in light of a corporation's strengths and weaknesses. Originally called business policy, strategic management incorporates such topics as long-range planning and strategy. *Business policy,* in contrast, has a general management orientation and tends primarily to look internally with a concern for properly integrating the corporation's many functional activities. Strategic management, as a field of study, incorporates the integrative concerns of business policy with a heavier environmental and strategic emphasis. Therefore, *strategic management* has tended to replace *business policy* as the preferred name of this field of study.

HOW HAS STRATEGIC MANAGEMENT EVOLVED?

Many of the concepts and techniques dealing with long-range (now called strategic) planning and strategic management have been developed and used successfully by business corporations such as General Electric and the Boston Consulting Group. Nevertheless, not all organizations use these tools or even attempt to manage strategically. Many are able to succeed for a while with unstated objectives and intuitive strategies. American Hospital Supply Corporation (AHS) was one such organization until Karl Bays became chief executive and introduced strategic planning to a sales-dominated management. Previously, the company's idea of long-range planning was "Maybe in December we should look at next year's budget," recalled a former AHS executive.[2]

From his extensive work in this field, Bruce Henderson of the Boston Consulting Group concluded that intuitive strategies cannot be continued successfully if (1) the corporation becomes large, (2) the layers of management increase, or (3) the environment changes substantially. The increasing risks of error, costly mistakes, and even economic ruin are causing professional managers to take strategic management seriously in order to keep their companies competitive in an increasingly volatile environment.

As top managers attempt to better deal with their changing world, strategic management within a firm generally evolves through four sequential phases:

Phase 1. Basic financial planning: Seeking better operational control by trying to meet budgets.

Phase 2. Forecast-based planning: Seeking more effective planning for growth by trying to predict the future beyond the next year.

Phase 3. Externally oriented planning (strategic planning): Seeking increased responsiveness to markets and competition by trying to think strategically.

Phase 4. Strategic management: Seeking a competitive advantage and a successful future by managing all resources.[3]

Phase 4 in the evolution of strategic management includes a consideration of strategy implementation and evaluation and control, in addition to the emphasis on strategic planning in Phase 3.

General Electric, one of the pioneers of strategic planning, led the transition from strategic planning to strategic management during the 1980s. By the 1990s, most corporations around the world had also begun the conversion to strategic management.

HAS LEARNING BECOME A PART OF STRATEGIC MANAGEMENT?

Strategic management has now evolved to the point that its primary value is to help the organization operate successfully in a dynamic, complex environment. Inland Steel Company, for example, uses strategic planning as a tool to drive organizational change. Managers at all levels are expected to continually analyze the changing steel industry in order to create or modify strategic plans throughout the year. To be competitive in dynamic environments, corporations are having to become less bureaucratic and more flexible. In stable environments such as those that have existed in the past, a competitive strategy simply involved defining a competitive position and then defending it. Because it takes less and less time for one product or technology to replace another, companies are finding that there is no such thing as a permanent competitive advantage. Many agree with Richard D'Aveni (in his book *HyperCompetition*) that any sustainable competitive advantage lies not in doggedly following a centrally managed 5-year plan, but in stringing together a series of strategic short-term thrusts (as Intel does by cutting into the sales of its own offerings with periodic introductions of new products).[4]

This means that corporations must develop strategic flexibility: the ability to shift from one dominant strategy to another. Strategic flexibility demands a long-term commitment to the development and nurturing of critical resources. It also demands that the company become a *learning organization*: an organization skilled at creating, acquiring, and transferring knowledge and at modifying its behavior to reflect new knowledge and insights. Learning organizations avoid stability through continuous self-examination and experimentation. People at all levels, not just top management, need to be involved in strategic management: scanning the environment for critical information, suggesting changes to strategies and programs to take advantage of environmental shifts, and working with others to continuously improve work methods, procedures, and evaluation techniques. At Xerox, for example, all employees have been trained in small-group activities and problem-solving techniques. They are expected to use the techniques at all meetings and at all levels, with no topic being off-limits.

WHAT IS THE IMPACT OF STRATEGIC MANAGEMENT ON PERFORMANCE?

Research has revealed that organizations that engage in strategic management generally outperform those that do not. The attainment of an appropriate match or "fit" between an organization's environment and its strategy, structure, and processes has positive effects on the organization's performance. For example, a study of the impact of deregulation on U.S. railroads found that railroads that changed their strategy as their environment changed outperformed those that did not change their strategies.[5]

Nevertheless, to be effective, strategic management need not always be a formal process. Studies of the planning practices of actual organizations suggest that the real value of strategic planning may be more in the future orientation of the planning process itself than in any resulting written strategic plan. Small companies, in particular, may plan informally and irregularly. The president and a handful of top managers might get together casually to resolve strategic issues and plan their next steps.

In large, multidivisional corporations, however, strategic planning can become complex and time-consuming. It often takes slightly more than 12 months for a large company to move from situation assessment to a final decision agreement. Because a strategic decision affects a relatively large number of people, a large firm needs a formalized, more sophisticated system to ensure that strategic planning leads to successful performance. Otherwise, top management becomes isolated from developments in the divisions and lower-level managers lose sight of the corporate mission.

1.2 INITIATION OF STRATEGY: TRIGGERING EVENTS

After much research, Henry Mintzberg discovered that strategy formulation is typically not a regular, continuous process: "It is most often an irregular, discontinuous process, proceeding in fits and starts. There are periods of stability in strategy development, but also there are periods of flux, of groping, of piecemeal change, and of global change."[6] This view of strategy formulation as an irregular process reflects the human tendency to continue on a particular course of action until something goes wrong or a person is forced to question his or her actions. This period of so-called strategic drift may simply be a result of the organization's inertia, or it may reflect the management's belief that the current strategy is still appropriate and needs only some fine-tuning. Most large organizations tend to follow a particular strategic orientation for about 15 to 20 years before they make a significant change in direction. After this rather long period of fine-tuning an existing strategy, some sort of shock to the system is needed to motivate management to seriously reassess the corporation's situation.

A *triggering event* is something that stimulates a change in strategy. Some of the possible triggering events are:

- **New CEO.** By asking a series of embarrassing questions, the new CEO cuts through the veil of complacency and forces people to question the very reason for the corporation's existence.

- **Intervention by an external institution.** The firm's bank suddenly refuses to agree to a new loan or suddenly calls for payment in full on an old one.
- **Threat of a change in ownership.** Another firm may initiate a takeover by buying the company's common stock.
- **Management's recognition of a performance gap.** A performance gap exists when performance does not meet expectations. Sales and profits either are no longer increasing or may even be falling.

Maytag Corporation is one example of a company in which a triggering event forced management to radically rethink its game plan. In 1978, Daniel Krumm, Maytag's CEO, asked three executives to serve as a strategic planning task force. Krumm posed the question: "If we keep doing what we're now doing, what will the Maytag Company look like in 5 years?" The question was a challenge to answer, especially because the company had never done financial modeling and none of the three executives knew much about strategic planning. The conclusion of the task force: A large part of Maytag's profits (the company at that time had the best profit margin in the industry) was coming from products and services with no future: repair parts, portable washers and dryers, and wringer washing machines. This report triggered Maytag's interest in strategic change. The company engaged in a series of acquisitions to broaden its product line and to give it a solid position in the industry.

1.3 BASIC MODEL OF STRATEGIC MANAGEMENT

Strategic management consists of four basic elements: (1) environmental scanning, (2) strategy formulation, (3) strategy implementation, and (4) evaluation and control. Figure 1.1 shows how these four elements interact. Management scans both the external environment for opportunities and threats and the internal environment for strengths and weaknesses. The following factors that are most important to the corporation's future are called **strategic factors:** strengths, weaknesses, opportunities, and threats (SWOT).

WHAT IS ENVIRONMENTAL SCANNING?

Environmental scanning is the monitoring, evaluating, and disseminating of information from the external and internal environments to key people within the corporation. The *external environment* consists of variables (opportunities and threats) that are outside the organization and not typically within the short-run control of top management. These variables form the context within which the corporation exists. They may be general forces and trends within the overall societal environment or specific factors that operate within an organization's specific task environment, often called its industry. (These external variables are defined and discussed in more detail in chapter 3.)

The *internal environment* of a corporation consists of variables (strengths and weaknesses) that are within the organization itself and are not usually within the short-run control of top management. These variables form the context in which work is done. They include the corporation's structure, culture, and resources. (These internal variables are defined and discussed in more detail in chapter 4.)

FIGURE 1.1 Basic Elements of the Strategic Management Process

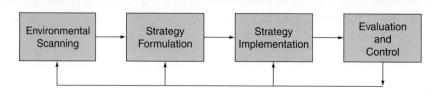

WHAT IS STRATEGY FORMULATION?

Strategy formulation is the development of long-range plans for the effective management of environmental opportunities and threats, taking into consideration corporate strengths and weaknesses. It includes defining the corporate mission, specifying achievable objectives, developing strategies, and setting policy guidelines.

WHAT IS A MISSION?

An organization's *mission* is its purpose, or the reason for its existence. It states what it is providing to society, for example, a service, such as housecleaning, or products, such as automobiles. A well-conceived mission statement defines the fundamental, unique purpose that sets a company apart from other firms of its type and identifies the scope of the company's operations in terms of products (including services) offered and markets served. It puts into words not only what the company is now, but what it wants to become: management's strategic vision of the firm's future. It promotes a sense of shared expectations in employees and communicates a public image to important stakeholder groups in the company's task environment. A mission statement reveals who the company is and what it does.

One example of a mission statement is the following by Maytag Corporation:

> To improve the quality of home life by designing, building, marketing, and servicing the best appliances in the world.

A mission may be defined narrowly or broadly. A *broad mission statement* is a vague and general statement of what the company is in business to do. One popular example is: "Serve the best interests of shareowners, customers, and employees." A broadly defined mission statement such as this keeps the company from restricting itself to one field or product line, but it fails to clearly identify either what it makes or which product or market it plans to emphasize. In contrast, a *narrow mission statement,* such as Maytag's statement, clearly states the organization's primary products and markets, but it may limit the scope of the firm's activities in terms of product or service offered, the technology used, and the market served.

WHAT ARE OBJECTIVES?

Objectives are the end results of planned activity. They state what is to be accomplished by when and should be quantified if possible. The achievement of corporate objectives should result in the fulfillment of the corporation's mission. Minnesota Mining & Manufacturing (3M), for example, has set very specific financial objectives for itself:

1. To achieve 10 percent annual growth in earnings per share.
2. To achieve 20–25 percent return on equity (ROE).
3. To achieve 27 percent return on capital employed.

The term *goal* is often confused with *objective*. In contrast to an objective, a *goal* is an open-ended statement of what one wishes to accomplish with no quantification of what is to be achieved and no time frame for completion.

Some of the areas in which a corporation might establish its goals and objectives are:

- Profitability (net profits)
- Efficiency (low costs, etc.)
- Growth (increase in total assets, sales, etc.)
- Stockholder wealth (dividends plus stock price appreciation)
- Utilization of resources (ROE or return on investment, ROI)
- Reputation (being considered a "top" firm)
- Contributions to employees (employment security, wages)
- Contributions to society (taxes paid, participation in charities, providing a needed product or service)
- Market leadership (market share)
- Technological leadership (innovations, creativity)
- Survival (avoiding bankruptcy)
- Personal needs of top management (using the firm for personal purposes, such as providing jobs for relatives)

WHAT ARE STRATEGIES?

A *strategy* of a corporation is a comprehensive master plan stating how the corporation will achieve its mission and objectives. It maximizes competitive advantage and minimizes competitive disadvantage. For example, after Rockwell International Corporation realized that it could no longer achieve its objectives by continuing with its strategy of diversification into multiple lines of businesses, it sold its aerospace and defense units to Boeing. Rockwell instead chose to concentrate on commercial electronics, an area that management felt had greater opportunities for growth.

The typical business firm usually considers three types of strategy: corporate, business, and functional.

1. Corporate strategy describes a company's overall direction in terms of its general attitude toward growth and the management of its various businesses and product lines. Corporate strategy is composed of directional strategy, portfolio analysis, and parenting strategy. Corporate directional strategy is conceptualized in terms of stability, growth, and retrenchment. For example, Maytag Corporation followed a corporate growth directional strategy by acquiring other appliance companies in order to have a full line of major home appliances.

2. Business strategy usually occurs at the business unit or product level, and it emphasizes improvement of the competitive position of a corporation's products or services in the specific industry or market segment served by that business unit. Business strategies are composed of competitive and cooperative strategies. For example, Maytag Corporation uses a differentiation competitive strategy that emphasizes quality for its

Maytag brand appliances, but it uses a low-cost competitive strategy for its Magic Chef brand appliances so that it can sell these appliances to cost-conscious home builders.

3. Functional strategy is the approach taken by a functional area, such as marketing or research and development, to achieve corporate and business unit objectives and strategies by maximizing resource productivity. It is concerned with developing and nurturing a distinctive competence to provide a company or business unit with a competitive advantage. An example of a functional strategy is America Online's marketing strategy of saturating the entire market with a low-priced product.

Business firms use all three types of strategy simultaneously. A *hierarchy of strategy* is the grouping of strategy types by level in the organization. This hierarchy of strategy is a nesting of one strategy within another so that they complement and support one another. (See Figure 1.2.) Functional strategies support business strategy, which, in turn, support the corporate strategy(ies).

Just as many firms often have no formally stated objectives, many CEOs have unstated, incremental, or intuitive strategies that have never been articulated or analyzed. Often the only way to spot the implicit strategies of a corporation is to examine not what management says, but what it does. Implicit strategies can be derived from corporation policies, programs approved (and disapproved), and authorized budgets. Programs and divisions favored by budget increases and staffed by managers who are considered to be on the fast promotion track reveal where the corporation is putting its money and its energy.

WHAT ARE POLICIES?

A *policy* is a broad guideline for decision making that links the formulation of strategy with its implementation. Companies use policies to make sure that employees throughout the firm make decisions and take actions that support the corporation's mission, its objectives, and its strategies. For example, consider the following company policies:

FIGURE 1.2 Hierarchy of Strategy

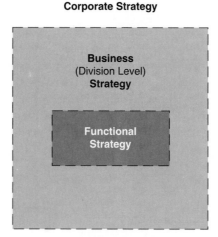

Corporate Strategy

Business
(Division Level)
Strategy

Functional
Strategy

- **Maytag Company.** Maytag will not approve any cost-reduction proposal if it reduces product quality in any way. (This policy supports Maytag's strategy of its Maytag brands competing on quality rather than on price.)
- **3M.** Researchers should spend 15 percent of their time working on something other than their primary project. (This supports 3M's strong product development strategy.)
- **Intel.** Cannibalize your product line (undercut the sales of your current products) with better products before a competitor does it to you. (This supports Intel's objective of market leadership.)
- **General Electric.** GE must be number one or two wherever it competes. (This supports GE's objective to be number one in market capitalization.)
- **America Online.** The company could have used a policy stating that a new marketing program would not be implemented until proper support was in place.

Policies like these provide clear guidance to managers throughout the organization. (Strategy formulation is discussed in greater detail in chapters 5, 6, and 7.)

WHAT IS STRATEGY IMPLEMENTATION?

Strategy implementation is the process by which strategies and policies are put into action through the development of programs, budgets, and procedures. This process might involve changes within the overall culture, structure, or management system of the entire organization, or within all of these areas. Except when such drastic corporate-wide changes are needed, middle- and lower-level managers typically implement strategy, with review by top management. Sometimes referred to as operational planning, strategy implementation often involves day-to-day decisions in resource allocation.

WHAT ARE PROGRAMS?

A *program* is a statement of the activities or steps needed to accomplish a single-use plan. It makes the strategy action-oriented. It may involve restructuring the corporation, changing the company's internal culture, or beginning a new research effort. For example, consider Intel Corporation, the microprocessor manufacturer. Realizing that Intel would not be able to continue its corporate growth strategy without the continuous development of new generations of microprocessors, management decided to implement a series of programs:

- They formed an alliance with Hewlett-Packard to develop the successor to the Pentium Pro chip.
- They assembled an elite team of engineers and scientists to do long-term, original research into computer chip design.

WHAT ARE BUDGETS USED FOR?

A *budget* is a statement of a corporation's programs in dollar terms. Used in planning and control, it lists the detailed cost of each program. Many corporations demand a certain percentage return on investment, often called a *hurdle rate*, before management will approve a new program. This ensures that the new program will significantly add to the corporation's profit performance and thus build stockholder value. The budget thus not only serves as a detailed plan of the new strategy in action, it also specifies through pro forma financial statements the expected impact on the firm's future financial future.

For example, to become a significant global competitor in the $250-billion-per-year market for telecommunications equipment, Cisco Systems had to compete with Nortel (twice as large as Cisco), Lucent (three times its size), and Siemens (seven times Cisco's sales). Cisco established a program to interest the large telephone companies in purchasing Cisco equipment. As part of the program, it launched an advertising campaign with the message that Cisco is the company that makes the Internet work. The 1999 budget for the commercials was $40 million in the United States and $20 million overseas.[7]

WHAT ARE PROCEDURES?

Procedures, sometimes termed *standard operating procedures* (SOP), are a system of sequential steps or techniques that describe in detail how a particular task or job is to be done. They typically detail the various activities that must be carried out for completion of the corporation's programs. For example, Delta Airlines used various procedures to cut costs. To reduce the number of employees, Delta asked technical experts in hydraulics, metal-working, avionics, and other trades to design cross-functional work teams. To cut marketing expenses, Delta instituted a cap on travel agent commissions and emphasized sales to bigger accounts. Delta also changed its purchasing and food service procedures. (Strategy implementation is discussed in more detail in chapters 8 and 9.)

WHAT IS EVALUATION AND CONTROL?

Evaluation and control is the process by which corporate activities and performance results are monitored so that actual performance can be compared with desired performance. Managers at all levels use the resulting information to take corrective action and resolve problems. Although evaluation and control is the final major element of strategic management, it also can pinpoint weaknesses in previously implemented strategic plans and thus stimulate the entire process to begin again.

For evaluation and control to be effective, managers must obtain clear, prompt, and unbiased information from the people below them in the corporation's hierarchy. Using this information, managers compare what is actually happening with what was originally planned in the formulation stage. For example, the success of Delta Airlines's turnaround strategy was evaluated in terms of the amount spent on each airplane seat per mile of flight. Before the "Leadership 7.5" program was instituted in April 1994, the cost per seat was 9.76¢. By the end of 1995, it was down to 8.4¢. The program seemed to be working, but it needed to reach 7.5¢ by June 1997 to achieve the company's objective of reducing annual expenses by $2.1 billion.

The evaluation and control of performance completes the strategic management model. Based on performance results, management may need to adjust its strategy formulation, implementation, or both. (Evaluation and control is discussed in more detail in chapter 10.)

DOES THE MODEL HAVE A FEEDBACK/LEARNING PROCESS?

The strategic management model depicted in Figure 1.1 includes a *feedback/learning process* in which information from each element of the process is used as a possible adjustment to each of the previous elements of the process. As the firm or business unit formulates and implements strategies, it must often go back to revise or correct decisions made earlier in the process. For example, poor performance (as measured in evaluation and control) usually indicates that something has gone wrong with either strategy formulation or implementation. It could also mean that a key variable, such a new competitor, was ignored during environmental scanning.

1.4 STRATEGIC DECISION MAKING

The distinguishing characteristic of strategic management is its emphasis on strategic decision making. As organizations grow larger and more complex with more uncertain environments, decisions become increasingly complicated and difficult to make. We propose a strategic decision-making framework that can help members of organizations make these types of decisions.

WHAT MAKES A DECISION STRATEGIC?

Unlike many other decisions, strategic decisions deal with the long-run future of the entire organization and have three characteristics:

1. **Rare.** Strategic decisions are unusual and typically have no precedent to follow.
2. **Consequential.** Strategic decisions commit substantial resources and demand a great deal of commitment.
3. **Directive.** Strategic decisions set precedents for lesser decisions and future actions throughout the organization.[8]

WHAT ARE MINTZBERG'S MODES
OF STRATEGIC DECISION MAKING?

Some strategic decisions are made in a flash by one person (often an entrepreneur or a powerful chief executive officer) who has a brilliant insight and is quickly able to convince others to follow this idea. Other strategic decisions seem to develop out of a series of small incremental choices that over time push the organization more in one direction than another. According to Henry Mintzberg, the most typical approaches or modes of strategic decision making are entrepreneurial, adaptive, and planning:[9]

- **Entrepreneurial mode.** In this mode of strategic decision making, the strategy is developed by one powerful individual. The focus is on opportunities, and problems are secondary. Strategy is guided by the founder's own vision of direction and is exemplified by large, bold decisions. The dominant goal is growth of the corporation. Bill Gates, founder and Chairman of Microsoft Corporation, embodies this mode of strategic decision making. The company reflects his vision of the personal computer industry. Although Microsoft's clear mission, competitiveness, tenacity, and technological self-confidence, which emanate from Gates, are certainly advantages of the entrepreneurial mode, Microsoft's tendency to introduce products before they are ready is a significant disadvantage.
- **Adaptive mode.** Sometimes referred to as "muddling through," this decision-making mode is characterized by reactive solutions to existing problems,

rather than a proactive search for new opportunities. Much bargaining concerning priorities of objectives occurs. Strategy is fragmented and is developed to move the corporation forward in incremental steps. This mode is typical of most universities, many large hospitals, a large number of governmental agencies, and a surprising number of large corporations.

- **Planning mode.** This mode of strategic decision making involves the systematic gathering of appropriate information for situation analysis, the generation of feasible alternative strategies, and the rational selection of the most appropriate strategy. This mode includes both the proactive search for new opportunities and the reactive solution of existing problems. Maytag Corporation uses the planning mode. After realizing how the major home

FIGURE 1.3   Strategic Decision-Making Process

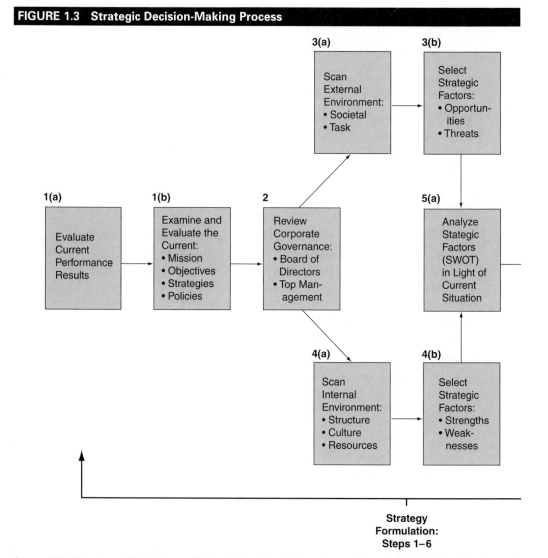

Source: T. L. Wheelen and J. D. Hunger, "Strategic Decision-Making Process." Copyright © 1994 by Wheelen and Hunger Associates. Reprinted by permission.

appliance industry was changing in the United States and throughout the world, Maytag's top management deliberately chose to transform the company from a high-quality niche producer of laundry appliances to a manufacturer of all types of major home appliances.

In some instances, a corporation might follow a fourth approach called *logical incrementalism,* which is a synthesis of the planning, adaptive, and to a lesser extent, the entrepreneurial modes of strategic decision making. As described by J. B. Quinn, top management might have a reasonably clear idea of the corporation's mission and objectives, but, in its development of strategies, it chooses to use "an interactive process in which the organization probes the future, experiments and learns from a series of

FIGURE 1.3   Continued

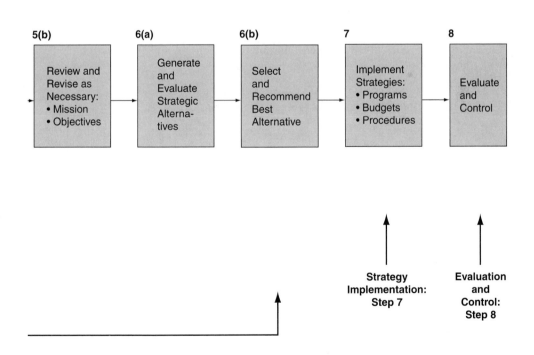

partial (incremental) commitments rather than through global formulations of total strategies."[10] This approach appears to be useful when the environment is changing rapidly and when it is important to build consensus and develop needed resources before committing the entire corporation to a specific strategy.

HOW CAN MANAGERS MAKE BETTER STRATEGIC DECISIONS?

Good arguments can be made for using either the entrepreneurial or adaptive modes (or logical incrementalism) in certain situations. In this book, however, we propose that in most situations the planning mode, which includes the basic elements of the strategic management process, is a more rational and thus better way of making strategic decisions. The planning mode is not only more analytical and less political than the other modes, but it is also more appropriate for dealing with complex, changing environments. We propose the following eight-step strategic decision-making process (which is also illustrated in Figure 1.3):

1. **Evaluate current performance results** in terms of (a) return on investment, profitability, and so forth, and (b) the current strategic posture of the company (mission, objectives, strategies, and policies).

2. **Review corporate governance,** that is, the performance of the firm's board of directors and top management.

3. **Scan the external environment** to locate strategic factors that pose opportunities and threats.

4. **Scan the internal corporate environment** to determine strategic factors that are strengths and weaknesses.

5. **Analyze strategic factors (SWOT)** to (a) pinpoint problem areas, and (b) review and revise the corporate mission and objectives as necessary.

6. **Generate, evaluate, and select the best alternative strategy** in light of the analysis conducted in Step 5.

7. **Implement selected strategies** via programs, budgets, and procedures.

8. **Evaluate implemented strategies** via feedback systems and the control of activities to ensure their minimum deviation from plans.

This rational approach to strategic decision making has been used successfully by corporations like Warner-Lambert, Dayton Hudson, Avon Products, Bechtel Group, Inc., and Taisei Corporation.

IN CONCLUSION

Nintendo of America struck gold with Pokemon! The strategic decision by President Arakawa to import the Pokemon video game with no adjustments for U.S. culture resulted in unprecedented growth in company sales and profits. Sales of Pokemon video games, the movie, cards, and a multitude of toys and other merchandise by Nintendo of America and its licensees surpassed $1 billion from its American launch in 1998 to the beginning of 2000. Praised by *Business Week* as one of the top 25 managers of the year, Minoru Arakawa modestly admits, "To be honest, I still don't understand the game."

Discussion Questions

1. Why has strategic management become so important to today's corporations?
2. How does strategic management typically evolve in a corporation?
3. What information is needed for the proper formulation of strategy?
4. Why are strategic decisions different from other kinds of decisions?
5. When is the planning mode of strategic decision making superior to the entrepreneurial and adaptive modes?

Key Terms (listed in order of appearance)

key strategic questions
strategic management
business policy
phases of development
learning organization
triggering events
strategic factors
SWOT
environmental scanning
external environment
internal environment
strategy formulation
mission
mission statements: broad and narrow
objectives
goals
strategy

corporate strategy
business strategy
functional strategy
hierarchy of strategy
policy
strategy implementation
program
budget
procedures
evaluation and control
strategic decisions
entrepreneurial mode
adaptive mode
planning mode
logical incrementalism
strategic decision-making process

Notes

1. "Pokemon Patriarch," *Business Week* (January 10, 2000): 70.
2. B. Lancaster, "American Hospital's Marketing Program Places Company Atop a Troubled Industry," *Wall Street Journal* (August 24, 1984): 19.
3. F. W. Gluck, S. P. Kaufman, and A. S. Walleck, "The Four Phases of Strategic Management," *Journal of Business Strategy* (winter 1982): 9–21.
4. R. A. D'Aveni, *Hypercompetition* (New York: Free Press, 1994). Hypercompetition is discussed in more detail in later chapters.
5. K. G. Smith, and C. M. Grimm, "Environmental Variation, Strategic Change and Firm Performance: A Study of Railroad Deregulation," *Strategic Management Journal* (July–August 1987): 363–76.

6. H. Mintzberg, "Planning on the Left Side and Managing on the Right," *Harvard Business Review* (July–August 1976): 56.

7. A. Kupfer, "The Real King of the Internet," *Fortune* (September 7, 1999): 85.

8. D. J. Hickson, R. J. Butler, D. Cray, G. R. Mallory, and D.C. Wilson, *Top Decisions: Strategic Decision-Making in Organiza-tions* (San Francisco: Jossey-Bass, 1986), 26–42.

9. H. Mintzberg, "Strategy-Making in Three Modes," *California Management Review* (winter 1973): 44–53.

10. J. B. Quinn, *Strategies for Change: Logical Incrementalism* (Homewood, IL.: Irwin, 1980), 58.

CHAPTER 2

CORPORATE GOVERNANCE
AND SOCIAL RESPONSIBILITY

At one time, the Eastman Kodak Company was one of the most respected companies in the United States and perhaps in the world. It was known for its excellent product quality and reliability. However, from 1983 to 1993, the company fell from the top 10 percent to the bottom 18 percent of admired companies. Industry analysts portrayed the firm as bloated, slow-moving, myopic, and incapable of dealing effectively with its falling share of the photographic film market. Top management made strategic decisions based on protecting current products instead of looking to develop future ones. For example, even though Kodak had been one of the first companies to develop a camcorder, management decided not to introduce it because it was costly and would possibly detract from the current sales of the company's amateur film products. Profits were consistently below expectations. The company incurred billions of dollars in repeated "one-time" charges as it undertook incremental efforts to streamline and improve its performance.

Kodak's board of directors was extremely concerned with the inability of Chief Executive Officer Kay Whitmore to turn the company around. Whitmore had joined Kodak in 1957 as an engineer, and he epitomized the company's cautious home-grown management. On August 6, 1993, Kodak's board of directors, led by a group of outside directors, fired Whitmore. Instead of looking internally for a replacement, the board offered the chief executive officer (CEO) position to George Fisher, then Chairman and CEO of Motorola, Inc. Motorola had long been regarded as a well-managed company, known for its dedication to hard work and quality. The board expected Fisher to deliver fast and deep cost cuts. Just 4 months later, however, Fisher stated that cost-cutting alone would not be the answer. He proposed to commit the entire company to imaging opportunities and to divest noncore businesses.

This example illustrates the impact of top management and the board of directors on a firm's performance. Kodak's top managers had traditionally been promoted from within. They had become so dedicated to the company's past in chemical imaging that they were unable to perceive a future in electronic imaging. As strategic managers, top management had failed to adjust to a changing environment. Although slow to react, the board of directors finally moved to hire managers from outside the company to foster a new perspective within the company.

2.1 CORPORATE GOVERNANCE: ROLE OF THE BOARD OF DIRECTORS

A *corporation* is a mechanism established to allow different parties to contribute capital, expertise, and labor for their mutual benefit. The investor or shareholder participates in the profits of the enterprise without taking responsibility for the operations. Management runs the company without being personally responsible for providing the funds. To make this possible, laws have been passed so that shareholders have limited liability and, correspondingly, limited involvement in a corporation's activities. That involvement does include, however, the right to elect directors who have a legal duty to represent the shareholders and protect their interests. As representatives of the shareholders, directors have both the authority and the responsibility to establish basic corporate policies and to ensure that they are followed.

The board of directors has, therefore, an obligation to approve all decisions that might affect the long-run performance of the corporation. This means that the corporation is fundamentally governed by the board of directors overseeing top management, with the concurrence of the shareholder. The term *corporate governance* refers to the relationship among these three groups (board of directors, management, and shareholders) in determining the direction and performance of the corporation.

Over the past decade, stockholders and various interest groups have seriously questioned the role of the board of directors in corporations. They are concerned that outside board members often lack sufficient knowledge, involvement, and enthusiasm to adequately provide guidance to top management. For example, when officials of the California Public Employees' Retirement System, a key stockholder group, criticized IBM's board of directors for not doing more to prevent the company's nosedive in earnings, the four outside members of the board's executive committee admitted that they did not know enough about the company's business to properly evaluate management. Like IBM's top management, they had missed the trend of moving away from mainframe computers toward personal computers. Board members actually admitted that none of them felt comfortable using a personal computer. According to one director, "Not one of us has a PC in our home or office."[1]

The general public has not only become more aware and more critical of the apparent lack of many boards of directors to assume responsibility for corporate activities, but it has also begun to push government to demand accountability. As a result, the board as a rubber stamp of the CEO or as a bastion of the "old boy" selection system is being replaced by more active, more professional boards.

WHAT ARE THE RESPONSIBILITIES OF THE BOARD?

Laws and standards defining the responsibilities of boards of directors vary from country to country. For example, board members in Ontario, Canada, face more than 100 provincial and federal laws governing director liability. The United States, however, has no clear national standards or federal laws. Specific requirements of board members (also called directors) vary, depending on the state in which the corporate charter is issued. There is, nevertheless, a developing worldwide consensus concerning the major responsibilities of a board. Interviews with 200 directors from eight countries (Canada, Finland, France, Germany, the Netherlands, Switzerland, the United Kingdom, and Venezuela) revealed strong agreement on the following five *board of director responsibilities,* listed in order of importance:

1. Setting corporate strategy, overall direction, mission, or vision.
2. Succession: hiring and firing the CEO and top management.
3. Controlling, monitoring, or supervising top management.
4. Reviewing and approving the use of resources.
5. Caring for stockholder interests.[2]

In addition to the aforementioned duties, directors in the United States must make certain that the corporation is managed in accordance with the laws of the state in which it is incorporated. They must also ensure management's adherence to laws and regulations such as those dealing with the issuance of securities, insider trading, and other conflict-of-interest situations. They must also be aware of the needs and demands of constituent groups so that they can achieve a judicious balance among the interests of these diverse groups while ensuring the continued functioning of the corporation.

In a legal sense, the board of directors is required to direct the affairs of the corporation but not to manage them. It is charged by law to act with *due care,* that is, to conscientiously carry out its responsibilities. If a director or the board as a whole fails to act with due care, and as a result, the corporation is in some way harmed, the careless director or directors can be held personally liable for the harm done.

WHAT IS THE ROLE OF THE BOARD
IN STRATEGIC MANAGEMENT?

How does a board of directors fulfill its many responsibilities? The role of the board in strategic management is to carry out three basic tasks:

- **Monitor.** By acting through its committees, a board can keep abreast of developments both inside and outside the corporation. It can thus bring to management's attention developments it might have overlooked. At a minimum, a board should carry out this task.
- **Evaluate and influence.** A board can examine management's proposals, decisions, and actions; agree or disagree with them; give advice and offer suggestions; and outline alternatives. More active boards do this in addition to monitoring management's activities.
- **Initiate and determine.** A board can delineate a corporation's mission and specify strategic options to its management. Only the most active boards take on this task in addition to the previous two.

IS THERE A BOARD OF DIRECTORS CONTINUUM?

A board of directors is involved in strategic management to the extent that it carries out the three tasks of monitoring, evaluating and influencing, and initiating and determining. The *board of directors continuum* shown in Figure 2.1 shows the possible degree of involvement (from low to high) in the strategic management process. Boards

FIGURE 2.1 Board of Directors Continuum

←————————————**DEGREE OF INVOLVEMENT IN STRATEGIC MANAGEMENT**————————————→

Low
(Passive)

High
(Active)

Phantom	Rubber Stamp	Minimal Review	Nominal Participation	Active Participation	Catalyst
Never knows what to do, if anything; no degree of involvement.	Permits officers to make all decisions. It votes as the officers recommend on action issues.	Formally reviews selected issues that officers bring to its attention.	Involved to a limited degree in the performance or review of selected key decisions, indicatiors, or programs of management.	Approves, questions, and makes final decisions on mission, strategy, policies and objectives. Has active board committees. Performs fiscal and management audits.	Takes the leading role in establishing and modifying the mission, objectives, strategy, and policies. It has a very active strategy committee.

Source: T. L. Wheelen and J. D. Hunger, "Board of Directors Continuum." Copyright © 1994 by Wheelen and Hunger Associates. Reprinted by permission.

can range from phantom boards with no real involvement to catalyst boards with a very high degree of involvement. Research does suggest that active board involvement in strategic management is positively related to corporate financial performance.

Highly involved boards tend to be very active. They take their tasks of monitoring, evaluating and influencing, and initiating and determining very seriously; they advise when necessary and keep management alert. As depicted in Figure 2.1, their heavy involvement in the strategic management process places them in the active participation or even catalyst position. At Control Data Corporation, for example, the board of directors spends the day before the official board meeting studying a business sector, such as computer peripherals, or an issue, such as efforts to improve quality. Other corporations with actively participating boards are Mead Corporation, Rolm and Haas, Whirlpool Corporation, Westinghouse, Dayton-Hudson, and General Motors.

As a board becomes less involved in the affairs of the corporation, it moves farther to the left on the continuum (see Figure 2.1). On the far left are passive phantom or rubber stamp boards that typically never initiate or determine strategy unless a crisis occurs. In these situations, the CEO also serves as Chairman of the Board and works to keep board members under his or her control by giving them the "mushroom treatment"(i. e., throw manure on them and keep them in the dark!*).*

Generally, the smaller the corporation is, the less active is its board of directors. The board tends to be dominated by directors who are also owner–managers of the company. Other directors are usually friends or family members. As the corporation grows and goes public, however, the boards become more active in terms of roles and responsibilities.

Most large, publicly owned corporations have boards that operate at some point between nominal and active participation. Few corporations have catalyst boards, except for those with major problems (that is, pending bankruptcies, mergers, or acquisitions). One study of boards ranging from hospitals to Fortune 500 firms found that:

- 30 percent of the boards actively worked with management to develop strategic direction (*active or catalyst*).
- 30 percent worked to revise as well as ratify management's proposals (*minimal or nominal participation*).
- 40 percent merely ratified management's strategic proposals (*phantom or rubber stamp*).[3]

WHO ARE MEMBERS OF A BOARD OF DIRECTORS?

The boards of most publicly owned corporations are composed of both inside and outside directors. *Inside directors* (sometimes called management directors) are typically officers or executives employed by the corporation. *Outside directors* may be executives of other firms but are not employees of the board's corporation. Although there is no clear evidence that a high proportion of outsiders on a board results in improved corporate performance, there is a trend in the United States to increase the number of outsiders on boards. The typical large U.S. corporation has an average of 11 directors, of whom 2 are insiders. Even though outsiders account for approximately 80 percent of the board members in these large U.S. corporations (approximately the same as in Canada), they only account for about 40 percent of board membership in small U.S. companies.

People who favor a high proportion of outsiders state that outside directors are less biased and more likely to evaluate management's performance objectively than inside directors. This is the main reason why the New York Stock Exchange requires that all companies listed on the exchange have an audit committee composed entirely of independent, outside members. This view is in agreement with *agency theory,* which states that problems arise in corporations because the agents (top management) are not willing to bear responsibility for their decisions unless they own a substantial amount of stock in the corporation. The theory suggests that a majority of a board needs to be from outside the firm so that top management is prevented from acting selfishly to the detriment of the shareholders.

In contrast, those who prefer inside directors over outside directors contend that outside directors are less effective than insiders because the outsiders are less likely to have the necessary interest, availability, or competency. Directors may sometimes serve on so many boards that they spread their time and interest too thinly to actively fulfill their responsibilities. They could also point out that the term *outsider* is too simplistic; some outsiders are not truly objective and should be considered more as insiders than as outsiders. Such outsiders may be *affiliated* directors who handle the legal or insurance work for the company, retired executives of the company, and family members of the founder of the firm.

The majority of outside directors are active or retired CEOs and chief operating officers (COOs) of other corporations. Others are academicians, attorneys, consultants, former government officials, major shareholders, and bankers. In Germany, bankers are represented on almost every board, primarily because they own large blocks of stock in German corporations. In Denmark, Sweden, Belgium, and Italy, however, investment companies assume this role. Of U.S. corporations in 1995, 69 percent of the boards had at least one woman director (33 percent had two), compared with 60 percent in 1992 and only 11 percent in 1972. Boards having at least one minority member increased from 9 percent in 1973 to 47 percent in 1995 (African-American: 34 percent; Latino: 9 percent; Asian: 4 percent). Around 1/3 of large U.S. corporations had international (non-U.S.) directors on their boards. Outside directors serving on the boards of large U.S. corporations annually earned on average $33,000.[4] Most companies also provided some form of payment through stock options. Directors serving on the boards of small companies usually received much less (around $10,000).

The vast majority of inside directors includes the chief executive officer, chief operating officer, and presidents or vice-presidents of key operating divisions or functional units. Few, if any, inside directors receive any extra compensation for assuming this extra duty. Very rarely does a U.S. board include any lower level operating employees. *Codetermination,* the inclusion of a corporation's workers on its board of directors, is more common in Europe. Critics of codetermination raise the issue of conflict of interest. Can a member of the board, who is privy to confidential managerial information, function, for example, as a union leader whose primary duty is to fight for the best benefits for the union members?

WHY ARE INTERLOCKING DIRECTORATES USEFUL?

CEOs often nominate chief executives (as well as board members) from other firms to membership on their own boards in order to create an interlocking directorate. A *direct interlocking directorate* occurs when two firms share a director or when an executive of one firm sits on the board of a second firm. An *indirect interlock* occurs when two corporations have directors who also serve on the board of a third firm, such as a bank.

Although the Clayton Act and the Banking Act of 1933 prohibit interlocking directorates by U.S. companies competing in the same industry, interlocking continues to occur in almost all corporations, especially large ones. Interlocking occurs because large firms have a significant impact on other corporations, and these other corporations, in turn, have some control over the firm's inputs and marketplace. Interlocking directorates are also a useful method for gaining both inside information about an uncertain environment and objective expertise about potential strategies and tactics. Family-owned corporations, however, are less likely to have interlocking directorates than corporations with highly dispersed stock ownership, probably because family-owned corporations do not like to dilute their corporate control by adding outsiders to boardroom discussions. Nevertheless, there is some evidence to indicate that well-interlocked corporations are better able to survive in a highly competitive environment.

HOW ARE PEOPLE NOMINATED AND ELECTED TO BOARDS?

Traditionally the CEO of the corporation decided whom to invite to board membership and merely asked the stockholders for approval. However, allowing the CEO free rein in nominating directors may be dangerous. The CEO might select only board members who, in the CEO's opinion, will not disturb the company's policies and functioning. Given that the average length of service of a U.S. board member is 8.4 years, CEO-friendly, passive boards are likely to result. Board members selected by the CEO often feel that they should go along with any proposals the CEO makes. Thus board members find themselves accountable to the very management they are charged to oversee. Because this is likely to happen, there is an increasing tendency for a special board committee to nominate new outside board members for election by the stockholders. Approximately 73 percent of large U.S. corporations now use nominating committees to identify potential directors.

Virtually every corporation whose board members serve terms of more than one year divides the board into classes and staggers elections so that only a portion of the board stands for election each year. Arguments in favor of this practice are that it provides continuity by reducing the chance of an abrupt turnover in membership and that it reduces the likelihood of electing people unfriendly to management (who might be interested in a hostile takeover) through cumulative voting.

HOW ARE BOARDS ORGANIZED?

The size of the board is determined by the corporation's charter and its bylaws in compliance with state laws. Although some states require a minimum number of board members, most corporations have quite a bit of discretion in determination of board size. The average large, publicly held firm has around 11 directors. The average small or medium privately held company has approximately seven to eight members.

Approximately 68 percent of the top executives of large, U.S. publicly held corporations hold the dual designation of chairman and CEO. This practice is being increasingly criticized because of the potential for conflict of interest. The CEO is supposed to concentrate on strategy, planning, external relations, and responsibility to the board. The chairman's responsibility is to ensure that the board and its committees perform their functions as stated in its charter. Further, the chairman schedules board meetings and presides over the annual stockholders' meeting. Critics of combining the two offices in one person ask how the board can properly oversee top management if the chairman is also top management. They recommend that outside directors elect a *lead director*, an outside director who conducts the annual evaluation of the CEO. The chairman and CEO roles are separated by law in Germany, the Netherlands, and Finland. A similar law is being considered in Britain and Australia. Recent research does suggest that firms that separate the two positions outperform financially those firms that combine the offices.[5]

The most effective boards accomplish much of their work through committees. Although the committees do not have legal duties, unless detailed in the bylaws, most committees are granted full power to act with the authority of the board between board meetings. Typical standing committees are the executive, audit, compensation, finance, and nominating committees. The executive committee is formed from local directors who can meet between board meetings to attend to matters that must be settled quickly. This committee acts as an extension of the board and, consequently, may have almost unrestricted authority in certain areas.

WHAT ARE THE TRENDS IN BOARDS OF DIRECTORS?

The board of directors is likely to play a more active role in the strategic management of the corporation in the future. The change, however, will probably be more evolutionary than radical or revolutionary. Different boards are at different levels of maturity and will not be changing in the same direction or at the same rate. Some of today's trends that are likely to continue include (1) increasing numbers of institutional investors (pension funds, etc.) and other outsiders on the board, (2) larger stock ownership by directors and executives, and (3) a greater willingness of the board to balance the economic goal of profitability with the social needs of society.

2.2 CORPORATE GOVERNANCE: THE ROLE OF TOP MANAGEMENT

The top management function is usually conducted by the CEO of the corporation in coordination with the COO or president, executive vice-president, and vice-presidents of divisions and functional areas. Even though strategic management involves everyone in the organization, the board of directors holds top management primarily responsible for the strategic management of the firm.

WHAT ARE THE RESPONSIBILITIES OF TOP MANAGEMENT?

Top management responsibilities, especially those of the CEO, involve getting things accomplished through and with others in order to meet the corporate objectives. Top management's job is thus multidimensional and is oriented toward the welfare of the total organization. Specific top management tasks vary from firm to firm and are developed from an analysis of the mission, objectives, strategies, and key activities of the corporation. The chief executive officer, in particular, must successfully handle two responsibilities crucial to the effective strategic management of the corporation: (1) provide executive leadership and a strategic vision, and (2) manage the strategic planning process.

WHAT ARE EXECUTIVE LEADERSHIP AND STRATEGIC VISION?

Executive leadership is the directing of activities toward the accomplishment of corporate objectives. Executive leadership is important because it sets the tone for the entire corporation. A *strategic vision* is a description of what the company is capable of becoming. It is often communicated in the mission statement. People in an organization want to have a sense of mission, but only top management is in the position to specify and communicate this strategic vision to the general workforce. Top management's enthusiasm (or lack of it) about the corporation tends to be contagious. The importance of executive leadership is illustrated by John Welch, Jr., the successful Chairman and CEO of General Electric Company (GE). According to Welch: "Good business leaders create a vision, articulate the vision, passionately own the vision, and relentlessly drive it to completion."[6]

Chief executive officers with a clear strategic vision are often perceived as dynamic and charismatic leaders. For instance, the positive attitudes characterizing many well-known industrial leaders, such as Bill Gates at Microsoft, Mary Kay Ash at Mary Kay

Cosmetics, Ted Turner at CNN, Herb Kelleher at Southwest Airlines, and Andy Grove at Intel, have energized their respective corporations. They are able to command respect and to influence strategy formulation and implementation because they tend to have three key characteristics:

1. The CEO articulates a strategic vision for the corporation. The CEO envisions the company not as it currently is, but as it can become. Because the CEO's vision puts activities and conflicts in a new perspective, it gives renewed meaning to everyone's work activities and enables employees to see beyond the details of their own jobs to the functioning of the total corporation.

2. The CEO presents a role for others to identify with and to follow. The CEO sets an example in terms of behavior and dress. The CEO's attitudes and values concerning the corporation's purpose and activities are clear cut and constantly communicated in words and deeds.

3. The CEO not only communicates high performance standards, but also shows confidence in the followers' abilities to meet these standards. No leader ever improved performance by setting easily attainable goals that provided no challenge. The CEO must be willing to follow through by coaching people.

How Does Top Management Manage the Strategic Planning Process?

As business corporations adopt more of the characteristics of the learning organization, strategic planning initiatives can now come from any part of an organization. However, unless top management encourages and supports the planning process, strategic management is not likely to result. In most corporations, top management must initiate and manage the strategic planning process. It may do so by first asking business units and functional areas to propose strategic plans for themselves, or it may begin by drafting an overall corporate plan within which the units can then build their own plans. Other organizations engage in concurrent strategic planning in which all the units of the organization draft plans for themselves after they have been provided with the overall mission and objectives of the organization.

Regardless of the approach taken, the typical board of directors expects top management to manage the overall strategic planning process so that the plans of all the units and functional areas fit together into an overall corporate plan. Therefore, top management's duties include the tasks of evaluating unit plans and providing feedback. To do this, top management may require each unit to justify its proposed objectives, strategies, and programs in terms of how well they satisfy the organization's overall objectives in light of available resources.

Many large organizations have a *strategic planning staff* charged with supporting both top management and the business units in the strategic planning process. This planning staff typically consists of just under 10 people, headed by a senior vice-president or director of corporate planning. The staff's major responsibilities are to (1) identify and analyze company-wide strategic issues and suggest corporate strategic alternatives to top management, and (2) work as facilitators with business units to guide them through the strategic planning process.

2.3 SOCIAL RESPONSIBILITIES OF STRATEGIC DECISION MAKERS

Should strategic decision makers be responsible only to stockholders or should they have broader responsibilities? The concept of *social responsibility* proposes that a private corporation has responsibilities to society that extend beyond making a profit. Strategic decisions often affect more than just the corporation. A decision to retrench by closing some plants and discontinuing product lines, for example, affects not only the firm's workforce but also communities where the plants are located and those customers who have no other source of the discontinued product. This brings into consideration the question of the appropriateness of certain missions, objectives, and strategies of business corporations. Some businesspeople believe profit maximization is the primary goal of their firm, whereas concerned interest groups argue that other goals should have a priority, such as the hiring of minorities and women, or community development. Strategic managers must be able to deal with these conflicting interests to formulate a viable strategic plan.

WHAT ARE THE RESPONSIBILITIES OF A BUSINESS FIRM?

What are the responsibilities of a business firm and how many of these responsibilities must strategic managers fulfill? Milton Friedman and Archie Carroll offer two contrasting views of the responsibilities of business firms to society.

WHAT IS FRIEDMAN'S TRADITIONAL VIEW OF BUSINESS RESPONSIBILITY?

Milton Friedman, in urging a return to a laissez-faire worldwide economy with a minimum of government regulation, argues against the concept of social responsibility. If a businessperson acts "responsibly" by cutting the price of the firm's product to prevent inflation, by making expenditures to reduce pollution, or by hiring the hard-core unemployed, that person, according to Friedman, is spending the stockholders' money for a general social interest. Even if the businessperson has stockholder permission or encouragement to do so, he or she is still acting from motives other than economic and may, in the long run, cause harm to the very society the firm is trying to help. By taking on the burden of these social costs, the business becomes less efficient: either prices go up to pay for the increased costs or investment in new activities and research is postponed. These results negatively, perhaps fatally, affect the long-term efficiency of a business. Friedman thus referred to the social responsibility of business as a "fundamentally subversive doctrine" and stated that "there is one and only one social responsibility of business—to use its resources and engage in activities designed to increase its profits so long as it stays within the rules of the game, which is to say, engages in open and free competition without deception or fraud."[7]

WHAT ARE CARROLL'S FOUR RESPONSIBILITIES OF BUSINESS?

Archie Carroll proposes that the managers of business organizations have four responsibilities: economic, legal, ethical, and discretionary.[8] These responsibilities are displayed in Figure 2.2 and are defined as follows:

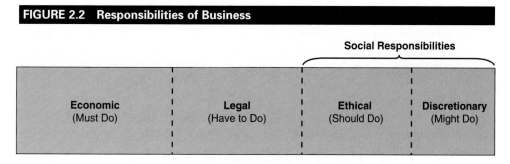

FIGURE 2.2   Responsibilities of Business

Source: Adapted from A. B. Carroll, "A Three Dimensional Conceptual Model of Corporate Performance," *Academy of Management Review* (October 1979), p. 499. Reprinted with permission.

1. Economic responsibilities are to produce goods and services of value to society so that the firm may repay its creditors and stockholders.

2. Legal responsibilities are defined by governments in laws that management is expected to obey.

3. Ethical responsibilities are to follow the generally held beliefs about how one should act in a society. For example, society generally expects firms to work with the employees and the community in planning for layoffs, even though there may be no law requiring this. The affected people can get very upset if an organization's management fails to act according to generally prevailing ethical values.

4. Discretionary responsibilities are the purely voluntary obligations a corporation assumes, for example, philanthropic contributions, training the hard-core unemployed, and providing day care centers. The difference between ethical and discretionary responsibilities is that few people expect an organization to fulfill discretionary responsibilities, whereas many expect an organization to fulfill ethical ones.

Carroll lists these four responsibilities in order of priority. A business firm must first make a profit to satisfy its economic responsibilities. To continue in existence, it must follow the laws, thus fulfilling its legal responsibilities. To this point Carroll and Friedman are in agreement. Carroll, however, goes further by arguing that business managers have responsibilities beyond economic and legal.

Once the two basic responsibilities are satisfied, according to Carroll, the firm should look to fulfilling its social responsibilities. Social responsibility, therefore, includes both ethical and discretionary, but not economic and legal responsibilities. A firm can fulfill its ethical responsibilities by doing those things that society tends to value but has not yet put into law. Once ethical responsibilities are satisfied, a firm can focus on discretionary responsibilities, purely voluntary actions that society has not yet decided are necessary.

The discretionary responsibilities of today may become the ethical responsibilities of tomorrow. The provision of day care facilities is, for example, moving rapidly from a discretionary to an ethical responsibility. Carroll suggests that to the extent that business corporations fail to acknowledge discretionary or ethical responsibilities, society, through government, will act, making them legal responsibilities. This may be done by government, moreover, without regard to an organization's economic responsibilities. As a result, the organization may have greater difficulty in earning a profit than it would have had in assuming voluntarily some ethical and discretionary responsibilities.

Both Friedman and Carroll argue their positions based on the impact of socially responsible actions on a firm's profits. Friedman says that socially responsible actions hurt a firm's efficiency. Carroll proposes that a lack of social responsibility results in an increase in government regulations, thus reducing a firm's efficiency. Research has failed, unfortunately, to consistently support either position. There is no clear relationship between social responsibility and financial performance, at least in the short run.[9]

WHO ARE CORPORATE STAKEHOLDERS?

The concept that business must be socially responsible sounds appealing until one asks, "Responsible to whom?" A corporation's task environment includes a large number of groups with interest in the activities of a business organization. These groups are called *stakeholders* because they are groups that affect or are affected by the achievement of the firm's objectives. Should a corporation be responsible only to some of these groups, or does business have an equal responsibility to all of them?

In any one strategic decision, the interests of one stakeholder group can conflict with another. For example, Maytag's reputation as a good corporate citizen was tarnished in some people's eyes when it announced the decision to move all dishwasher manufacturing from Iowa to Tennessee in order to consolidate the manufacturing of all of its brands of dishwashers into one large, highly efficient plant. The union protested the move out of state. The president of the union local asked: "Where is their commitment to the community and the state of Iowa?" On the one hand, stockholders were generally pleased with the decision because it would lower costs. On the other hand, Iowa officials and the local union were very unhappy at what they called "community cannibalism" in which Tennessee would gain jobs at Iowa's expense. Which group's interests should have priority?

Given the wide range of interests and concerns present in any organization's task environment, one or more groups, at any one time, probably will be dissatisfied with an organization's activities, even if management is trying to be socially responsible. Therefore, strategic managers must realize that before making a strategic decision, they should consider how each alternative will affect important stakeholder groups. What seems at first to be the best decision because it appears to be the most profitable may actually result in the worst set of consequences to the corporation. A decision now to continue legal but unsafe conditions to avoid the cost of repair may keep costs low temporarily, but it could result in a very expensive lawsuit in the future.

IN CONCLUSION

Strategic managers can have a huge impact on the entire corporation through their values and their vision. For example, when Kay Anderson founded the Medical Graphics Corporation in St. Paul, Minnesota, she acted out of a desire to achieve more than just profits. Concerned with improving medical diagnostics since her father died suddenly of a heart attack when she was 13 years old, Kay had a personal mission to help save lives. She used Medical Graphics to help achieve that mission. After Kay had done everything from building the equipment, to writing software, to visiting hospitals to demonstrate and sell her products, the corporation's sales climbed to almost $10 million annually. In her words: "I was on a crusade to save lives by inventing and perfecting a technology that would aid the early detection and diagnosis of heart and lung disease . . . It was a crusade and I was its driving force." In all her actions as CEO, Kay showed that the real mission of the corporation was to prevent heart and lung disease in people like her father. To her surprise, her employees also identified with this mission and were energized by it. "It turned out that all of us were in it for something more than money," concluded Kay.[10]

Discussion Questions

1. Does a corporation really need a board of directors?
2. How does a strategic vision differ from a corporation's mission?
3. What recommendations would you make to improve corporate governance?
4. Do you agree with economist Milton Friedman that social responsibility is a "fundamentally subversive doctrine" that will only hurt a business corporation's long-term efficiency?
5. Should a company be concerned if some of its suppliers in developing countries are abusing their workers, employing child labor, and paying near-starvation wages?

Key Terms (listed in order of appearance)

corporation
corporate governance
board of director responsibilities
due care
role of the board
board of directors continuum
inside directors
outside directors
agency theory
codetermination
interlocking directorate: direct and indirect

lead director
top management responsibilities
executive leadership
strategic vision
strategic planning staff
social responsibility
economic responsibilities
legal responsibilities
ethical responsibilities
discretionary responsibilities
stakeholders

Notes

1. J. H. Dobrzynski, "These Board Members Aren't IBM-Compatible," *Business Week* (August 2, 1992): 23.
2. A. Demb, and F. F. Neubauer, "The Corporate Board: Confronting the Paradoxes," *Long Range Planning* (June 1992): 13.
3. W. Q. Judge Jr., and C. P. Zeithaml, "Institutional and Strategic Choice Perspectives on Board Involvement in the Strategic Decision Process," *Academy of Management Journal* (October 1992): 766–794.
4. Reported by Korn/Ferry International and J. S. Lublin, "Survey Finds More Fortune 500 Firms Have at Least Two Female Directors," *Wall Street Journal* (September 25, 1995): A5.

5. P. L. Rechner, and D. R. Dalton, "CEO Duality and Organizational Performance: A Longitudinal Analysis," *Strategic Management Journal* (February 1991): 155–160; P. L. Rechner, and D. R. Dalton, "The Link Between Financial Performance and Board Leadership Structure," *Handbook of Business Strategy, 1992/93 Yearbook,* edited by H. E. Glass and M. A. Hovde (Boston: Warren, Gorham, and Lamont, 1992), 20.1–20.7.

6. N. Tichy, and R. Charan, "Speed, Simplicity, Self-Confidence: An Interview with Jack Welch," *Harvard Business Review* (September–October 1989): 113.

7. M. Friedman, "The Social Responsibility of Business Is to Increase Its Profits," *New York Times Magazine* (September 13, 1970), pp. 30, 126–127; and *Capitalism and Free-dom* (Chicago: University of Chicago Press, 1963), 133.

8. A. B. Carroll, "A Three-Dimensional Conceptual Model of Corporate Performance," *Academy of Management Review* (October 1979): 497–505.

9. P. Rechner, and K. Roth, "Social Responsibility and Financial Performance: A Structural Equation Methodology," *International Journal of Management* (December 1990): 382–391; K. E. Aupperle, A. B. Carroll, and J. D. Hatfield, "An Empirical Examination of the Relationship Between Corporate Social Responsibility and Profitability," *Academy of Management Journal* (June 1985): 459.

10. K. Anderson, "The Purpose at the Heart of Management," *Harvard Business Review* (May–June 1992): 52–62.

CHAPTER 3

ENVIRONMENTAL SCANNING AND INDUSTRY ANALYSIS

Chefs Unlimited was founded by Dodd and Michelle Aldred of Raleigh, North Carolina. As husband and wife veterans of the restaurant industry, they knew how difficult it was to work long hours and still allow time to prepare home-cooked meals. That was one reason why people were spending more at restaurants during the 1990s. (The percentage of food dollars spent away from home increased from 36 percent in 1980 to 44 percent in 1995.) The Aldreds felt that many people were beginning to tire of eating out and would be willing to pay for a quality meal eaten in their own home. They offered people the opportunity to order entrees for either a 1- or 2-week period. Doing their own cooking in a 3,000 square foot commercial kitchen, the Aldreds delivered meals to customers for subsequent reheating. Although more expensive, these meals were of higher quality than the typical frozen dinner. In just 4 years Chefs Unlimited was so successful catering to modern families that the Aldreds were planning to air express their meals to a nationwide audience the next year. Meanwhile, the U.S. Personal Chef Association was predicting a 5-fold increase in the number of personal chef entrepreneurs in the United States and Canada..

Pioneering companies have gone out of business because of their failure to adapt to environmental change or, even worse, by failing to create change. For example, Baldwin Locomotive, the major manufacturer of steam locomotives, was very slow in making the switch to diesel locomotives. General Electric and General Motors soon dominated the diesel locomotive business. The dominant manufacturers of vacuum tubes failed to make the change to transistors and consequently lost this market. Failure to adapt is, however, only one side of the coin. The aforementioned Chefs Unlimited example shows how a changing environment can create new opportunities at the same time it destroys old ones. The lesson is simple. To be successful over time, an organization needs to be in tune with its external environment. There must be a strategic fit between what the environment wants and what the corporation has to offer, as well as between what the corporation needs and what the environment can provide.

Current predictions are that the environment for all organizations will become even more uncertain in the twenty-first century. *Environmental uncertainty* is the degree of complexity plus the degree of change existing in an organization's external environment. On the one hand, environmental uncertainty is a threat to strategic managers because it hampers their ability to develop long-range plans and to make strategic decisions to keep the corporation in equilibrium with its external environment. On the other hand, environmental uncertainty is an opportunity because it creates a new playing field in which creativity and innovation can play a major part in strategic decisions.

3.1 ENVIRONMENTAL SCANNING

Before an organization can begin strategy formulation, it must scan the external environment to identify possible opportunities and threats and its internal environment for strengths and weaknesses. *Environmental scanning* is the monitoring, evaluating, and disseminating of information from the external and internal environments to key people within the corporation. It is a tool that a corporation uses to avoid strategic surprise and to ensure long-term health. Research has found a positive relationship between environmental scanning and profits.[1]

WHAT EXTERNAL ENVIRONMENTAL VARIABLES SHOULD BE SCANNED?

In undertaking environmental scanning, strategic managers must first be aware of the many variables within a corporation's societal and task environments. The *societal environment* includes general forces that do not directly touch on the short-run activities of the organization but that can, and often do, influence its long-run decisions. These forces, shown in Figure 3.1, are as follows:

- **Economic** forces regulate the exchange of materials, money, energy, and information.
- **Technological** forces generate problem-solving inventions.
- **Political–legal** forces allocate power and provide constraining and protecting laws and regulations.
- **Sociocultural** forces regulate the values, mores, and customs of society.

The *task environment* includes those elements or groups that directly affect the corporation and, in turn, are affected by it. These groups include governments, local communities, suppliers, competitors, customers, creditors, employees and labor unions, special-interest groups, and trade associations. A corporation's task environment can be thought of as the industry within which it operates. *Industry analysis* refers to an in-depth examination of key factors within a corporation's task environment. Both the societal and task environments must be monitored so that strategic factors that are likely to have a strong impact on corporate success or failure can be detected.

WHAT SHOULD BE SCANNED IN THE SOCIETAL ENVIRONMENT?

The societal environment contains many possible strategic factors. The number of factors becomes enormous when one realizes that, generally speaking, each country in the world can be represented by its own unique set of societal forces, some of which are very similar to neighboring countries and some of which are very different. For

FIGURE 3.1   Environmental Variables

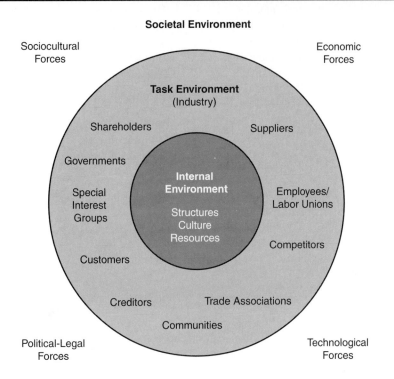

example, even though Austria and the Czech Republic share borders in Central Europe, the Czech Republic's recent history as a communist-bloc country means that in the 1990s it had none of the commercial infrastructure to support the transition from a centrally planned to a free market economy. Consequently, starting a business in Austria was significantly easier than in the Czech Republic where the old lethargic, state-controlled companies were neither able to quickly produce needed supplies nor able to distribute products effectively. Nevertheless, excellent school systems in both countries have produced well-educated and cultured consumers and employees.

How Should Societal Trends Be Monitored?   As noted in Table 3.1, large corporations categorize the societal environment in any one geographic region into four areas and focus their scanning in each area on trends with corporate-wide relevance. Obviously, trends in any one area may be very important to the firms in one industry but of lesser importance to firms in other industries.

Trends in the *economic* part of the societal environment can have an obvious impact on business activity. For example, an increase in interest rates means fewer sales of major home appliances because a rising interest rate tends to be reflected in higher mortgage rates. Because higher mortgage rates increase the cost of buying a house, the demand for new and used houses tends to fall. Because most major home appliances are sold when people change houses, a reduction in house sales soon translates into a decline in sales of refrigerators, stoves, and dishwashers, and reduced profits for everyone in that industry.

TABLE 3.1 Some Important Variables in the Societal Environment			
Economic	*Technological*	*Political–Legal*	*Sociocultural*
GDP Trends	Total government spending for R&D	Antitrust regulations	Lifestyle changes
Interest rates		Environmental protection laws	Career expectations
Money supply	Total industry spending for R&D		Consumer activism
Inflation rates		Tax laws	Rate of family formation
Unemployment levels	Focus of technological efforts	Special incentives	
Wage/price controls	Patent protection	Foreign trade regulations	Growth rate of population
Devalation/revaluation	New products	Attitudes toward foreign companies	Age distribution of population
Energy availability and cost	New developments in technology transfer from lab to marketplace	Laws on hiring and promotion	Regional shifts in population
Disposable and discretionary income	Productivity improvements through automation	Stability of government	Life expectancies
			Birth rates

Changes in the *technological* part of the societal environment can also have a great impact on multiple industries. For example, improvements in computer microprocessors have not only led to the widespread use of home computers, but also to better automobile engine performance in terms of power and fuel economy through the use of microprocessors to monitor fuel injection.

Trends in the *political–legal* part of the societal environment have a significant impact on business firms. For example, periods of strict enforcement of U.S. antitrust laws directly affect corporate growth strategy. As large companies find it more difficult to acquire another firm in the same or in a related industry, they are typically driven to diversify into unrelated industries. In Europe, the formation of the European Union has led to an increase in merger activity across national boundaries.

Demographic trends are part of the *sociocultural* aspect of the societal environment. The demographic bulge in the U.S. population caused by the "baby boom" in the 1950s strongly affects market demand in many industries. For example, between 1995 and 2005, an average of 4,400 Americans are turning 50 every day. This over-50 age group has become the fastest growing age group in all developed countries. Companies with an eye on the future can find many opportunities offering products and services to the growing number of "woofies" (well-off old folks), which is defined as people over 50 with money to spend. These people are very likely to purchase recreational vehicles, take ocean cruises, and enjoy leisure sports such as boating, fishing, and bowling, in addition to needing financial services and health care.

This trend can mean increasing sales for firms like Winnebago (RVs), Carnival Cruise Lines, and Brunswick (sports equipment), among others. To attract older customers, retailers will need to place seats in their larger stores so aging shoppers can rest. Washrooms need to be more accessible. Signs need to be larger. Restaurants need to raise the level of lighting so people can read their menus. Home appliances need simpler and larger controls. Already, the market for upright road bikes is declining as sales for recumbant bikes, tread mills, and massagers for aching muscles increase.

Following are seven sociocultural trends in the United States that are helping to define what North America and the world will look like over the next few years.

1. An increase in environmental awareness.
2. Growth of markets aimed toward senior citizens.
3. The Generation Y boomlet will crest at 30.8 million births by 2005.
4. Decline of the mass market and growth of niche markets served by mass customization manufacturing.
5. Faster pace of life via cell phones, telecommuting, and marketing through the Internet.
6. Single-person households and married couples with no children are becoming the most common household type.
7. An increase in diversity of workforce and markets.

What Are International Societal Considerations? For each country or group of countries in which a company operates, management must face a whole new societal environment having different economic, technological, political–legal, and sociocultural variables. This is especially an issue for a *multinational corporation* (MNC), a company having significant manufacturing and marketing operations in multiple countries. International societal environments vary so widely that a corporation's internal environment and strategic management process must be very flexible. Cultural trends in Germany, for example, have resulted in the inclusion of worker representatives in corporate strategic planning. Differences in societal environments strongly affect the ways in which an MNC conducts its marketing, financial, manufacturing, and other functional activities. For example, the existence of regional associations like the European Union, the North American Free Trade Zone, and Mercosur in South America have a significant impact on the competitive "rules of the game" for both those MNCs operating within and those MNCs that want to enter these areas. To account for the many differences among societal environments from one country to another, Table 3.1 would need to be changed to include such variables as currency convertibility, climate, and regional associations under the Economic category; natural resource availability, transportation network, and communication infrastructure under the Technological category; form of government, regulations on foreign ownership, and terrorist activity under the Political–legal category; and language, social institutions, and attitudes toward foreigners under the Sociocultural category.

Before a company plans its strategy for a particular international location, it must scan the particular country environment(s) in question for opportunities and threats and compare them to its own organizational strengths and weaknesses. For example, if a company wants to operate successfully in a global industry such as automobiles, tires, electronics, or watches, it must be prepared to establish a significant presence in the "triad." Coined by Kenichi Ohmae, the *triad* refers to the three developed regions of Japan, North America, and Western Europe, which now form a single market with common needs.[2] Focusing on the triad is essential for an MNC pursuing success in a global industry, according to Ohmae, because close to 90 percent of all high-value-added, high-technology manufactured goods are produced and consumed in North America, Western Europe, and Japan. Ideally a company should have a significant presence in each of these regions so that it can produce and market its products simultaneously in all three areas. Otherwise, it will lose competitive advantage to triad-oriented MNCs. No longer can an MNC develop and market a new product in one part of the world before it exports it to other developed countries.

WHAT SHOULD BE SCANNED IN THE TASK ENVIRONMENT?

As shown in Figure 3.2, a corporation's scanning of the environment should include analyses of all the relevant elements in the task environment. These analyses take the form of individual reports written by various people in different parts of the firm. At Procter & Gamble (P&G), for example, each quarter, people from each of the brand management teams work with key people from the sales and market research departments to research and write a "competitive activity report" on each of the product categories in which P&G competes. People in purchasing write similar reports concerning new developments in the industries that supply P&G. These and other reports are then summarized and transmitted up the corporate hierarchy for top management to use in strategic decision making. If a new development is reported regarding a particular product category, top management may then send memos to people throughout the organization to watch for and report on developments in related product areas. The many reports resulting from these scanning efforts, when boiled down to their essentials, act as a detailed list of external strategic factors.

FIGURE 3.2 Scanning the External Environment

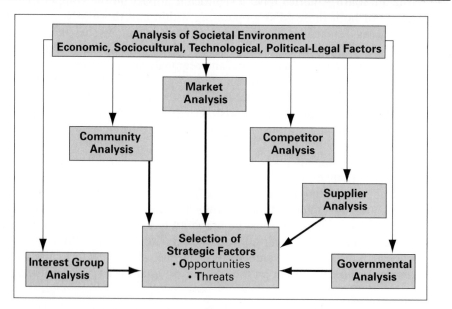

How Can Managers Identify External Strategic Factors?

Companies often respond differently to the same environmental changes because of differences in the ability of managers to recognize and understand external strategic issues and factors. Few firms can successfully monitor all important external variables. Even though managers agree that strategic importance determines which variables are consistently tracked, they sometimes miss or choose to ignore crucial new developments. Personal values of a corporation's managers and the success of current strategies are likely to bias both their perception of what is important to monitor in the external environment and their interpretations of what they perceive. This is known as *strategic myopia:* the willingness to reject unfamiliar as well as negative information. If a firm needs to change its strategy, it might not be gathering the appropriate external information to change strategies successfully.

One way to identify and analyze developments in the external environment is to use the *issues priority matrix* (provided in Figure 3.3) as follows.

1. Identify a number of likely trends emerging in the societal and task environments. These are strategic environmental issues: those important trends that, if they happen, will determine what various industries will look like.
2. Assess the probability (from low to high) of these trends actually occurring.
3. Attempt to ascertain the likely impact (from low to high) of each of these trends on the corporation.

The issues priority matrix can be used to help managers decide which environmental trends should be merely scanned (low priority) and which should be monitored

FIGURE 3.3   Issues Priority Matrix

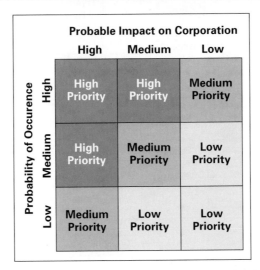

Source: Adapted from L. L. Lederman, "Foresight Activities in the U.S.A.: Time for a Re-Assessment?" *Long-Range Planning* (June 1984), p. 46. Copyright © 1984 by Pergamon Press, Ltd. Reprinted by permission.

as strategic factors (high priority). The *external strategic factors* of a corporation are those environmental trends that are judged to have both a medium to high probability of occurrence and a medium to high probability of impact on the corporation. Those environmental trends judged to be a corporation's strategic factors are then categorized as potential opportunities and threats and are included in strategy formulation.

3.2 INDUSTRY ANALYSIS: ANALYZING THE TASK ENVIRONMENT

An *industry* is a group of firms producing a similar product or service, such as financial services or soft drinks. An examination of the important stakeholder groups, such as suppliers and customers, in the task environment of a particular corporation is a part of industry analysis.

WHAT IS MICHAEL PORTER'S APPROACH TO INDUSTRY ANALYSIS?

Michael Porter, an authority on competitive strategy, contends that a corporation is most concerned with the intensity of competition within its industry. Basic competitive forces, which are depicted in Figure 3.4, determine the intensity level. "The collective strength of these forces," he contends, "determines the ultimate profit potential in the

FIGURE 3.4 Forces Driving Industry Competition

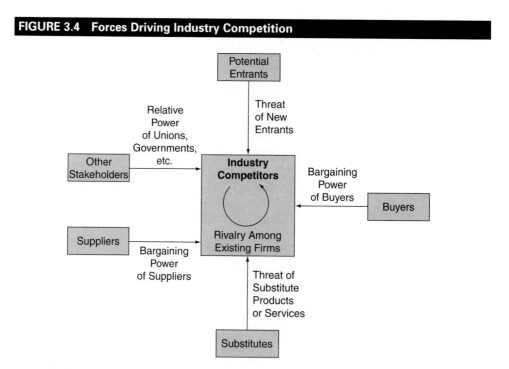

Source: Adapted/reprinted with permission of The Free Press, an imprint of Simon & Schuster, from *Competitive Strategy, Techniques for Analyzing Industries and Competitors* by Michael E. Porter. Copyright © 1980 by The Free Press.

industry, where profit potential is measured in terms of long-run return on invested capital."[3] The stronger each of these forces is, the more companies are limited in their ability to raise prices and earn greater profits. Although Porter mentions only five forces, a sixth, other stakeholders, is added here to reflect the power that governments, local communities, and other groups from the task environment wield over industry activities.

Using the model in Figure 3.4, a strong force can be regarded as a threat because it is likely to reduce profits. In contrast, a weak force can be viewed as an opportunity because it may allow the company to earn greater profits. In the short run, these forces act as constraints on a company's activities. In the long run, however, it may be possible for a company, through its choice of strategy, to change the strength of one or more of the forces to the company's advantage.

In carefully scanning its industry, the corporation must assess the importance to its success of each of the following six forces: threat of new entrants, rivalry among existing firms, threat of substitute products, bargaining power of buyers, bargaining power of suppliers, and relative power of other stakeholders.[4]

WHAT IS THE THREAT OF NEW ENTRANTS?

New entrants are newcomers to an existing industry. They typically bring new capacity, a desire to gain market share, and substantial resources. Therefore they are threats to an established corporation. The threat of entry depends on the presence of entry barriers and the reaction that can be expected from existing competitors. An *entry barrier* is an obstruction that makes it difficult for a company to enter an industry. For example, no new domestic automobile companies have been successfully established in the United States since the 1930s because of the high capital requirements to build production facilities and to develop a dealer distribution network. Some of the possible barriers to entry are the following:

- **Economies of Scale.** Scale economies in the production and sale of mainframe computers, for example, gave IBM a significant cost advantage over any new rival.
- **Product Differentiation.** Corporations like Procter & Gamble and General Mills, which manufacture products like Tide and Cheerios, create high entry barriers through their high levels of advertising and promotion.
- **Capital Requirements.** The need to invest huge financial resources in manufacturing facilities in order to produce computer microprocessors creates a significant barrier to entry to any competitor for Intel.
- **Switching Costs.** Once a software program like Excel or Word becomes established in an office, office managers are very reluctant to switch to a new program because of the high training costs.
- **Access to Distribution Channels.** Small entrepreneurs often have difficulty obtaining supermarket shelf space for their goods because large retailers charge for space on their shelves and give priority to the established firms who can pay for the advertising needed to generate high customer demand.
- **Cost Disadvantages Independent of Size.** Microsoft's development of the first widely adopted operating system (MS-DOS) for the IBM-type personal computer gave it a significant advantage over potential competitors. Its introduction of Windows helped to cement that advantage.

- **Government Policy.** Governments can limit entry into an industry through licensing requirements by restricting access to raw materials, such as off-shore oil drilling sites.

WHAT IS RIVALRY AMONG EXISTING FIRMS?

Rivalry is the amount of direct competition in an industry. In most industries, corporations are mutually dependent. A competitive move by one firm can be expected to have a noticeable effect on its competitors and thus may cause retaliation or counter efforts. For example, the entry by mail order companies such as Dell and Gateway into a PC industry previously dominated by IBM, Apple, and Compaq increased the level of competitive activity to such an extent that any price reduction or new product introduction is now quickly followed by similar moves from other PC makers. According to Porter, intense rivalry is related to the presence of the following factors:

- **Number of Competitors.** When competitors are few and roughly equal in size, such as in the U.S. auto and major home appliance industries, they watch each other carefully to make sure that any move by another firm is matched by an equal countermove.
- **Rate of Industry Growth.** Any slowing in passenger traffic tends to set off price wars in the airline industry because the only path to growth is to take sales away from a competitor.
- **Product or Service Characteristics.** Many people choose a videotape rental store based on location, variety of selection, and pricing because they view videotapes as a *commodity*: a product whose characteristics are the same regardless of who sells it.
- **Amount of Fixed Costs.** Because airlines must fly their planes on a schedule regardless of the number of paying passengers for any one flight, they offer cheap standby fares whenever a plane has empty seats.
- **Capacity.** If the only way a manufacturer can increase capacity is in a large increment by building a new plant (as in the paper industry), it will run that new plant at full capacity to keep its unit costs as low as possible, thus producing so much that the selling price falls throughout the industry.
- **Height of Exit Barriers.** Exit barriers keep a company from leaving an industry. The brewing industry, for example, has a low percentage of companies that leave the industry because breweries are specialized assets with few uses except for making beer.
- **Diversity of Rivals.** Rivals that have very different ideas of how to compete are likely to often cross paths and unknowingly challenge each other's position.

WHAT IS THE THREAT OF SUBSTITUTE PRODUCTS OR SERVICES?

Substitute products are those products that appear to be different but can satisfy the same need as another product. According to Porter, "Substitutes limit the potential returns of an industry by placing a ceiling on the prices firms in the industry can profitably charge."[5] To the extent that switching costs are low, substitutes may have a strong effect on an industry. Tea can be considered a substitute for coffee. If the price of coffee goes up high enough, coffee drinkers will slowly begin switching to tea. The price of tea thus puts a price ceiling on the price of coffee. Sometimes a difficult task, the identification of possible substitute products or services means searching for products or services that can perform the same function, even though they may not appear to be easily substitutable.

WHAT IS THE BARGAINING POWER OF BUYERS?

Buyers affect an industry through their ability to force down prices, bargain for higher quality or more services, and play competitors against each other. A buyer or distributor is powerful if some of the following factors hold true:

- A buyer purchases a large proportion of the seller's product or service (for example, oil filters purchased by a major automaker).
- A buyer has the potential to integrate backward by producing the product itself (for example, a newspaper chain could make its own paper).
- Alternative suppliers are plentiful because the product is standard or undifferentiated (for example, motorists can choose among many gas stations).
- Changing suppliers costs very little (for example, office supplies are easy to find).
- The purchased product represents a high percentage of a buyer's costs, thus providing an incentive to shop around for a lower price (for example, gasoline purchased for resale by convenience stores makes up half their costs).
- A buyer earns low profits and is thus very sensitive to costs and service differences (for example, grocery stores have very small margins).
- The purchased product is unimportant to the final quality or price of a buyer's products or services and thus can be easily substituted without adversely affecting the final product (for example, electric wire bought for use in lamps).

WHAT IS THE BARGAINING POWER OF SUPPLIERS?

Suppliers can affect an industry through their ability to raise prices or reduce the quality of purchased goods and services. A supplier or supplier group is powerful if some of the following factors apply:

- The supplier industry is dominated by a few companies, but it sells to many (for example, the petroleum industry).
- Its product or service is unique or it has built up switching costs (for example, word processing software).
- Substitutes are not readily available (for example, electricity).
- Suppliers are able to integrate forward and compete directly with their present customers (for example, a microprocessor producer like Intel can make PCs).
- A purchasing industry buys only a small portion of the supplier group's goods and services and is thus unimportant to the supplier (for example, sales of lawn mower tires are less important to the tire industry than are sales of auto tires).

WHAT IS THE RELATIVE POWER OF OTHER STAKEHOLDERS?

A sixth force should be added to Porter's list to include a variety of stakeholder groups from the task environment. Some of these other stakeholders are governments (if not explicitly included elsewhere), local communities, creditors (if not included with suppliers), trade associations, special-interest groups, and shareholders. The importance of these stakeholders varies by industry. For example, environmental groups in Maine, Michigan, Oregon, and Iowa successfully fought to pass bills outlawing disposable bottles and cans, and thus deposits for most drink containers are now required. This effectively raised costs across the board, with the most impact on the marginal producers who could not internally absorb all of these costs.

DO INDUSTRIES EVOLVE OVER TIME?

Most industries evolve over time through a series of stages from growth through maturity to eventual decline. The strength of each of the six competitive forces described in the preceding section varies according to the stage of industry evolution. The industry life cycle is useful for explaining and predicting trends among the six forces that drive industry competition. For example, when an industry is new, people often buy the product regardless of price because it fulfills a unique need. This is probably a *fragmented industry*: an industry in which no firm has large market share and each firm serves only a small piece of the total market in competition with others (for example, Chinese restaurants). As new competitors enter the industry, prices drop as a result of competition. Companies use the experience curve (discussed in chapter 4) and economies of scale to reduce costs faster than their competition. Companies integrate to reduce costs even further by acquiring their suppliers and distributors. Competitors try to differentiate their products from one another to avoid the fierce price competition common to a maturing industry.

By the time an industry enters maturity, products tend to become more like commodities. This is now a *consolidated industry*: an industry dominated by a few large firms, each of which struggles to differentiate its products from the competition. As buyers become more sophisticated over time, they base their purchasing decisions on better information. Products become more like commodities in which price becomes a dominant concern given a minimum level of quality and features. One example of this trend is the videocassette recorder (VCR) industry. By the 1990s, VCRs had reached the point that there were few major differences among them. Consumers realized that, because slight improvements cost significantly more money, it made little sense to pay more than the minimum for a VCR. The same is true of gasoline.

As an industry moves through maturity toward possible decline, the growth rate of its products' sales slows and may even begin to decrease. To the extent that exit barriers are low, firms will begin converting their facilities to alternative uses or will sell them to another firm. The industry tends to consolidate around fewer but larger competitors. The U.S. major home appliance industry, for example, changed from being a fragmented industry (pure competition) composed of hundreds of appliance manufacturers in the 1940s to a consolidated industry (mature oligopoly) composed of five companies controlling over 98 percent of U.S. major home appliance sales by the end of the century. A similar consolidation occurred in the European major home appliance industry during the 1990s.

HOW ARE INTERNATIONAL INDUSTRIES CATEGORIZED?

World industries vary on a continuum from multidomestic to global (see Figure 3.5).[6] A *multidomestic industry* is a collection of essentially domestic industries, like retailing and insurance, in which products or services are tailored specifically for a particular country. The activities in a subsidiary of an MNC in this type of industry are essentially independent of the activities of the MNC's subsidiaries in other countries. In each country, the MNC tailors its products or services to the very specific needs of consumers in that particular country. A *global industry,* in contrast, operates worldwide, with MNCs making only small adjustments for country-specific circumstances. A global industry is one in which the activities of an MNC in one country are significantly affected by its activities in other countries. MNCs produce products or services in various locations throughout the world and sell them all over the world, making only minor adjustments for specific country requirements. Examples of global industries are commercial aircraft, television sets, semiconductors, copiers, automobiles, watches, and tires. The largest industrial corporations in the world in terms of dollar sales are, for the most part, multinational corporations operating in global industries.

The factors that tend to determine whether an industry will be primarily multidomestic or primarily global are (1) the *pressure for coordination* within the multinational corporations operating in that industry and (2) the *pressure for local responsiveness* on the part of individual country markets. To the extent that the pressure for coordination is strong and the pressure for local responsiveness is weak for multinational corporations within a particular industry, that industry will tend to become global. In contrast, when the pressure for local responsiveness is strong and the pressure for coordination is weak for multinational corporations in an industry, that industry will tend to become multidomestic. Between these two extremes lie a number of industries with varying characteristics of both multidomestic and global industries.

WHAT IS A STRATEGIC GROUP?

A *strategic group* is a set of business units or firms that "pursue similar strategies with similar resources."[7] Categorizing firms in any one industry into a set of strategic groups is very useful to strategic managers as a way of better understanding the competitive environment. Because a corporation's structure and culture tend to reflect the kinds of strategies it follows, companies or business units belonging to a particular strategic group within the same industry tend to be strong rivals and more similar to each other than to competitors in other strategic groups within the same industry. For example,

---

FIGURE 3.5 Continuum of International Industries

Multidomestic ←————————————————————————————→ *Global*

Industry in which companies tailor their products to the specific needs of consumers in a particular country.	Industry in which companies manufacture and sell the same products, with only minor adjustments made for individual countries around the world.
• Retailing • Insurance • Banking	• Automobiles • Tires • Television sets

although McDonald's and Olive Garden are a part of the same restaurant industry, they have different missions, objectives, and strategies and thus belong to different strategic groups. They generally have very little in common and pay little attention to each other when planning competitive actions. Burger King and Hardee's, however, have a great deal in common with McDonald's in terms of their similar strategy of producing a high volume of low-priced meals targeted for sale to the average family. Consequently they are strong rivals and are organized to operate in a similar fashion.

Strategic groups in a particular industry can be mapped by plotting the market positions of industry competitors on a two-dimensional graph using two strategic variables as the vertical and horizontal axes. (See Figure 3.6.) First, select two broad characteristics, such as price and menu, that differentiate the companies in an industry from

FIGURE 3.6 Mapping Strategic Groups in the U.S. Restaurant Chain Industry

one another. Second, plot the firms using these two characteristics as the dimensions. Third, draw a circle around those companies that are closest to one another as one strategic group, varying the size of the circle in proportion to the group's share of total industry sales. Name each strategic group in the restaurant industry with an identifying title, such as quick fast food or buffet-style service. Other dimensions, such as quality and degree of vertical integration, can also be used in additional graphs of the restaurant industry to show how the various firms in the industry compete.

WHAT ARE STRATEGIC TYPES?

In analyzing the level of competitive intensity within a particular industry or strategic group, it is useful to characterize the various competitors for predictive purposes. A *strategic type* is a category of firms based on a common strategic orientation and a combination of structure, culture, and processes consistent with that strategy. According to Miles and Snow, competing firms within a single industry can be categorized on the basis of their general strategic orientation into one of four basic types, defenders, prospectors, analyzers, and reactors.[8] This distinction helps explain why companies facing similar situations behave differently and why they continue to do so over a long period of time. These general types have the following characteristics:

- **Defenders** are companies with a limited product line that focus on improving the efficiency of their existing operations. This cost orientation makes them unlikely to innovate in new areas. An example is the Adolph Coors Company, which for many years emphasized production efficiency in its one Colorado brewery and virtually ignored marketing.
- **Prospectors** are companies with fairly broad product lines that focus on product innovation and market opportunities. This sales orientation makes them somewhat inefficient. They tend to emphasize creativity over efficiency. An example is the Miller Brewing Company, which successfully promoted "light" beer and generated aggressive, innovative advertising campaigns, but had to close a brand-new brewery when management overestimated market demand.
- **Analyzers** are companies that operate in at least two different product-market areas, one stable and one variable. In the stable areas, efficiency is emphasized; in the variable areas, innovation is emphasized. An example is Anheuser-Busch, which can take a defender orientation to protect its massive market share in U.S. beer and a prospector orientation to generate sales in its amusement parks.
- **Reactors** are companies that lack a consistent strategy–structure–culture relationship. Their (often ineffective) responses to environmental pressures tend to be piecemeal strategic changes. An example is the Pabst Brewing Company, which because of numerous takeover attempts has been unable to generate a consistent strategy to keep its sales from dropping.

Dividing the competition into these four categories enables the strategic manager not only to monitor the effectiveness of certain strategic orientations, but also to develop scenarios of future industry developments (discussed later in this chapter).

WHAT IS HYPERCOMPETITION?

Hypercompetition describes an industry undergoing an ever-increasing level of environmental uncertainty in which competitive advantage is only temporary. For example, industries that were once multidomestic (like major home appliances) are becoming global. New flexible, aggressive, innovative competitors are moving into established markets to rapidly erode the advantages of large previously dominant firms. Distribution channels vary from country to country and are being altered daily through the use of sophisticated information systems. Closer relationships with suppliers are being forged to reduce costs, increase quality, and gain access to new technology. According to D'Aveni, "Market stability is threatened by short product life cycles, short product design cycles, new technologies, frequent entry by unexpected outsiders, repositioning by incumbents, and tactical redefinitions of market boundaries as diverse industries merge."[9] Companies learn to quickly imitate the successful strategies of market leaders, and it becomes harder to sustain any competitive advantage for very long.

In hypercompetitive industries such as computers, competitive advantage comes from an up-to-date knowledge of environmental trends and competitive activity coupled with a willingness to risk a current advantage for a possible new advantage. Companies must be willing to *cannibalize* their own products (to replace popular products before competitors do so) in order to sustain their competitive advantage. As a result, industry or competitive intelligence has never been more important.

WHAT IS THE VALUE OF AN INDUSTRY MATRIX?

An *industry matrix* summarizes the external strategic factors (opportunities and threats) that face a particular industry. As shown in Table 3.2, the matrix gives a weight for each factor based on how important that factor is to the future of the industry. The

TABLE 3.2 Industry Matrix

Strategic Factors	Weight	Company A Rating	Company A Weighted Score	Company B Rating	Company B Weighted Score
1	*2*	*3*	*4*	*5*	*6*
Total	1.00				

Source: T. L. Wheelen and J. D. Hunger, "Industry Matrix." Copyright © 1997 by Wheelen and Hunger Associates. Reprinted by permission.

matrix also specifies how well various competitors in the industry are responding to each factor. To generate an industry matrix using two industry competitors (called A and B), complete the following steps for the industry being analyzed:

- In column 1 (*Strategic Factors*), list the 8 to 10 most important opportunities and threats facing the industry as a whole.
- In column 2 (*Weight*), assign a weight to each factor from 1.0 (*Most Important*) to 0.0 (*Not Important*) based on that factor's probable impact on the overall future success of the industry. (All weights must sum to 1.0 regardless of the number of strategic factors.)
- In column 3 (*Company A Rating*), examine a particular company within the industry; for example, Company A. Using your best judgment, assign a rating to each factor from 5 (*Outstanding*) to 1 (*Poor*) based on Company A's current way of managing a particular factor.

5	4	3	2	1
Out-standing	Above Average	Average	Below Average	Poor

- In column 4 (*Company A Weighted Score*), multiply the weight in column 2 for each factor times its rating in column 3 to obtain that factor's weighted score for Company A. This results in a weighted score for each factor ranging from 5.0 (outstanding) to 1.0 (poor) with 3.0 as average.
- In column 5 (*Company B Rating*), examine a second company within the industry; in this case, Company B. Assign a rating to each factor from 5 (outstanding) to 1 (poor) based on Company B's current response to each particular factor.
- In column 6 (*Company B Weighted Score*), multiply the weight in column 2 for each factor times its rating in column 5 to obtain that factor's weighted score for Company B.
- Finally, add the weighted scores for all the factors in columns 4 and 6 to determine the total weighted scores for Companies A and B. The total weighted score indicates how well each company is responding to current and expected factors in the industry's environment.

The industry matrix can be expanded to include all the major competitors within an industry simply by adding two additional columns for each additional competitor.

3.3 COMPETITIVE INTELLIGENCE

Much external environmental scanning is done on an informal and individual basis. Information is obtained from a variety of sources, such as customers, suppliers, bankers, consultants, publications, personal observations, subordinates, superiors, and peers. For example, R&D scientists and engineers can learn about new products and competitors' ideas at professional meetings; someone from the purchasing department may uncover valuable bits of information about a competitor by speaking with supplier representatives. A study of product innovation in the scientific instrument and machine tool industries found that customers initiated 80 percent of all product innovations with their inquiries and complaints.[10] In these industries, the sales force and service departments must be especially vigilant.

Competitive intelligence is a formal program of gathering information on a company's competitors. Only 7 percent of U.S. corporations have fully developed intelligence programs. In contrast, all Japanese corporations involved in international business and over half of German and Swedish companies have active intelligence programs. This situation is changing, however. At General Mills, for example, all employees of the company have been trained to recognize and tap sources of competitive information. Janitors no longer simply place orders with suppliers of cleaning materials, they also ask about relevant practices at competing firms.

Most corporations rely on outside organizations to provide them with environmental data. Firms such as A. C. Nielsen Co. provide subscribers with bimonthly data on brand share, retail prices, percentages of stores stocking an item, and percentages of stock-out stores. Strategists can use these data to spot regional and national trends as well as to assess market share. "Information brokers" such as FIND/SVP and Finsbury Data Services sell information on market conditions, government regulations, competitors, and new products. Company and industry profiles are generally available from Hoover's On-line Web site (http://www.hoovers.com) and other internet sites. Many business corporations have established their own in-house libraries and computerized information systems to deal with the growing mass of available information.

Some companies, however, choose to use industrial espionage or other intelligence-gathering techniques to get their information straight from their competitors. For example, Avon Products hired private investigators to retrieve documents (some of them shredded) that Mary Kay Corporation had thrown away in a public dumpster. Even Procter & Gamble, which defends itself like a fortress from information leaks, is vulnerable. A competitor was able to learn the precise launch date of a concentrated laundry detergent in Europe when one of its employees visited the factory where machines were being made. Simply asking a few questions about what a certain machine did, for whom it was being built, and when it would be delivered was all that was necessary.

3.4 FORECASTING

Environmental scanning provides reasonably hard data on the present situation and current trends, but intuition and luck are needed to accurately predict if these trends will continue. The resulting forecasts are, however, usually based on a set of assumptions that may or may not be valid.

WHY CAN ASSUMPTIONS BE DANGEROUS?

Faulty underlying assumptions are the most frequent cause of forecasting errors. Nevertheless many managers who formulate and implement strategic plans rarely consider that their success is based on a series of assumptions. Many long-range plans are simply based on projections of the current situation. One example of what can happen when a corporate strategy rests on the very questionable assumption that the future will simply be an extension of the present is that of Tupperware, the maker of plastic refrigerator containers. Management not only assumed in the 1960s and 1970s that Tupperware parties would continue being an excellent distribution channel, but its faith in this assumption also blinded it to information about America's changing lifestyles and their likely impact on sales. Even in the 1990s, when Tupperware executives realized that their extrapolated sales forecasts were no longer justified, they were unable to improve their forecasting techniques until they changed their assumptions.

WHAT FORECASTING TECHNIQUES ARE AVAILABLE?

Various techniques are used to forecast future situations, and each has its proponents and critics. A study of nearly 500 of the world's largest corporations revealed trend extrapolation to be the most widely practiced form of forecasting; over 70 percent use this technique either occasionally or frequently.[11] Simply stated, *extrapolation* is the extension of present trends into the future. It rests on the assumption that the world is reasonably consistent and changes slowly in the short run. Approaches of this type include time-series methods, which attempt to carry a series of historical events forward into the future. The basic problem with extrapolation is that a historical trend is based on a series of patterns or relationships among so many different variables that a change in any one can drastically alter the future direction of the trend. As a rule of thumb, the further into the past one can find relevant data supporting the trend, the more confidence one can have in the prediction.

Brainstorming and statistical modeling are also popular forecasting techniques. *Brainstorming* is a nonquantitative approach in which ideas are proposed without first mentally screening them and without criticism by others. All that is required is the presence of people with some knowledge of the situation to be predicted. Ideas tend to build on previous ideas until a consensus is reached. This is a good technique to use with operating managers who have more faith in "gut feeling" than in quantitative "number-crunching" techniques. *Statistical modeling* is a quantitative technique that attempts to discover causal or at least explanatory factors that link two or more time series together. Examples of statistical modeling are regression analysis and other econometric methods. Although very useful in the grasping of historic trends, statistical modeling, like trend extrapolation, is based on historical data. As the patterns of relationships change, the accuracy of the forecast deteriorates.

Scenarios are focused descriptions of different likely futures presented in a narrative fashion. Scenario writing appears to be the most widely used forecasting technique after trend extrapolation. The scenario thus may be merely a written description of some future state, in terms of key variables and issues, or it may be generated in combination with other forecasting techniques.

An *industry scenario* is a forecasted description of a particular industry's likely future. It is a scenario that is developed by analyzing the probable impact of future societal forces on key groups in a particular industry. The process may operate as follows:[12]

1. Examine possible shifts in the societal variables.
2. Identify uncertainties in each of the six forces of the task environment (e.g., potential entrants, competitors, likely substitutes, buyers, suppliers, and other key stakeholders).
3. Make a range of plausible assumptions about future trends.
4. Combine assumptions about individual trends into internally consistent scenarios.
5. Analyze the industry situation that would prevail under each scenario.
6. Determine the sources of competitive advantage under each scenario.
7. Predict competitors' behavior under each scenario.
8. Select those scenarios that are either most likely to occur or are most likely to have a strong impact on the future of the company. Use these in strategy formulation.

3.5 SYNTHESIS OF EXTERNAL FACTORS: EFAS

After strategists have scanned the societal and task environments and identified a number of likely external factors for their particular corporation, they may want to refine their analysis of these factors using a form such as that given in Table 3.3. The External Factors Analysis Summary (EFAS) Table is one way to organize the external factors into the generally accepted categories of opportunities and threats as well as to analyze how well a particular company's management (rating) is responding to these specific factors in light of the perceived importance (weight) of these factors to the company. To generate an EFAS Table, complete the following steps for the company being analyzed:

- In column 1 (*External Factors*), list the 8 to 10 most important opportunities and threats facing the company.
- In column 2 (*Weight*), assign a weight to each factor from 1.0 (most important) to 0.0 (not important) based on that factor's probable impact on a particular company's current strategic position. The higher the weight, the more important this factor is to the current and future success of the company. (All weights must sum to 1.00 regardless of the number of factors.)
- In column 3 (*Rating*), assign a rating to each factor from 5 (outstanding) to 1 (poor) based on that particular company's current response to that particular factor. Each rating is a judgment regarding how well the company is currently dealing with each external factor.

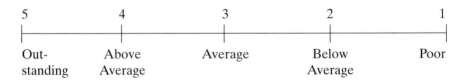

5	4	3	2	1
Out-standing	Above Average	Average	Below Average	Poor

- In column 4 (*Weighted Score*), multiply the weight in column 2 for each factor times its rating in column 3 to obtain that factor's weighted score. This results in a weighted score for each factor ranging from 5.0 (outstanding) to 1.0 (poor) with 3.0 as average.

- In column 5 (*Comments*), note why a particular factor was selected and how its weight and rating were estimated.
- Finally, add the weighted scores for all the external factors in column 4 to determine the *total weighted score* for that particular company. The total weighted score indicates how well a particular company is responding to current and expected factors in its external environment. The score can be used to compare that firm to other firms in its industry. The total weighted score for an average firm in an industry is always 3.0.

As an example of this procedure, Table 3.3 includes a number of external factors for Maytag Corporation with corresponding weights, ratings, and weighted scores provided.

TABLE 3.3   External Factor Analysis Summary (EFAS): Maytag as Example

External Factors	Weight	Rating	Weighted Score	Comments
	1	2	3	4	5
Opportunities				
• Economic integration of European Community	.20	4	.80	Acquisition of Hoover
• Demographics favor quality appliances	.10	5	.50	Maytag quality
• Economic development of Asia	.05	1	.05	Low Maytag presence
• Opening of Eastern Europe	.05	2	.10	Will take time
• Trend to "Super Stores"	.10	2	.20	Maytag weak in this channel
Threats				
• Increasing government regulations	.10	4	.40	Well positioned
• Strong U.S. competition	.10	4	.40	Well positioned
• Whirlpool and Electrolux strong globally	.15	3	.45	Hoover weak globally
• New product advances	.05	1	.05	Questionable
• Japanese appliance companies	.10	2	.20	Only Asian presence is Australia
Total	1.00		3.15	

Notes:

1. List opportunities and threats (5–10 each) in Column 1.

2. Weight each factor from 1.0 (Most Important) to 0.0 (Not Important) in Column 2 based on that factor's probable impact on the company's strategic position. The total weights must sum to 1.00.

3. Rate each factor from 5 (Outstanding) to 1 (Poor) in Column 3 based on the company's response to that factor.

4. Multiply each factor's weight times its rating to obtain each factor's weighted score in Column 4.

5. Use Column 5 (comments) for rationale used for each factor.

6. Add the weighted scores to obtain the total weighted score for the company in Column 4. This tells how well the company is responding to the factors in its external environment.

Source: T. L. Wheelen and J. D. Hunger, "External Factor Analysis Summary (EFAS)." Copyright © 1991 by Wheelen and Hunger Associates. Reprinted by permission.

IN CONCLUSION

When Wal-Mart comes to town, it is not always appreciated. In fact, it is sometimes referred to as the "Merchant of Death." Wal-Mart earned that reputation when small town merchants were unable to compete with the newcomer's wide selection and low prices and went out of business. When Fred Nelson, owner of Nelson Mill & Agri-Center in Viroqua, Wisconsin, learned that Wal-Mart was planning to come to town, he did something about it. He took six employees on a spying mission to visit the discounter 140 miles away in Anamosa, Iowa. After checking prices and service at the Wal-Mart, Nelson talked with the manager of the farm store next door to learn how he responded to the new neighbor. Nelson learned that he couldn't match Wal-Mart's prices because it buys in such large quantities, but he could focus on available niches. Returning home to Viroqua, Nelson reduced his inventories of toys and housewares and eliminated health and beauty aids entirely. He focused on clothing, tools, and giftwares and stocked better quality brands and a broader range than Wal-Mart. He expanded his repair and parts-ordering services, liberalized his returns policy, and extended his hours. He stressed his service to his main clientele, local farmers. He expanded his farm supply department and priced basics like WD-40 at Wal-Mart levels. Thanks to his environmental scanning efforts, Fred Nelson's new strategy has resulted in stable profits and annual sales in excess of $8 million, up from $6.8 million before Wal-Mart came to town.

Discussion Questions

1. Discuss how a development in a corporation's societal environment can affect the corporation through its task environment.
2. According to Porter, what determines the level of competitive intensity in an industry?
3. According to Porter's discussion of industry analysis, is Pepsi Cola a substitute for Coca-Cola?
4. How can a strategic decision maker identify strategic factors in the corporation's external environment?
5. Compare and contrast trend extrapolation with the writing of scenarios as forecasting techniques.

Key Terms (listed in order of appearance)

environmental uncertainty
environmental scanning
societal environment
task environment
industry analysis
multinational corporation (MNC)
triad
strategic myopia
issues priority matrix
external strategic factors

industry
new entrants
entry barriers
rivalry
substitute products
bargaining power of buyers & suppliers
bargaining power of other stakeholders
fragmented industries
consolidated industries
multidomestic industry

global industry
strategic group
strategic type
hypercompetition
industry matrix
competitive intelligence

extrapolation
brainstorming
statistical modeling
scenarios
industry scenario
EFAS Table

Notes

1. J. B. Thomas, S. M. Clark, and D. A. Gioia, "Strategic Sensemaking and Organizational Performance: Linkages Among Scanning, Interpretation, Action, and Outcomes," *Academy of Management Journal* (April 1993): 239–270.
2. K. Ohmae, "The Triad World View," *Journal of Business Strategy* (spring 1987): 8–19
3. M. E. Porter, *Competitive Strategy* (New York: Free Press, 1980), 3.
4. This summary of the forces driving competitive strategy is taken from Porter, *Competitive Strategy,* pp. 7–29
5. Ibid., p. 23.
6. M. E. Porter, "Changing Patterns of International Competition," *California Management Review* (winter 1986): 9–40.
7. K. J. Hatten, and M. L. Hatten, "Strategic Groups, Asymmetrical Mobility Barriers,
   and Contestability," *Strategic Management Journal* (July–August 1987): 329.
8. R. E. Miles, and C. C. Snow, *Organizational Strategy, Structure, and Process* (New York: McGraw-Hill, 1978).
9. R. A. D'Aveni, *Hypercompetition* (New York: Free Press, 1994), xii–xiv.
10. R. T. Pascale, "Perspective on Strategy: The Real Story Behind Honda's Success," *California Management Review* (spring 1981): 70.
11. H. E. Klein, and R. E. Linneman, "Environmental Assessment: An International Study of Corporate Practices," *Journal of Business Strategy* (summer 1984): 72.
12. This process of scenario development is adapted from M. E. Porter, *Competitive Advantage* (New York: Free Press, 1985), 448–470.

CHAPTER 4

INTERNAL SCANNING: ORGANIZATIONAL ANALYSIS

A man stands before his mirror and, as he does many times a week, prepares to shave. After applying shaving cream, he deliberately shaves only one side of his face. He then changes razors to do the other side. He runs his fingers over his cheeks to check the closeness of the shave. "That's the only way to really compare shaves," he comments. This is a typical morning for Alfred Zeien, Chairman and Chief Executive Officer of Gillette Company, who routinely tests his company's razors against those of his competition.

Gillette is a company obsessed with shaving and with making the best razors. It routinely spends large amounts of money on research and development. At any given time, Gillette is working on as many as 20 experimental razors. Why does this company spend so much time and money on a product so simple and as mundane as a razor? The answer lies in Gillette's dedication to being not only the best in its field, but also in designing razors that are difficult for its competitors to copy. In the days of the double-edge razor, others could make blades that fit Gillette's, as well as their own, razors relatively easily. Trac II and the Sensor razor changed things; it took some time for rivals to imitate these products. The Sensor design, in particular, was very difficult to copy, partially because the manufacturing equipment needed to produce it was so expensive and complicated. This gave Gillette the competitive advantage it needed to dominate the marketplace.

4.1 RESOURCE-BASED VIEW OF THE FIRM

Scanning and analyzing the external environment for opportunities and threats is not enough to provide an organization a competitive advantage. Strategic managers must also look within the corporation itself to identify *internal strategic factors:* those critical strengths and weaknesses that are likely to determine if the firm will be able to take advantage of opportunities while avoiding threats. This internal scanning is often referred to as *organizational analysis* and is concerned with identifying and developing an organization's resources.

HOW DO RESOURCES DETERMINE COMPETITIVE ADVANTAGE?

Proposing that a company's sustained competitive advantage is primarily determined by its resource endowments, Grant proposes a five-step, resource-based approach to strategy analysis:

1. Identify and classify the firm's resources in terms of strengths and weaknesses.
2. Combine the firm's strengths into specific capabilities. These are *core competencies:* the things that a corporation can do exceedingly well.
3. Appraise the profit potential of these resources and competencies in terms of their potential for sustainable competitive advantage and the ability to harvest the profits resulting from the use of these resources and capabilities.
4. Select the strategy that best exploits the firm's resources and competencies relative to external opportunities.
5. Identify resource gaps and invest in upgrading weaknesses.[1]

When an organization's resources are combined into capabilities, they form a number of core competencies. In the example provided earlier, Gillette has two identifiable resources: (1) the technology itself, and (2) the capability for developing and using new technological resources. These formed Gillette's core competency of product development. A *distinctive competency* is a core competency that is superior to those of the competition. Since Gillette's ability to develop new products was superior to any of its competitors, its product development was also a distinctive competency.

WHAT DETERMINES THE SUSTAINABILITY OF AN ADVANTAGE?

The ability of a firm to use its resources and capabilities to develop a competitive advantage through distinctive competencies does not mean it will be able to sustain it. Two basic characteristics determine the sustainability of a firm's distinctive competencies: durability and imitability.

Durability is the rate at which a firm's underlying resources and capabilities (core competencies) depreciate or become obsolete. New technology can make a company's core competency obsolete or irrelevant. For example, Intel's skills in using basic technology developed by others to manufacture and market quality microprocessors was a crucial capability until management realized that the firm had taken current technology as far as possible with the Pentium chip. Without basic R&D of its own, it would slowly lose its competitive advantage to others.

Imitability is the rate at which a firm's underlying resources and capabilities (core competencies) can be duplicated by others. To the extent that a firm's distinctive competency gives it competitive advantage in the marketplace, competitors will do what they can to imitate that set of skills and capabilities. Competitors' efforts may range from reverse engineering to hiring employees from the competitor to outright patent infringement. A core competency can be easily imitated to the extent that it is transparent, transferable, and replicable.

- **Transparency.** The speed with which other firms can understand the relationship of resources and capabilities supporting a successful firm's strategy. For example, Gillette has always supported its dominance in the marketing of razors with excellent R&D. A competitor could never understand how the Sensor razor was produced simply by taking one apart. Gillette's Sensor razor design was very difficult to copy, partially because the manufacturing equipment needed to produce it was so expensive and complicated.
- **Transferability.** The ability of competitors to gather the resources and capabilities necessary to support a competitive challenge. For example, it may be very difficult for a wine maker to duplicate a French winery's key resources of land and climate, especially if the imitator is located in Iowa.
- **Replicability.** The ability of competitors to use duplicated resources and capabilities to imitate the other firm's success. For example, even though many companies have tried to imitate the success of Procter & Gamble (P&G) with brand management by hiring brand managers away from P&G, they have often failed to duplicate P&G's success. The competitors failed to identify less visible P&G coordination mechanisms or to realize that P&G's brand management style conflicted with the competitor's own corporate culture.

A *continuum of resource sustainability* is composed of an organization's resources and capabilities characterized by their durability and imitability (that is, they aren't transparent, transferable, or replicable). This continuum is depicted in Figure 4.1. At one extreme are slow-cycle resources, which are sustainable because they are shielded by patents, geography, strong brand names, and the like. These resources and capabilities are distinctive competencies because they provide a sustainable competitive advantage. Gillette's Sensor razor is a good example of a product built around slow-cycle resources.

FIGURE 4.1 Continuum of Resource Sustainability

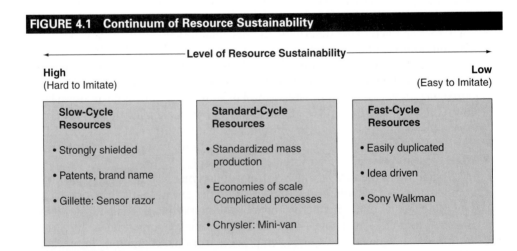

Source: Suggested by J. R. Williams, "How Sustainable Is Your Competitive Advantage?" *California Management Review* (Spring 1992), p. 33.

The other extreme includes fast-cycle resources, which face the highest imitation pressures because they are based on a concept or technology that can be easily duplicated, such as Sony's Walkman. To the extent that a company has fast-cycle resources, the primary way it can compete successfully is through increased speed from lab to marketplace. Otherwise, it has no real sustainable competitive advantage.

With its low-cost position, reputation for safe, on-time flights, and its dedicated workforce, Southwest Airlines has successfully built a sustainable competitive advantage based on relatively slow-cycle resources: resources that are durable and cannot be easily imitated because they lack transparency, transferability, and replicability.

4.2 VALUE-CHAIN ANALYSIS

A *value chain* is a linked set of value-creating activities beginning with basic raw materials coming from suppliers, moving on to a series of value-added activities involved in producing and marketing a product or service, and ending with distributors getting the final goods into the hands of the ultimate consumer. See Figure 4.2 for an example of a typical value chain for a manufactured product. The focus of value-chain analysis is to examine the corporation in the context of the overall chain of value-creating activities, of which the firm may only be a small part.

INDUSTRY VALUE-CHAIN ANALYSIS

The value chains of most industries can be split into two segments, upstream and downstream halves. In the petroleum industry, for example, upstream refers to oil exploration, drilling, and moving the crude oil to the refinery, whereas downstream refers to refining the oil plus the transporting and marketing of gasoline and refined oil to distributors and gas station retailers. Even though most large oil companies are completely integrated, they often vary in the amount of expertise they have at each part of the value chain. Texaco, for example, has its greatest expertise downstream in marketing and retailing. Others, such as British Petroleum, are more dominant in upstream activities like exploration.

In analyzing the complete value chain of a product, note that even if a firm operates up and down the entire industry chain, it usually has an area of primary expertise where its primary activities lie. A company's *center of gravity* is that part of the chain that is most important to the company and the point where its greatest expertise and capabilities, its core competencies, lie. According to Galbraith, a company's center of

---

FIGURE 4.2   Typical Value Chain for a Manufactured Product

Raw Materials → Primary Manufacturing → Fabrication → Product Producer → Distributor → Retailer

Source: Suggested by J. R. Galbraith, "Strategy and Organization Planning," in *The Strategy Process: Concepts, Contexts, Cases,* 2nd ed., edited by H. Mintzberg and J. B. Quinn (Englewood Cliffs, N.J.: Prentice Hall, 1991), p. 316

gravity is usually the point at which the company started.[2] After a firm successfully establishes itself at this point by obtaining a competitive advantage, one of its first strategic moves is to move forward or backward along the value chain in order to reduce costs, guarantee access to key raw materials, or to guarantee distribution. This process is called vertical integration.

CORPORATE VALUE-CHAIN ANALYSIS

Each corporation has its own internal value chain of activities. Porter proposes that a manufacturing firm's primary activities usually begin with inbound logistics (raw materials handling and warehousing), go through an operations process in which a product is manufactured, and continue on to outbound logistics (warehousing and distribution), marketing and sales, and finally to service (installation, repair, and sale of parts). Several support activities, such as procurement (purchasing), technology development (R&D), human resource management, and firm infrastructure (accounting, finance, strategic planning), ensure that the primary value-chain activities operate effectively and efficiently. Each of a company's product lines has its own distinctive value chain. Because most corporations make several different products or services, an internal analysis of the firm involves analyzing a series of different value chains.

The systematic examination of individual value activities can lead to a better understanding of a corporation's strengths and weaknesses. According to Porter, "Differences among competitor value chains are a key source of competitive advantage."[3] Corporate value-chain analysis involves the following steps:

1. Examine each product line's value chain in terms of the various activities involved in producing that product or service. Which activities can be considered strengths or weaknesses?

2. Examine the "linkages" within each product line's value chain. *Linkages* are the connections between the way one value activity (for example, marketing) is performed and the cost of performance of another activity (for example, quality control). In seeking ways for a corporation to gain competitive advantage in the marketplace, the same function can be performed in different ways with different results. For example, quality inspection of 100 percent of output by the workers themselves instead of the usual 10 percent by quality control inspectors might increase production costs, but that increase could be more than offset by the savings obtained from reducing the number of repair people needed to fix defective products and increasing the amount of time devoted by salespeople to selling instead of exchanging already-sold, but defective, products.

3. Examine the potential synergies among the value chains of different product lines or business units. Each value element, such as advertising or manufacturing, has an inherent economy of scale in which activities are conducted at their lowest possible cost per unit of output. If a particular product is not being produced at a high enough level to reach economies of scale in distribution, another product could be used to share the same distribution channel. This is a way to achieve economies of scope (defined later in the chapter). For example, the cost of joint production of multiple products can be less than the cost of separate production.

4.3 SCANNING INTERNAL RESOURCES

The simplest way to begin an analysis of a corporation's value chain is by carefully examining its traditional functional areas for strengths and weaknesses. Functional resources include not only the financial, physical, and human assets in each area, but also the ability of the people in each area to formulate and implement the necessary functional objectives, strategies, and policies. The resources include the knowledge of analytical concepts and procedural techniques common to each area and the ability of the people in each area to use them effectively. If used properly, these resources serve as strengths to carry out value-added activities and support strategic decisions. In addition to the usual business functions of marketing, finance, R&D, operations, human resources, and information systems, we also discuss structure and culture as key parts of a business corporation's value chain.

A functional resource is a strength if it provides a company with a competitive advantage. It is something the firm does or has the potential to do particularly well relative to the abilities of existing or potential competitors. A functional resource is a weakness if it is something the corporation does poorly or doesn't have the capacity to do although its competitors have that capacity. Evaluate the importance of these resources to ascertain if they are internal strategic factors, the particular strengths and weaknesses that will help determine the future of the company. This can be done by comparing measures of these variables with measures of (1) the company's past performance, (2) the company's key competitors, and (3) the industry as a whole. To the extent that a functional resource (such as a firm's financial situation) is significantly different than it was in the firm's past, from its key competitors, or from the industry average, that variable is likely to be a strategic factor and should be considered in strategic decisions.

WHAT ARE THE TYPICAL ORGANIZATIONAL STRUCTURES?

Although an almost infinite variety of structural forms are possible, certain basic types predominate in modern complex organizations. Figure 4.3 illustrates three basic structures: simple, functional, and divisional. Strategic business units and the conglomerate structure are variants of divisional structure and are thus not depicted. Generally speaking, each structure tends to support some corporate strategies over others.

- **Simple structure** has no functional or product categories and is appropriate for a small, entrepreneur-dominated company with one or two product lines that operates in a reasonably small, easily identifiable market niche. Employees tend to be generalists and jacks-of-all-trades.
- **Functional structure** is appropriate for a medium-sized firm with several product lines in one industry. Employees tend to be specialists in the business functions important to that industry, such as manufacturing, marketing, finance, and human resources.
- **Divisional structure** is appropriate for a large corporation with many product lines in several related industries. Employees tend to be functional specialists organized according to product/market distinctions. General Motors, for example, groups its various auto lines into the separate divisions of

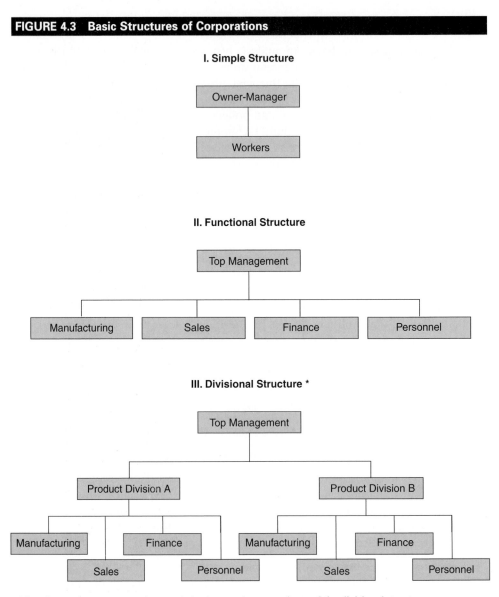

FIGURE 4.3 Basic Structures of Corporations

*Conglomerate structure and strategic business units are variants of the divisional structure.

Chevrolet, Pontiac, Oldsmobile, Buick, and Cadillac. Management attempts to find some synergy among divisional activities through the use of committees and horizontal linkages.

- **Strategic business units (SBUs)** are a recent modification to the divisional structure. Strategic business units are divisions or groups of divisions composed of independent product-market segments that are given primary responsibility and authority for the management of their own functional areas. An SBU may be of any size or level, but it must have (1) a unique mission, (2) identifiable competitors, (3) an external market focus, and (4) control of its business functions.[4] The idea is to decentralize on the basis of strategic elements rather than on the basis of size, product characteristics, or span of control and to create horizontal linkages among units previously kept separate. For example, rather than organize products on the basis of packaging technology like frozen foods, canned foods, and bagged foods, General Foods organized its products into SBUs on the basis of consumer-oriented menu segments: breakfast food, beverage, main meal, dessert, and pet foods.

- **Conglomerate structure** is appropriate for a large corporation with many product lines in several unrelated industries. A variant of the divisional structure, the conglomerate structure (sometimes called a holding company) is typically an assemblage of legally independent firms (subsidiaries) operating under one corporate umbrella but controlled through the respective subsidiaries' boards of directors. The unrelated nature of the subsidiaries prevents any attempt at gaining synergy among them.

If the current basic structure of a corporation does not easily support a strategy under consideration, top management must decide if the proposed strategy is feasible or if the structure should be changed to a more advanced structure such as the matrix or network. (Advanced structural designs are discussed in chapter 8.)

WHAT IS CORPORATE CULTURE?

Corporate culture is the collection of beliefs, expectations, and values learned and shared by a corporation's members and transmitted from one generation of employees to another. The term corporate culture generally reflects the values of the founder(s) and the mission of the firm. It gives a company a sense of identity: "This is who we are. This is what we do. This is what we stand for." The culture includes the dominant orientation of the company, such as research and development at Hewlett-Packard, customer service at Nordstrom's, or product quality at Maytag.

Corporate culture has two distinct attributes, intensity and integration.[5] *Cultural intensity* (or depth) is the degree to which members of a unit accept the norms, values, or other culture content associated with the unit. Organizations with strong norms promoting a particular value, such as quality at Maytag, have intensive cultures, whereas new firms (or those in transition) have weaker, less intensive cultures. Employees of a company with an intensive culture tend to exhibit consistency in behavior, that is, they tend to act similarly over time. *Cultural integration* (or breadth) is the extent to which units throughout an organization share a common culture. Organizations with a pervasive dominant culture, such as a military unit, may be hierarchically controlled and power oriented and have highly integrated cultures. All employees tend to hold the same cultural values and norms. In contrast, a company that is structured into diverse units by functions or divisions usually exhibits some strong subcultures (e.g., R&D versus manufacturing) and an overall weaker corporate culture.

Corporate culture fulfills several important functions in an organization:

1. Culture conveys a sense of identity for employees.
2. Culture helps generate employees' commitment to something greater than themselves.
3. Culture adds to the stability of the organization as a social system.
4. Culture serves as a frame of reference for employees to use to make sense out of organizational activities and to use as a guide for appropriate behavior.[6]

Corporate culture shapes the behavior of people in the corporation. Because these cultures have a powerful influence on the behavior of managers at all levels, they can strongly affect a corporation's ability to shift its strategic direction. A strong culture should not only promote survival, but should also create the basis for a superior competitive position. To the extent that a critical capability is embedded in an organization's culture, it will be very hard for a competitor to duplicate it.

A change in mission, objectives, strategies, or policies is not likely to be successful if it goes against the firm's accepted culture. Foot-dragging and even sabotage may result, as employees fight to resist a radical change in corporate philosophy. Like structure, if an organization's culture is compatible with a new strategy, it is an internal strength. But if the corporate culture is not compatible with the proposed strategy, it is a serious weakness.

WHAT ARE THE STRATEGIC MARKETING ISSUES?

The marketing manager is the company's primary link to the customer and the competition. The manager must therefore be especially concerned with the firm's market position and marketing mix.

WHAT ARE MARKET POSITION AND SEGMENTATION?

Market position refers to the selection of specific areas for marketing concentration and can be expressed in terms of market, product, and geographical locations. Through market research, corporations are able to practice *market segmentation*: tailoring products for specific market niches.

WHAT IS MARKETING MIX?

The *marketing mix* is the particular combination of key variables under the corporation's control that it can use to affect demand and to gain competitive advantage. These variables are product, place, promotion, and price. Within each of these four variables are several subvariables, listed in Table 4.1, that should be analyzed in terms of their effects on divisional and corporate performance.

WHAT IS THE PRODUCT LIFE CYCLE?

One of the most useful concepts in marketing insofar as strategic management is concerned is that of the product life cycle. As depicted in Figure 4.4, the *product life cycle* is a graph showing time plotted against the dollar sales of a product as it moves from introduction through growth and maturity to decline. This concept enables a marketing manager to examine the marketing mix of a particular product or group of products in terms of its position in its life cycle.

TABLE 4.1 Marketing Mix Variables			
Product	*Place*	*Promotion*	*Price*
Quality	Channels	Advertising	List price
Features	Coverage	Personal selling	Discounts
Options	Locations	Sales promotion	Allowances
Style	Inventory	Publicity	Payment periods
Brand name	Transport		Credit terms
Packaging			
Sizes			
Services			
Warranties			
Returns			

Source: Philip Kotler, *Marketing Management: Analysis, Planning, and Control,* 4th ed. (Englewood Cliffs, N.J.: Prentice-Hall, 1980), p. 89. Copyright (c) 1980. Reprinted by permission of Prentice-Hall, Inc.

WHAT ARE THE STRATEGIC FINANCIAL ISSUES?

The financial manager must ascertain the best sources of funds, uses of funds, and control of funds. Cash must be raised from internal or external sources and allocated for different uses. The flow of funds in the operations of the organization must be monitored. To the extent that a corporation is involved in international activities, currency fluctuations must be dealt with to ensure that profits aren't wiped out by the rise or fall

FIGURE 4.4   The Product Life Cycle

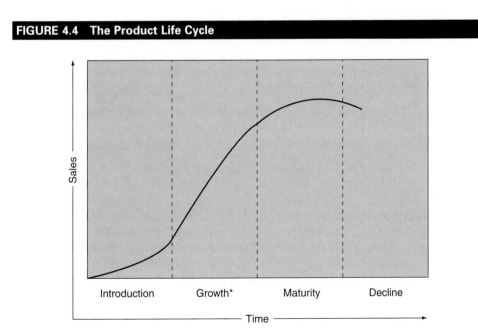

*The right end of the Growth stage is often called Competitive Turbulence because of price and distribution competition that shakes out the weaker competitors. For further information, see C. R. Wasson, *Dynamic Competitive Strategy and Product Life Cycles,* 3rd ed. (Austin, Tex.: Austin Press, 1978).

of the dollar versus the yen, Deutsche mark, and other currencies. Benefits, in the form of returns, repayments, or products and services, must be given to the sources of outside financing. All these tasks must be handled in a way that complements and supports overall corporate strategy.

WHAT IS FINANCIAL LEVERAGE?

The mix of externally generated short-term and long-term funds in relation to the amount and timing of internally generated funds should be appropriate to the corporate objectives, strategies, and policies. The concept of *financial leverage* (the ratio of total debt to total assets) helps describe the use of debt (versus equity) to finance the company's programs from outside. Financing company activities by selling bonds or notes instead of through issuing stock boosts earnings per share: the interest paid on the debt reduces taxable income, but fewer stockholders share the profits. The debt, however, does raise the firm's break-even point above what it would have been if the firm had financed from internally generated funds only. High leverage may therefore be perceived as a corporate strength in times of prosperity and ever-increasing sales or as a weakness in times of a recession and falling sales because leverage magnifies the effect of an increase or decrease in dollar sales on earnings per share.

WHAT IS CAPITAL BUDGETING?

Capital budgeting is the analyzing and ranking of possible investments in fixed assets such as land, buildings, and equipment in terms of the additional outlays and additional receipts that will result from each investment. A good finance department will be able to prepare such capital budgets and to rank them on the basis of some accepted criteria or hurdle rate (for example, years to pay back investment, rate of return, or time to break-even point) for the purpose of strategic decision making.

WHAT ARE THE STRATEGIC RESEARCH AND DEVELOPMENT (R&D) ISSUES?

The R&D manager is responsible for suggesting and implementing a company's technological strategy in light of its corporate objectives and policies. The manager's job therefore involves (1) choosing among alternative new technologies to use within the corporation, (2) developing methods of embodying the new technology in new products and processes, and (3) deploying resources so that the new technology can be successfully implemented.

WHAT ARE R&D INTENSITY, TECHNOLOGICAL COMPETENCE, AND TECHNOLOGY TRANSFER?

The company must make available the resources necessary for effective research and development. A company's *R&D intensity* (its spending on R&D as a percentage of sales revenue) is a principal means of gaining market share in global competition. The amount spent on R&D often varies by industry. For example, the computer software and drug industries spend an average of 13.2 percent and 11.5 percent, respectively, of their sales dollar for R&D. A good rule of thumb for R&D spending is that a corporation should spend at a "normal" rate for that particular industry.

Simply spending money on R&D or new projects does not mean, however, that the money will produce useful results. A company's R&D unit should be evaluated for *technological competence,* the proper management of technology, in both the development and the use of innovative technology. Not only should the corporation make a consistent research effort (as measured by reasonably constant corporate expenditures that result in usable innovations), it should also be proficient in managing research personnel and integrating their innovations into its day-to-day operations. If a company is not proficient in *technology transfer,* the process of taking a new technology from the laboratory to the marketplace, it will not gain much advantage from new technological advances. For example, Xerox Corporation has been criticized because it failed to take advantage of various innovations (such as the mouse and the graphical user interface for personal computers) developed originally in its sophisticated Palo Alto Research Center.

WHAT IS THE R&D MIX?

Research and development includes basic, product, and engineering or process R&D. *Basic R&D* focuses on theoretical problem areas and is typically undertaken by scientists in well-equipped laboratories. The best indicators of a company's capability in this area are its patents and research publications. *Product R&D* concentrates on marketing and is concerned with product or product-packaging improvements. The best measurements of ability in this area are the number of successful new products introduced and the percentage of total sales and profits coming from products introduced within the past 5 years. *Engineering or process R&D* is concerned with engineering and concentrates on improving quality control, design specifications, and production equipment. A company's capability in this area can be measured by consistent reductions in unit manufacturing costs and product defects. Most corporations have a mix of basic, product, and process R&D, which varies by industry, company, and product line. The *R&D mix* is the balance of the three types of research. The mix should be appropriate to the strategy being considered and to each product's life cycle. For example, it is generally accepted that product R&D normally dominates the early stages of a product's life cycle (when the product's optimal form and features are still being debated), whereas process R&D becomes especially important in the later stages (when the product's design is solidified and the emphasis is on reducing costs and improving quality).

WHAT IS THE IMPACT OF TECHNOLOGICAL DISCONTINUITY ON STRATEGY?

The R&D manager must determine when to abandon present technology and when to develop or adopt new technology. According to Richard Foster of McKinsey and Company, *technological discontinuity* is the displacement of one technology by another. It is a frequent and strategically important phenomenon. Such a discontinuity occurs when a new technology cannot simply be used to enhance the current technology but actually substitutes for that technology to yield better performance. For each technology within a given field or industry, according to Foster, the plotting of product performance against research effort and expenditures on a graph results in an S-shaped curve. He describes the process depicted in Figure 4.5 as follows:

> Early in the development of the technology a knowledge base is being
> built and progress requires a relatively large amount of effort. Later,
> progress comes more easily. And then, as the limits of that technology are
> approached, progress becomes slow and expensive. That is when R&D

FIGURE 4.5 Technological Discontinuity

What the S-Curves Reveal

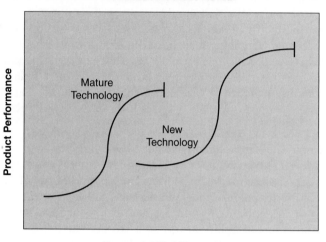

In the corporate planning process, it is generally assumed that incremental progress in technology will occur. But past developments in a given technology cannot be extrapolated into the future, because every technology has its limits. The key to competitiveness is to determine when to shift resources to a technology with more potential.

Source: P. Pascarella, "Are You Investing in the Wrong Technology?" *Industry Week* (July 25, 1983), p. 38. Copyright © 1983 Penton/IPC. All rights reserved. Reprinted by permission.

dollars should be allocated to technology with more potential. That is also—not so incidentally—when a competitor who has bet on a new technology can sweep away your business or topple an entire industry.[7]

The presence of a technological discontinuity in the world's steel industry during the 1960s explains why the large capital expenditures by U.S. steel companies failed to keep them competitive with the Japanese firms, which adopted the new technologies. As Foster points out, "History has shown that as one technology nears the end of its S curve, competitive leadership in a market generally changes hands."[8]

WHAT ARE THE STRATEGIC OPERATIONS ISSUES?

The primary task of the operations (manufacturing or service) manager is to develop and operate a system that will produce the required number of products or services, with a certain quality, at a given cost, within an allotted time. Many of the key concepts and techniques popularly used in manufacturing can be applied to service businesses. In general terms, manufacturing can be intermittent or continuous. In *intermittent systems* (job shops), the item is normally processed sequentially, but the work and sequence of the process vary. At each location, the tasks determine the details of processing and the time required for them. In contrast, *continuous systems* are those laid out as lines on which products can be continuously assembled or processed. An example is an automobile assembly line.

The type of manufacturing system that a corporation uses determines divisional or corporate strategy. It makes no sense, for example, to plan to increase sales by saturating the market with low-priced products if the company's manufacturing process was designed as an intermittent job shop system that produces one-time-only products to a customer's specifications. Conversely, a plan to produce several specialty products might not be economically feasible if the manufacturing process was designed to be a mass-producing, continuous system using low-skilled labor or special-purpose robots.

WHAT IS THE EXPERIENCE CURVE?

A conceptual framework that many large corporations have used successfully is the experience curve (originally called the learning curve). The *experience curve* suggests that unit production costs decline by some fixed percentage (commonly 20–30 percent) each time the total accumulated volume of production (in units) doubles. The actual percentage varies by industry and is based on many variables: the amount of time it takes a person to learn a new task, scale economies, product and process improvements, and lower raw materials costs, among others. For example, in an industry with an 85 percent experience curve, a corporation might expect a 15 percent reduction in costs for every doubling of volume. The total costs per unit can be expected to drop from $100 when the total production is 10 units, to $85 ($100 × 85 percent) when production increases to 20 units, and to $72.25 ($85 × 85 percent) when it reaches 40 units. Achieving these results often means investing in R&D and fixed assets, resulting in higher operating leverage and less flexibility. Nevertheless, the manufacturing strategy is to build capacity ahead of demand in order to achieve the lower unit costs that develop from the experience curve. On the basis of some future point on the experience curve, the product or service should be priced very low to preempt competition and increase market demand. The resulting high number of units sold and high market share should result in high profits, based on the low unit costs.

Management commonly uses the experience curve to estimate the production costs of (1) a product never before made with the present techniques and processes or (2) current products produced by newly introduced techniques or processes. The concept was first applied in the airframe industry and can be applied in the service industry as well. Although many firms have used experience curves extensively, an unquestioning acceptance of the industry norm (such as 80 percent for the airframe industry or 70 percent for integrated circuits) is risky. The experience curve of the industry as a whole might not hold true for a particular company for a variety of reasons.

WHAT IS FLEXIBLE MANUFACTURING?

The use of large mass-production facilities to take advantage of experience-curve economies has been criticized. The use of Computer-Assisted Design and Computer-Assisted Manufacturing (CAD/CAM) and robot technology allows learning times to be shorter and products to be economically manufactured in small, customized batches. *Economies of scope* (in which common parts of the manufacturing activities of various products are combined to gain economies even though small numbers of each product are made) replace *economies of scale* (in which unit costs are reduced by making large numbers of the same product) in flexible manufacturing. *Flexible manufacturing* permits the low-volume output of custom-tailored products at relatively low unit costs through economies of scope. It is thus possible to have the cost advantages of continuous systems with the customer-oriented advantages of intermittent systems.

WHAT ARE THE STRATEGIC HUMAN RESOURCE ISSUES?

The primary task of the manager of human resources is to improve the match between individuals and jobs. A good human resource management (HRM) department should know how to use attitude surveys and other feedback devices to assess employees' satisfaction with their jobs and with the corporation as a whole. HRM managers should also use job analysis to obtain job description information about what each job needs to accomplish in terms of quality and quantity. Up-to-date job descriptions are essential not only for proper employee selection, appraisal, training, and development; wage and salary administration; and labor negotiations; but also for summarizing the corporate-wide human resources in terms of employee-skill categories. Just as a company must know the number, type, and quality of its manufacturing facilities, it must also know the kinds of people it employs and the skills they possess. The best strategies are meaningless if employees do not have the skills to carry them out or if jobs cannot be designed to accommodate the available workers. Hewlett-Packard, for example, uses employee profiles to ensure that it has the right mix of talents for implementing its planned strategies.

HOW SHOULD TEAMS BE USED?

Management is beginning to realize that it must be more flexible in its utilization of employees in order for human resources to be a strength. Human resource managers therefore need to be knowledgeable about work options such as part-time work, job sharing, flextime, extended leaves, contract work, and especially in the proper use of teams. Over two-thirds of large U.S. companies are successfully using *autonomous work teams* in which a group of people work together without a supervisor to plan, coordinate, and evaluate their own work. Nevertheless, only 10 percent of the workers of these companies are currently in these teams.[9] Productivity and quality increased to such an extent at Northern Telecom that the company was able to reduce the number of quality inspectors by 40 percent.[10]

As a way to move a product more quickly through its development stage, companies like Motorola, Chrysler, NCR, Boeing, and General Electric have begun using *cross-functional* work teams. Instead of developing products in a series of steps, beginning with a request from sales, which leads to design, to engineering, to purchasing, and finally to manufacturing (often resulting in customer rejection of a costly product), companies are tearing down the traditional walls separating departments so that people from each discipline can get involved in projects early on. In a process called *concurrent engineering,* the once-isolated specialists now work side by side and compare notes constantly in an effort to design cost-effective products with features customers want.

HOW IMPORTANT ARE UNION RELATIONS?

If the corporation is unionized, a good human resource manager should be able to work closely with the union. Although union membership in the United States in the mid-1990s had dropped to less than 10 percent of private-sector workers from over 23 percent in the 1970s, unions still represented around 20 percent of workers in the manufacturing industry in the United States.[11] To save jobs, U.S. unions are increasingly willing to support employee involvement programs designed to increase worker participation in decision making. Outside the United States, however, the average proportion of unionized workers among major industrialized nations is around 50 percent. These differences have significant implications for the management of multinational corporations.

How Important Is Diversity?

Human diversity is the mix in the workplace of people from different races, cultures, and backgrounds. This is a hot issue in HRM. Realizing that the demographics are changing toward an increasing percentage of minorities and women in the U.S. workforce, companies are now concerned with hiring and promoting people without regard to ethnic background. Good human resource managers should be working to ensure that people are treated fairly on the job and not harassed by prejudiced co-workers or managers.

An organization's human resources are especially important in today's world of global communication and transportation systems. Competitors around the world copy advances in technology almost immediately. Because people are not as willing to move to other companies in other countries, the only long-term resource advantage remaining to corporations operating in the industrialized nations may lie in the area of skilled human resources.

What Are the Strategic Information Systems Issues?

The primary task of the manager of information systems (also called information technology) is to design and manage the flow of information in an organization in ways that improve productivity and decision making. Information must be collected, stored, and synthesized in such a manner that it can answer important operating and strategic questions. This function is growing in importance.

A corporation's information system can be a strength or a weakness in all three elements of strategic management. Not only can it aid in environmental scanning and in controlling a company's many activities, it can also be used as a strategic weapon in gaining competitive advantage. For example, American Hospital Supply (AHS), a leading manufacturer and distributor of a broad line of products for doctors, laboratories, and hospitals, developed an order-entry distribution system that directly linked the majority of its customers to AHS computers. The system was successful because it simplified ordering processes for customers, reduced costs for both AHS and the customer, and allowed AHS to provide pricing incentives to the customer. As a result, customer loyalty was high and AHS's share of the market grew.

A trend in corporate information systems is the increasing use of the *internet* (electronic communication between people and organizations via the World Wide Web) for marketing and intranets for internal communication. For example, Federal Express found that by allowing customers to directly access its package-tracking database via the FedEx Web site instead of having to ask a human operator, the company saved up to $2 million annually. An *intranet* is an information network within an organization that also has access to the external worldwide internet. The percentage of large and midsize firms using an intranet has soared to beyond 55 percent from just 11 percent in 1995. Intranets typically begin as ways to provide employees with company information such as lists of product prices, fringe benefits, and company policies. The networks are then gradually extended to major suppliers and customers so as to include key players in a product's value chain. More companies are taking the next step: to allow employees, customers, and suppliers to conduct business on the Internet in a completely automated manner. By connecting these groups, companies hope to obtain a competitive advantage by reducing the time needed to design and bring new products to market, slashing inventories, customizing manufacturing, and entering new markets.

4.4 SYNTHESIS OF INTERNAL FACTORS: IFAS

Once strategists have scanned the internal organizational environment and identified factors for their particular corporation, they may wish to summarize their analysis of these factors using a form such as that given in Table 4.2. This Internal Factor Analysis Summary (IFAS) Table is one way to organize the internal factors into the generally accepted categories of strengths and weaknesses and to analyze how well a particular

TABLE 4.2 Internal Factor Analysis Summary (IFAS): Maytag as Example

Internal Factors	1	Weight 2	Rating 3	Weighted Score 4	Weighted Comments	5
Strengths						
• Quality Maytag culture		.15	5	.75	Quality key to success	
• Experienced top management		.05	4	.20	Know appliances	
• Vertical integration		.10	4	.40	Dedicated factories	
• Employee relations		.05	3	.15	Good, but deteriorating	
• Hoover's international orientation		.15	3	.45	Hoover name in cleaners	
Weaknesses						
• Process-oriented R&D		.05	2	.10	Slow on new products	
• Distribution channels		.05	2	.10	Superstores replacing small dealers	
• Financial position		.15	2	.30	High debt load	
• Global positioning		.20	2	.40	Hoover weak outside the United Kingdom and Australia	
• Manufacturing facilities		.05	4	.20	Investing now	
Total		1.00		3.05		

Notes:

1. List strengths and weaknesses (5-10 each) in Column 1.

2. Weight each factor from 1.0 (Most Important) to 0.0 (Not Important) in Column 2 based on that factor's probable impact on the company's stategic position. The total weight must sum to 1.00.

3. Rate each factor from 5 (Outstanding) to 1 (Poor) in Column 3 based on the company's response to that factor.

4. Multiply each factor's weight times its rating to obtain each factor's weighted score in Column 4.

5. Use Column 5 (comments) for rationale used for each factor.

6. Add the weighted scores to obtain the total weighted score for the company in Column 4. This tells how well the company is responding to the factors in its internal environment.

Source: T. L. Wheelen and J. D. Hunger, "Internal Factor Analysis Summary (IFAS)." Copyright © 1991 by Wheelen and Hunger Associates. Reprinted by permission.

company's management is responding to these specific factors in light of the perceived importance of these factors to the company. To use the IFAS Matrix, complete the following steps for the company being analyzed:

- In column 1 (*Internal Factors*), list the 8 to 10 most important strengths and weaknesses facing the company.
- In column 2 (*Weight*), assign a weight to each factor from 1.0 (most important) to 0.0 (not important) based on that factor's probable impact on a particular company's current strategic position. The higher the weight, the more important this factor is to the current and future success of the company. (All weights must sum to 1.00 regardless of the number of strategic factors.)
- In column 3 (*Rating*), assign a rating to each factor from 5 (outstanding) to 1 (poor) based on management's current response to that particular factor. Each rating is a judgment regarding how well the company's management is currently managing each internal factor.

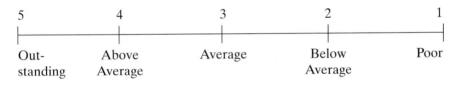

- In column 4 (*Weighted Score*), multiply the weight in column 2 for each factor times its rating in column 3 to obtain that factor's *weighted score*. This results in a weighted score for each factor ranging from 5.0 (outstanding) to 1.0 (poor) with 3.0 as average.
- In column 5 (*Comments*), note why a particular factor was selected and how its weight and rating were estimated.
- Finally, add the weighted scores for all the internal factors in column 4 to determine the *total weighted score* for that particular company. The total weighted score indicates how well a particular company is managing current and expected factors in its internal environment. The score can be used to compare that firm to other firms in its industry. The total weighted score for an average firm in an industry is always 3.0.

As an example of this procedure, Table 4.2 includes a number of internal factors for Maytag Corporation with corresponding weights, ratings, and weighted scores provided. It is thus very similar to the EFAS Table (Table 3.3, chapter 3, this book) that summarized external factors. Note that Maytag's total weighted score is 3.05, meaning that the corporation is about average compared to the strengths and weaknesses of other competitors in the U.S. major home appliance industry.

IN CONCLUSION

Animation has always been a distinctive competency at Walt Disney Productions. It has given the company a sustainable competitive advantage over the years because this capability is durable and hard for competitors to imitate. Thanks to its founder, this competency has become embedded in the corporate culture and has become a part of the firm's very identity. Even though the company had expanded from simple cartoons into theme parks and hotels, Walt Disney had always pointed to animation (and especially to Mickey Mouse, his personal creation) as a strategic factor for the company. One of his favorite expressions was "Remember, it all started with a mouse."

Discussion Questions

1. What is the relevance of the resource-based view of the firm to strategic management?

2. In what ways can a corporation's structure and culture be internal strengths or weaknesses?

3. What kind of internal factors help managers decide whether a firm should emphasize the production and sales of a large number of low-priced products or a small number of high-priced products?

4. What are the pros and cons of management's using the experience curve to determine strategy?

5. How might a firm's management decide whether it should continue to invest in current known technology or in new, but untested technology? What factors might encourage or discourage such a shift?

Key Terms (listed in order of appearance)

internal strategic factors
organizational analysis
core competencies
distinctive competence
durability
imitability
continuum of resource sustainability
value chain (industry and corporate)
center of gravity
linkages
simple structure
functional structure
divisional structure
strategic business units
conglomerate structure
corporate culture
cultural intensity
cultural integration
market position
market segmentation
marketing mix

product life cycle
financial leverage
capital budgeting
R&D intensity
technological competence
technology transfer
basic R&D
product R&D
process R&D
R&D mix
technological discontinuity
intermittent systems
continuous systems
experience curve
flexible manufacturing
economies of scale
economies of scope
autonomous work teams
human diversity
Internet/intranet
IFAS Table

Notes

1. R.M. Grant, "The Resource-Based Theory of Competitive Advantage: Implications for Strategy Formulation." *California Management Review* (spring 1991): 114–135.

2. J. R. Galbraith, "Strategy and Organization Planning," in *The Strategy Process: Concepts, Contexts, and Cases,* 2nd ed., edited by H. Mintzberg and J. B. Quinn (Englewood Cliffs, NJ: Prentice Hall, 1991), 315–324.

3. M. Porter, *Competitive Advantage: Creating and Sustaining Superior Performance* (New York: Free Press, 1985), 36.

4. M. Leontiades, "A Diagnostic Framework for Planning," *Strategic Management Journal* (January–March 1983): 14.

5. D. M. Rousseau, "Assessing Organizational Culture: The Case for Multiple Methods," in *Organizational Climate and Culture,* edited by B. Schneider (San Francisco: Jossey-Bass, 1990), 153–192.

6. L. Smircich, "Concepts of Culture and Organizational Analysis," *Administrative Science Quarterly* (September 1983): 345–346.

7. P. Pascarella, "Are You Investing in the Wrong Technology?" *Industry Week* (July 25, 1983): 37.

8. Ibid., p. 38.

9. B. Dumaine, "The Trouble with Teams," *Fortune* (September 5, 1994): 86.

10. A. Versteeg, "Self-Directed Work Teams Yield Long-Term Benefits," *Journal of Business Strategy* (November–December 1990): 9–12.

11. The percentage of unionized government workers is 38.7 percent. See "Uncle Sam Gompers," *Wall Street Journal* (October 25, 1994): A20.

CHAPTER 5

STRATEGY FORMULATION:
SITUATION ANALYSIS
AND BUSINESS STRATEGY

When Donald Lamberti incorporated Casey's General Stores in 1967 in Des Moines, Iowa, he formulated a strategy unknown at that time in the convenience store industry. Instead of targeting the large, growing metropolitan areas of the eastern, western, and southern United States where potential sales were high, he chose to focus on the small towns in the agricultural heartland of the Midwest. Contrary to all the conventional wisdom arguing against beginning a business in a declining market, Lamberti avoided direct competition with Seven-Eleven and moved into these increasingly ignored small markets. The company expanded its offerings from just gasoline and basic groceries to include fast food and bakeries. In many small midwestern towns, Casey's was now the only retail business left. These were towns too small for even Wal-Mart to covet. Like any convenience store, prices were somewhat higher than in larger, more specialized stores in the cities. But small-town people did not want to have to drive 10 to 20 miles for a loaf of bread or a pizza.

By 2000, Casey's had opened 1,118 convenience stores in the upper midwestern United States. At a time when other convenience stores were struggling to show a profit and avoid bankruptcy, Casey's recorded continuing growth and profitability. (For further information, see http://www.caseys.com.)

Casey's General Stores is successful because its management formulated a new strategy designed to give it an advantage in a very competitive industry. Casey's is an example of a differentiation focus competitive strategy in which a company focuses on a particular market area to provide a differentiated product or service. This strategy is one of the business competitive strategies discussed in this chapter.

5.1 SITUATIONAL (SWOT) ANALYSIS

Strategy formulation is often referred to as strategic planning or long-range planning and is concerned with developing a corporation's mission, objectives, strategies, and policies. It begins with situation analysis: the process of finding a strategic fit between external opportunities and internal strengths while working around external threats and internal weaknesses. The following factors summarize the strategic factors for a specific company: strengths, weaknesses, opportunities, and threats (SWOT). SWOT analysis should not only result in the identification of a corporation's distinctive competencies, the particular capabilities and resources a firm possesses and the superior way in which they are used, but also in the identification of opportunities that the firm is not currently able to take advantage of due to a lack of appropriate resources.

HOW GENERATE A STRATEGIC FACTORS ANALYSIS SUMMARY (SFAS)TABLE ?

The strategic factors analysis summary (SFAS) Table summarizes a corporation's strategic factors by combining the *external* factors from the EFAS Table with the *internal* factors from the IFAS Tables. The EFAS and IFAS examples given of Maytag Corporation in Tables 3.3 (chapter 3, this book) and 4.2 (chapter 4, this book) list a total of 20 internal and external factors. These are too many factors for most people to use in strategy formulation. The SFAS Table requires the strategic decision maker to condense these strengths, weaknesses, opportunities, and threats into 10 or fewer strategic factors. This is done by reviewing each of the weights for the individual factors in the EFAS and IFAS Tables. The highest weighted EFAS and IFAS factors should appear in the SFAS Table.

As shown in Figure 5.1, you can create an SFAS Table by following these steps:

- In the *Strategic Factors* column (column 1), list the most important EFAS and IFAS items. After each factor, indicate whether it is a strength (S), weakness (W), opportunity (O), or threat (T).
- In the *Weight* column (column 2), enter the weights for all of the internal and external strategic factors. As with the EFAS and IFAS Tables presented earlier, the weight column must still total 1.00. This means that the weights calculated earlier for EFAS and IFAS will probably have to be adjusted.
- In the *Rating* column (column 3), enter the ratings of how the company's management is responding to each of the strategic factors. These ratings will probably (but not always) be the same as those listed in the EFAS and IFAS Tables.
- In the *Weighted Score* column (column 4), calculate the weighted scores as done earlier for EFAS and IFAS.
- In the new *Duration* column (column 5), depicted in Figure 5.1, indicate short-term (less than 1 year), intermediate-term (1–3 years), or long-term (3 years and beyond).
- In the *Comments* column (column 6), repeat or revise your comments for each strategic factor from the previous EFAS and IFAS Tables.

TABLE 4.2   Internal Factor Analysis Summary (IFAS): Maytag as Example

Internal Factors	Weight	Rating	Weighted Score	Comments
	1	2	3	4
Strengths				
• Quality Maytag culture	.15	5	.75	Quality key to success
• Experienced top management	.05	4	.20	Know appliances
• Vertical integration	.10	4	.40	Dedicated factories
• Employee relations	.05	3	.15	Good, but deteriorating
• Hoover's international orientation	.15	3	.45	Hoover name in cleaners
Weaknesses				
• Process-oriented R&D	.05	2	.10	Slow on new products
• Distribution channels	.05	2	.10	Superstores replacing small dealers
• Financial position	.15	2	.30	High debt load
• Global positioning	.20	2	.40	Hoover weak outside the United Kingdom and Australia
• Manufacturing facilities	.05	4	.20	Investing now
Total	**1.00**		**3.05**	

TABLE 3.3   External Factor Analysis Summary (EFAS): Maytag as Example

External Factors	Weight	Rating	Weighted Score	Comments
	1	2	3	4
Opportunities				
• Economic integration of European Community	.20	4	.80	Acquisition of Hoover
• Demographics favor quality appliances	.10	5	.50	Maytag quality
• Economic development of Asia	.05	1	.05	Low Maytag presence
• Opening of Eastern Europe	.05	2	.10	Will take time
• Trend to "Super Stores"	.10	2	.20	Maytag weak in this channel
Threats				
• Increasing government regulations	.10	4	.40	Well positioned
• Strong U.S. competition	.10	4	.40	Well positioned
• Whirlpool and Electrolux strong globally	.15	3	.45	Hoover weak globally
• New product advances	.05	1	.05	Questionable
• Japanese appliance companies	.10	2	.20	Only Asian presence is Australia
Total	**1.00**		**3.15**	

FIGURE 5.1 Strategic Factor Analysis Summary (SFAS) Matrix

	1	2	3	4	5 Duration			6
Strategic Factors (Select the most important opportunities/threats from EFAS, Table 3.3 and the most important strengths and weaknesses from IFAS, Table 4.2)		**Weight**	**Rating**	**Weighted Score**	**Short**	**Intermediate**	**Long**	**Comments**
• Quality Maytag culture (S)		.10	5	.5			X	Quality key to success
• Hoover's international orientation (S)		.10	3	.3		X		Name recognition
• Financial position (W)		.10	2	.2		X		High debt
• Global positioning (W)		.15	2	.3			X	Only in N.A., U.K., and Australia
• Economic integration of European Community (O)		.10	4	.4			X	Acquisition of Hoover
• Demographics favor quality (O)		.10	5	.5		X		Maytag quality
• Trend to super stores (O + T)		.10	2	.2	X			Weak in this channel
• Whirlpool and Electrolux (T)		.15	3	.45	X			Dominate industry
• Japanese appliance companies (T)		.10	2	.2			X	Asian presence
Total		1.00		3.05				

Notes:

1. List each of the strategic factors developed in your IFAS and EFAS tables in Column 1.

2. Weight each factor from 1.0 (Most Important) to 0.0 (Not Important) in Column 2 based on that factor's probable impact on the company's strategic position. **The total weights must sum to 1.00.**

3. Rate each factor from 5 (Outstanding) to 1 (Poor) in Column 3 based on the company's response to that factor.

4. Multiply each factor's weight times its rating to obtain each factor's weighted score in Column 4.

5. For duration in Column 5, check appropriate column (short term—less than 1 year; intermediate—1 to 3 years; long term—over 3 years.)

6. Use Column 6 (comments) for rationale used for each factor.

7. Add the weighted scores to obtain the total weighted score for the company in Column 4. This tells how well the company is dealing with its strategic factors.

Source: T. J. Wheelen and J. D. Hunger. "Strategic Factor Analysis Summary (SFAS)." Copyright © 1993 by Wheelen and Hunger Associates. Reprinted by permission.

The resulting SFAS Table is a listing of the firm's external and internal strategic factors in one table. The SFAS Table includes only the most important factors and provides the basis for strategy formulation.

WHAT IS THE VALUE OF A PROPITIOUS NICHE?

One desired outcome of analyzing strategic factors is identifying a propitious niche where an organization could use its distinctive competence to take advantage of a particular opportunity. A *propitious niche* is a company's specific competitive role that is so well suited to the firm's internal and external environment that other corporations are not likely to challenge or dislodge it.[1]

Finding such a niche is not always easy. A firm's management must be always looking for *strategic windows,* that is, unique market opportunities at a particular time. The first one through the strategic window can occupy a propitious niche and discourage competition (if the firm has the required internal strengths). One company that has successfully found a propitious niche is Frank J. Zamboni & Company, the manufacturer of the machines that smooth the ice at skating and hockey rinks. Frank Zamboni invented the unique tractor-like machine in 1949, and no one has found a substitute for what it does. Before the machine was invented, people had to clean and scrape the ice by hand to prepare the surface for skating. Now hockey fans look forward to intermissions just to watch "the Zamboni" slowly drive up and down the ice rink turning rough, scraped ice into a smooth mirror surface. As long as the Zamboni company is able to produce the machines in the quantity and quality desired at a reasonable price, it's not worth another company's time to go after Frank Zamboni & Company's propitious niche.

5.2 REVIEW OF MISSION AND OBJECTIVES

A corporation must reexamine its current mission and objectives before it can generate and evaluate alternative strategies. Even when formulating strategy, managers tend to concentrate on the alternatives, the action possibilities, rather than on a mission to fulfill and the objectives to achieve. This tendency is so attractive because it is much easier to deal with alternative courses of action that exist in the present than to really think about what the corporation wants to accomplish in the future. In the end, managers often choose strategies that set their objectives for them, rather than having their choices incorporate clear objectives and a mission statement.

Problems in performance can derive from an inappropriate mission statement that is too narrow or too broad. If the mission does not provide a common thread (a unifying theme) for a corporation's businesses, managers may be unclear about where the company is heading. Objectives and strategies might be in conflict with each other. To the detriment of the corporation as a whole, divisions might be competing against one another rather than against outside competition.

A company's objectives can also be inappropriately stated. They can either focus too much on short-term operational goals or be so general that they provide little real guidance. A gap may exist between planned and achieved objectives. When such a strategic gap occurs, either the strategies have to be changed to improve performance or the objectives need to be adjusted downward to be more realistic. Consequently objectives should be constantly reviewed to ensure their usefulness. Ford Motor Company did just that after management realized that Ford had the potential to be first in sales worldwide. No longer content with being in second place, Alexander Trotman, Ford's Chairman of the Board, contended: "Have you ever seen a team run out on the field and say, 'We're going to be No. 2'?"[2]

5.3 GENERATING ALTERNATIVE STRATEGIES USING A TOWS MATRIX

Thus far we have discussed how a firm uses SWOT analysis to assess its situation. SWOT can also be used to generate a number of possible alternative strategies. The *TOWS* (SWOT backwards) *Matrix* illustrates how the external opportunities and threats facing a particular corporation can be matched with that company's internal strengths and weaknesses to result in four sets of possible strategic alternatives. (See Figure 5.2.) This is a good way to use brainstorming to create alternative strategies that might not otherwise be considered. It forces strategic managers to create various kinds of growth as well as retrenchment strategies. It can be used to generate corporate as well as business and functional strategies.

To generate a TOWS Matrix for Maytag Corporation, for example, use the *External Factor Analysis Summary* (EFAS) listed in Table 3.3 from chapter 3 (this book) and the *Internal Factor Analysis Summary* (IFAS) listed in Table 4.2 from chapter 4 (this book). To build Figure 5.2, take the following steps:

1. In the *Opportunities* (O) block, list the external opportunities available in the company's or business unit's current and future environment from the EFAS Table (Table 3.3, chapter 3, this book).

2. In the *Threats* (T) block, list the external threats facing the corporation now and in the future from EFAS Table.

3. In the *Strengths* (S) block, list the specific areas of current and future strength for the corporation from the IFAS Table (Table 4.2, chapter 4, this book).

4. In the *Weaknesses* (W) block, list the specific areas of current and future weakness for the corporation from the IFAS Table.

5. Generate a series of possible strategies for the corporation under consideration based on particular combinations of the four sets of strategic factors:

- **SO Strategies** are generated by thinking of ways a corporation could choose to use its strengths to take advantage of opportunities.
- **ST Strategies** consider a corporation's strengths as a way to avoid threats.
- **WO Strategies** attempt to take advantage of opportunities by overcoming weaknesses.
- **WT Strategies** are basically defensive and primarily act to minimize weaknesses and avoid threats.

TABLE 4.2 Internal Factor Analysis Summary (IFAS): Maytag as Example

Internal Factors	Weight	Rating	Weighted Score	Comments
Strengths	1	2	3	4	5
• Quality Maytag culture	.15	5	.75	Quality key to success
• Experienced top management	.05	4	.20	Know appliances
• Vertical integration	.10	4	.40	Dedicated factories
• Employee relations	.05	3	.15	Good, but deteriorating
• Hoover's international orientation	.15	3	.45	Hoover name in cleaners
Weaknesses				
• Process-oriented R&D	.05	2	.10	Slow on new products
• Distribution channels	.05	2	.10	Superstores replacing small dealers
• Financial position	.15	2	.30	High debt load
• Global positioning	.20	2	.40	Hoover weak outside the United Kingdom and Australia
• Manufacturing facilities	.05	4	.20	Investing now
Total	**1.00**		**3.05**	

TABLE 3.3 External Factor Analysis Summary (EFAS): Maytag as Example

External Factors	Weight	Rating	Weighted Score	Comments
Opportunities	1	2	3	4	5
• Economic integration of European Community	.20	4	.80	Acquisition of Hoover
• Demographics favor quality appliances	.10	5	.50	Maytag quality
• Economic development of Asia	.05	1	.05	Low Maytag presence
• Opening of Eastern Europe	.05	2	.10	Will take time
• Trend to "Super Stores"	.10	2	.20	Maytag weak in this channel
Threats				
• Increasing government regulations	.10	4	.40	Well positioned
• Strong U.S. competition	.10	4	.40	Well positioned
• Whirlpool and Electrolux strong globally	.15	3	.45	Hoover weak globally
• New product advances	.05	1	.05	Questionable
• Japanese appliance companies	.10	2	.20	Only Asian presence is Australia
Total	**1.00**		**3.15**	

FIGURE 5.2   Generating a TOWS Matrix for Maytag Corporation

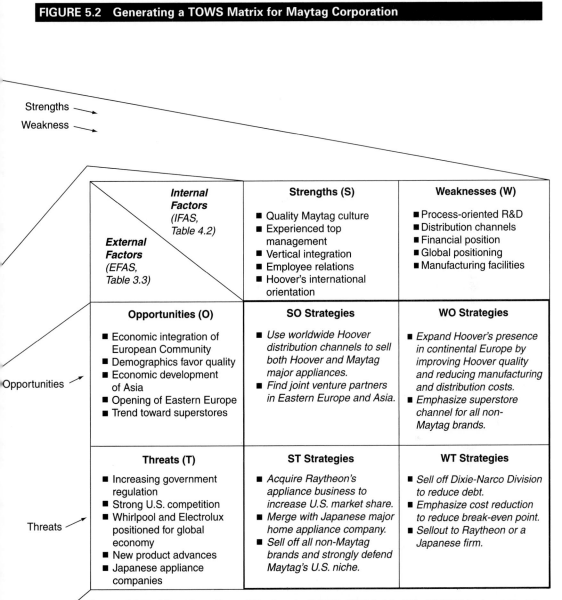

	Strengths (S)	Weaknesses (W)
Internal Factors (IFAS, Table 4.2) / **External Factors** (EFAS, Table 3.3)	■ Quality Maytag culture ■ Experienced top management ■ Vertical integration ■ Employee relations ■ Hoover's international orientation	■ Process-oriented R&D ■ Distribution channels ■ Financial position ■ Global positioning ■ Manufacturing facilities
Opportunities (O) ■ Economic integration of European Community ■ Demographics favor quality ■ Economic development of Asia ■ Opening of Eastern Europe ■ Trend toward superstores	**SO Strategies** ■ *Use worldwide Hoover distribution channels to sell both Hoover and Maytag major appliances.* ■ *Find joint venture partners in Eastern Europe and Asia.*	**WO Strategies** ■ *Expand Hoover's presence in continental Europe by improving Hoover quality and reducing manufacturing and distribution costs.* ■ *Emphasize superstore channel for all non-Maytag brands.*
Threats (T) ■ Increasing government regulation ■ Strong U.S. competition ■ Whirlpool and Electrolux positioned for global economy ■ New product advances ■ Japanese appliance companies	**ST Strategies** ■ *Acquire Raytheon's appliance business to increase U.S. market share.* ■ *Merge with Japanese major home appliance company.* ■ *Sell off all non-Maytag brands and strongly defend Maytag's U.S. niche.*	**WT Strategies** ■ *Sell off Dixie-Narco Division to reduce debt.* ■ *Emphasize cost reduction to reduce break-even point.* ■ *Sellout to Raytheon or a Japanese firm.*

Source: Adapted from *Long-Range Planning*, April 1982, H. Weihrich, "The TOWS Matrix - A Tool for Situational Analysis" p. 60. Copyright ©1982, with kind permission from H. Weihrich and Elsevier Ltd., The Boulevard, Langford Lane, Kidlington OX5 1 GB, UK.

5.4 BUSINESS STRATEGY

Business strategy focuses on improving the competitive position of a company's or business unit's products or services within the specific industry or market segment that the company or business unit serves. Business strategy can be *competitive* (battling against all competitors for advantage) or *cooperative* (working with one or more competitors to gain advantage against other competitors), or both. Business strategy asks how the company or its units should compete or cooperate in a particular industry.

WHAT ARE COMPETITIVE STRATEGIES?

Competitive strategy creates a defendable position in an industry so that a firm can outperform competitors. It raises the following questions:

- Should we compete on the basis of low cost (and thus price), or should we differentiate our products or services on some basis other than cost, such as quality or service?
- Should we compete head-to-head with our major competitors for the biggest but most sought-after share of the market, or should we focus on a niche in which we can satisfy a less sought-after but also profitable segment of the market?

Michael Porter proposes two "generic" competitive strategies for outperforming other corporations in a particular industry: lower cost and differentiation.[3] These strategies are called generic because they can be pursued by any type or size of business firm, even by not-for-profit organizations.

- *Lower cost strategy* is the ability of a company or a business unit to design, produce, and market a comparable product more efficiently than its competitors.
- *Differentiation strategy* is the ability to provide unique and superior value to the buyer in terms of product quality, special features, or after-sale service.

Porter further proposes that a firm's competitive advantage in an industry is determined by its *competitive scope,* that is, the breadth of the target market of the company or business unit. Before using one of the two generic competitive strategies (lower cost or differentiation), the firm or unit must choose the range of product varieties it will produce, the distribution channels it will employ, the types of buyers it will serve, the geographic areas in which it will sell, and the array of related industries in which it will also compete. This should reflect an understanding of the firm's unique resources. Simply put, a company or business unit can choose a *broad target* (that is, aim at the middle of the mass market) or a *narrow target* (that is, aim at a market niche). Combining these two types of target markets with the two competitive strategies results in the four variations of generic strategies depicted in Figure 5.3. When the lower cost and differentiation strategies have a broad mass-market target, they are simply called *cost leadership* and *differentiation*. When the strategies are focused on a market niche (narrow target), however, they are called *cost focus* and *differentiation focus.*

Cost leadership is a low-cost competitive strategy that aims at the broad mass market and requires "aggressive construction of efficient-scale facilities, vigorous pursuit

FIGURE 5.3   Porter's Generic Competitive Strategies

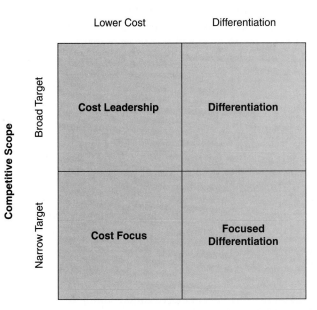

Source: Reprinted with permission of The Free Press, a division of Simon & Schuster, from *The Competitive Advantage of Nations* by Michael E. Porter. Copyright © 1990 by Michael E. Porter.

of cost reductions from experience, tight cost and overhead control, avoidance of marginal customer accounts, and cost minimization in areas like R&D, service, sales force, advertising, and so on."[4] Because of its lower costs, the cost leader is able to charge a lower price for its products than its competitors and still make a satisfactory profit. Some companies successfully following this strategy are Wal-Mart, Alamo Rent-A-Car, Southwest Airlines, Timex, and Gateway 2000. Having a low-cost position also gives a company or business unit a defense against rivals. Its lower costs allow it to continue to earn profits during times of heavy competition. Its high market share means that it will have high bargaining power relative to its suppliers (because it buys in large quantities). Its low price will also serve as a barrier to entry because few new entrants will be able to match the leader's cost advantage. As a result, cost leaders are likely to earn above-average returns on investment.

Differentiation is aimed at the broad mass market and involves the creation of a product or service that is perceived throughout its industry as unique. The company or business unit may then charge a premium for its product. This specialty can be associated with design or brand image, technology, features, dealer network, or customer service. Differentiation is a viable strategy for earning above-average returns in a specific business because the resulting brand loyalty lowers customers' sensitivity to price. Increased costs can usually be passed on to the buyers. Buyer loyalty also serves as an entry barrier: new firms must develop their own distinctive competence to differentiate their products in some way in order to compete successfully. Examples of companies that have successfully used a differentiation strategy are Walt Disney Productions, Maytag appliances, Nike athletic shoes, and Mercedes-Benz automobiles. Research does suggest that a differentiation strategy is more likely to generate higher profits than is a low-cost strategy because differentiation creates a better entry barrier. A lowercost strategy is more likely, however, to generate increases in market share.[5]

Cost focus is a lower cost competitive strategy that focuses on a particular buyer group or geographic market and attempts to serve only this niche, to the exclusion of others. In using cost focus, the company or business unit seeks a cost advantage in its target segment. A good example of this strategy is Fadal Engineering. Fadal focuses its efforts on building and selling no-frills machine tools to small manufacturers. Fadal achieved cost focus by keeping overhead and R&D to a minimum and by focusing its marketing efforts strictly on its market niche. The cost focus strategy is valued by those who believe that a company or business unit that focuses its efforts is better able to serve its narrow strategic target more efficiently than can its competition. It does, however, require a tradeoff between profitability and overall market share.

Differentiation focus is a differentiation strategy that concentrates on a particular buyer group, product line segment, or geographic market. This is the strategy successfully followed by Casey's General Stores, Morgan Motor Car Company (manufacturer of classic British sports cars), and local health food stores. In using differentiation focus, the company or business unit seeks differentiation in a targeted market segment. This strategy is valued by those who believe that a company or a unit that focuses its efforts is better able to serve the special needs of a narrow strategic target more *effectively* than can its competition.

WHAT RISKS ARE ASSOCIATED WITH COMPETITIVE STRATEGIES?

No specific competitive strategy is guaranteed to achieve success, and some companies that have successfully implemented one of Porter's competitive strategies have found that they could not sustain the strategy. Each of the generic strategies has its risks. For one thing, cost leadership can be imitated by competitors, especially when technology changes. Differentiation can also be imitated by competition, especially when the basis for differentiation becomes less important to buyers. For example, a company that follows a differentiation strategy must ensure that the higher price it charges for its higher quality is not priced too far above the competition or else customers will not see the extra quality as worth the extra cost. Focusers may be able to achieve better differentiation or lower cost in market segments, but they may also lose to broadly targeted competitors when the segment's uniqueness fades or demand disappears.

WHAT ARE THE ISSUES IN COMPETITIVE STRATEGIES?

Porter argues that to be successful, a company or business unit must achieve one of the generic competitive strategies. Otherwise, the company or business unit is *stuck in the middle* of the competitive marketplace with no competitive advantage and is doomed to below-average performance. An example of a company stuck in the middle is Tandy Corporation, the owner of Radio Shack stores. Tandy's strategy of selling personal computers to the average person had failed to generate the large amount of sales and profits that top management had desired. Its computers had neither the exciting new features found on Compaq's products nor the low price of the PC clones like those sold through the mail by Dell or Gateway. Sales were stagnating. Attempting to increase its sales to business through its GRiD Systems subsidiary while keeping up its Radio Shack sales, Tandy was confronted with the dilemma of trying to be all things to all people—and failing. Deciding at last that computers were distracting from its primary business of consumer electronics retailing, management finally sold the company's computer operations to AST Research.

Research generally supports Porter's contention that a firm that fails to achieve a generic strategy is going to be stuck in the middle with no competitive advantage. But what about companies that attempt to achieve both a lower cost and a differentiation position? The Japanese auto companies of Toyota, Nissan, and Honda are often presented as examples of successful firms able to achieve both of these generic strategies. Although Porter agrees that a company or a business unit may achieve lower cost and differentiation simultaneously, he argues that this state is often temporary. Porter does admit, however, that many different kinds of potentially profitable competitive strategies are possible. Although only one company can successfully pursue the mass market cost leadership strategy (because it is so dependent on achieving dominant market share), others can pursue an almost unlimited number of differentiation and focus strategies (depending on the range of possible desirable features and the number of identifiable market niches).

WHAT IS THE RELATIONSHIP BETWEEN INDUSTRY STRUCTURE AND COMPETITIVE STRATEGY?

Although each of Porter's generic competitive strategies may be used in any industry, in some instances certain strategies are more likely to succeed than others. In a fragmented industry, for example, in which many small and medium-sized local companies compete for relatively small shares of the total market, focus strategies will likely predominate. Fragmented industries are typical for products in the early stages of their life cycle and for products that are adapted to local tastes. If few economies are to be gained through size, no large firms will emerge and entry barriers will be low, allowing a stream of new entrants into the industry. If a company can overcome the limitations of a fragmented market, however, it can reap the benefits of a cost leadership or differentiation strategy. Until Pizza Hut used advertising to differentiate itself from local competitors, the pizza fast-food business was a fragmented industry composed primarily of locally owned pizza parlors, each with its own distinctive product and service offering. Subsequently Domino's used the cost leader strategy to achieve U.S. national market share.

As an industry matures, fragmentation is overcome and the industry tends to become a consolidated industry dominated by a small number of large companies. Although many industries begin by being fragmented, battles for market share and creative attempts to overcome local or niche market boundaries often result in a few companies' obtaining increasingly larger market shares. When product standards become established for minimum quality and features, competition shifts to a greater emphasis on cost and service. Slower growth combined with overcapacity and knowledgeable buyers put a premium on a firm's ability to achieve cost leadership or differentiation along the dimensions most desired by the market. Research and development shifts from product to process improvements. Overall product quality improves and costs are reduced significantly. This is the type of industry in which cost leadership and differentiation tend to be combined to various degrees. A firm can no longer gain high market share simply through low price. The buyers are more sophisticated and demand a certain minimum level of quality for the price paid. The same is true for firms emphasizing high quality. Either the quality must be high enough and valued by the customer enough to justify the higher price or the price must be dropped (through lowering costs) to compete effectively with the lower-priced products. This consolidation is taking place worldwide in the automobile, airline, and home appliance industries.

HOW DOES HYPERCOMPETITION AFFECT COMPETITIVE STRATEGY?

In his book *Hypercompetition,* D'Aveni proposes that it is becoming increasingly difficult to sustain a competitive advantage for very long. "Market stability is threatened by short product life cycles, short product design cycles, new technologies, frequent entry by unexpected outsiders, repositioning by incumbents, and tactical redefinitions of market boundaries as diverse industries merge."[6] Consequently a company or business unit must constantly work to improve its competitive advantage. It is not enough to be just the lowest cost competitor. Through continuous improvement programs, competitors are usually working to lower their costs as well. Firms must find new ways to not only reduce costs further, but to also add value to the product or service being provided.

The same is true of a firm or unit that is following a differentiation strategy. Maytag Company (a unit of Maytag Corporation), for example, was successful for many years by offering the most durable brand in major home appliances. It was able to charge the highest prices for Maytag brand washing machines. When other competitors improved the quality of their products, however, it became increasingly harder for customers to justify Maytag's significantly higher price. Consequently Maytag Company was forced not only to add new features to its products, but also to reduce costs through improved manufacturing processes so that its prices were no longer out of line with those of the competition.

D'Aveni contends that when industries become hypercompetitive, they tend to go through escalating stages of competition. Firms initially compete on cost or quality until an abundance of high-quality, low-priced goods result. This occurred in the U.S. major home appliance industry by 1980. In a second stage of competition, the competitors move into untapped markets. Others usually imitate these moves until the moves become too risky or expensive. This epitomized the major home appliance industry during the 1980s and 1990s as firms moved first to Europe and then into Asia and South America.

According to D'Aveni, firms then raise entry barriers to limit competitors. Economies of scale, distribution agreements, and strategic alliances now make it all but impossible for a new firm to enter the major home appliance industry. After the established players have entered and consolidated all new markets, the next stage is for the remaining firms to attack and destroy the strongholds of other firms. Maytag's 1995 decision to divest its European division and concentrate on improving its position in North America was a prelude to building a North American stronghold while Whirlpool, GE, and Electrolux were distracted by European and worldwide investments. Eventually, according to D'Aveni, the remaining large global competitors work their way to a situation of perfect competition in which no one has any advantage and profits are minimal.

Before hypercompetition, strategic initiatives provided competitive advantage for many years, perhaps for decades. This is no longer the case. According to D'Aveni, as industries become hypercompetitive, there is no such thing as a sustainable competitive advantage. Successful strategic initiatives in this type of industry typically last only months to a few years. According to D'Aveni, the only way a firm in this kind of dynamic industry can sustain any competitive advantage is through a continuous series of multiple short-term initiatives aimed at replacing a firm's current successful products with the next generation of products before the competitors can do so. Intel and Microsoft are taking this approach in the hypercompetitive computer industry.

Hypercompetition views competition, in effect, as a distinct series of ocean waves on what used to be a fairly calm stretch of water. As industry competition becomes more intense, the waves grow higher and require more dexterity to handle. Although a strategy is still needed to sail from point A to point B, more turbulent water means that a craft must continually adjust course to suit each new large wave. One danger of D'Aveni's concept of hypercompetition, however, is that it may lead to an overemphasis on short-term tactics (to be discussed in the next section) over long-term strategy. Too much of an orientation on the individual waves of hypercompetition could cause a company to focus too much on short-term temporary advantage and not enough on achieving its long-term objectives through building sustainable competitive advantage.

WHAT ARE COMPETITIVE TACTICS?

A *tactic* is a specific operating plan detailing how a strategy is to be implemented in terms of when and where it is to be put into action. By their nature, tactics are narrower in their scope and shorter in their time horizon than are strategies. Tactics may therefore be viewed (like policies) as a link between the formulation and implementation of strategy. Some of the tactics available to implement competitive strategies are those dealing with timing (when) and market location (where).

WHAT ARE TIMING TACTICS?

A *first mover* (pioneer) is the first company to manufacture and sell a new product or service. Some of the advantages of being a first mover are that the company is able to establish a reputation as a leader in the industry, move down the learning curve to assume the cost leader position, and earn temporarily high profits from buyers who value the product or service very highly. Being a first mover does, however, have its disadvantages. These disadvantages are, conversely, advantages enjoyed by late mover firms. *Late movers* are those firms that enter the market only after product demand has been established. They may be able to imitate others' technological advances (and thus keep R&D costs low), minimize risks by waiting until a new market is established, and take advantage of the natural inclination of the first mover to ignore market segments.

WHAT ARE MARKET LOCATION TACTICS?

A company or business unit can implement a competitive strategy either offensively or defensively. An *offensive tactic* attempts to take market share from an established competitor. It usually takes place in an established competitor's market location. A *defensive tactic,* in contrast, attempts to keep a competitor from taking away one's market share. It usually takes place within a company's current market position as a defense against possible attack by a rival.[7]

Offensive Tactics. Some of the methods used to attack a competitor's position are:

- **Frontal Assault.** The attacking firm goes head-to-head with its competitor. It matches the competitor in every category from price to promotion to distribution channel. To be successful, the attacker must not only have superior resources, but it must also be willing to persevere. This tactic is generally very expensive and may serve to awaken a sleeping giant (as MCI and Sprint did to AT&T in long-distance telephone service), depressing profits for all in the industry.
- **Flanking Maneuver.** Rather than going straight for a competitor's position of strength with a frontal assault, a firm may attack a part of the market where the competitor is weak. Cyrix Corporation followed this tactic with its entry into the microprocessor market, a market then almost totally dominated by Intel. Rather than going directly after Intel's microprocessor business, Cyrix developed a math coprocessor for Intel's 386 chip that would run 20 times faster than Intel's microprocessor. To be successful, the flanker must be patient and willing to carefully expand out of the relatively undefended market niche or else face retaliation by an established competitor.
- **Encirclement.** Usually evolving from a frontal assault or flanking maneuver, encirclement occurs as an attacking company or business unit encircles the competitor's position in terms of products or markets or both. The encircler has greater product variety (a complete product line ranging from low to high price) or serves more markets (it dominates every secondary market), or both. Honda successfully took this approach in motorcycles by taking every market segment except for the heavyweight segment in the United States controlled by Harley-Davidson. To be successful, the encircler must have the wide variety of abilities and resources necessary to attack multiple market segments.
- **Bypass Attack.** Rather than directly attacking the established competitor frontally or on its flanks, a company or business unit may choose to change the rules of the game. This tactic attempts to cut the market out from under the established defender by offering a new type of product that makes the competitor's product unnecessary. For example, instead of competing directly against Microsoft's Windows 95/97/NT operating systems, Netscape chose to use Java "applets" in its Internet browser so that an operating system and specialized programs were no longer necessary to run applications on a personal computer.
- **Guerrilla Warfare.** Instead of a continual and extensive resource-expensive attack on a competitor, a firm or business unit may choose to "hit and run." Guerrilla warfare involves small, intermittent assaults on a competitor's different market segments. In this way, a new entrant or small firm can make some gains without seriously threatening a large, established competitor and evoking some form of retaliation. To be successful, the firm or unit con-

ducting guerrilla warfare must be patient enough to accept small gains and to avoid pushing the established competitor to the point that it must make a response or else lose face. Microbreweries, which make beer for sale to local customers, use this tactic against national brewers like Anheuser-Busch.

Defensive Tactics. According to Porter, defensive tactics aim to lower the probability of attack, divert attacks to less-threatening avenues, or lessen the intensity of an attack. Instead of increasing competitive advantage per se, they make a company's or business unit's competitive advantage more sustainable by causing a challenger to conclude that an attack is unattractive. These tactics deliberately reduce short-term profitability to ensure long-term profitability. [8]

- **Raise Structural Barriers.** Entry barriers act to block a challenger's logical avenues of attack. According to Porter, some of the most important are to (1) offer a full line of products in every profitable market segment to close off any entry points, (2) block channel access by signing exclusive agreements with distributors, (3) raise buyer switching costs by offering low-cost training to users, (4) raise the cost of gaining trial users by keeping prices low on items new users most likely will purchase, (5) increase scale economies to reduce unit costs, (6) foreclose alternative technologies through patenting or licensing, (7) limit outside access to facilities and personnel, (8) tie up suppliers by obtaining exclusive contracts or purchasing key locations, (9) avoid suppliers that also serve competitors, and (10) encourage the government to raise barriers such as safety and pollution standards or favorable trade policies.
- **Increase Expected Retaliation.** This tactic is an action that increases the perceived threat of retaliation for an attack. For example, management may strongly defend any erosion of market share by drastically cutting prices or matching a challenger's promotion through a policy of accepting any price-reduction coupons for a competitor's product. This counterattack is especially important in markets that are important to the defending company or business unit. For example, when Clorox Company challenged Procter & Gamble Company in the detergent market with Clorox Super Detergent, P&G retaliated by test marketing its liquid bleach Lemon Fresh Comet in an attempt to scare Clorox into retreating from the detergent market.
- **Lower the Inducement for Attack.** This third tactic reduces a challenger's expectations of future profits in the industry. Like Southwest Airlines, a company can deliberately keep prices low and constantly invest in cost-reducing measures. Keeping prices very low gives a new entrant little profit incentive.

Before selecting one of the generic competitive strategies and the appropriate competitive tactic for a company or business unit, management should assess their feasibility in terms of company or business unit resources and capabilities. Does the company have the necessary resources to carry out the chosen competitive strategy and tactic? If not, can it acquire or develop them? This is discussed in more detail in chapter 7.

WHAT ARE COOPERATIVE STRATEGIES?

Competitive strategies and tactics are used to gain competitive advantage within an industry by battling against other firms. These are not, however, the only business strategy options available to a company or business unit for competing successfully within an industry. *Cooperative strategies* are those strategies used to gain competitive advantage within an industry by working with rather than against other firms. Other than collusion, which is illegal, the primary type of cooperative strategy is the strategic alliance.

A *strategic alliance* is a partnership of two or more corporations or business units formed to achieve strategically significant objectives that are mutually beneficial. Alliances between companies or business units have become a fact of life in modern business. Some alliances are very short-term, only lasting long enough for one partner to establish a beachhead in a new market. Others are longer lasting and may even be the prelude to a full merger between two companies.

Companies or business units may form a strategic alliance for a number of reasons, such as to obtain technology or manufacturing capabilitiesand access to specific markets, to reduce financial or political risk, and to achieve competitive advantage.

Cooperative arrangements between companies and business units fall along a continuum from weak and distant to strong and close. (See Figure 5.4.) The types of alliances range from mutual service consortia to joint ventures and licensing arrangements to value-chain partnerships.[9]

WHAT IS A MUTUAL SERVICE CONSORTIUM?

A *mutual service consortium* is a partnership of similar companies in similar industries who pool their resources to gain a benefit that is too expensive to develop alone, such as access to advanced technology. For example, IBM of the United States, Toshiba of Japan, and Siemens of Germany formed a consortium to develop new generations of computer chips. As part of this alliance, IBM offered Toshiba its expertise in chemical mechanical polishing to help develop a new manufacturing process using ultraviolet lithography to etch tiny circuits in silicon chips. IBM then transferred the new technology to a facility in the United States. The mutual service consortium is a fairly weak and distant alliance. There is very little interaction or communication among the partners.

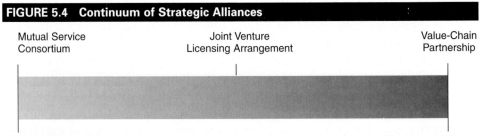

FIGURE 5.4   Continuum of Strategic Alliances

Mutual Service Consortium	Joint Venture Licensing Arrangement	Value-Chain Partnership

Weak and Distant   **Strong and Close**

Source: Suggested by R. M. Kanter, "Collaborative Advantage: The Art of Alliances," *Harvard Business Review* (July–August 1994), pp. 96–108.

WHAT IS A JOINT VENTURE?

A *joint venture* is a cooperative business activity, formed by two or more separate organizations for strategic purposes, that creates an independent business entity and allocates ownership, operational responsibilities, and financial risks and rewards to each member, while preserving their separate identity and autonomy. Along with licensing arrangements, joint ventures lay at the midpoint of the continuum and are formed to pursue an opportunity that needs a capability from two companies or business units, such as the technology of one and the distribution channels of another.

Joint ventures are the most popular form of strategic alliance. They often occur because the companies involved do not want to or cannot legally merge permanently. Joint ventures provide a way to temporarily combine the different strengths of partners to achieve an outcome of value to both. For example, the pharmaceutical firm Merck & Company agreed with the chemical giant DuPont Company to form, under joint ownership, a new company called DuPont Merck Pharmaceutical Company. Merck provided the new company with its foreign marketing rights to some prescription medicines plus some cash. In return, Merck got access to all of DuPont's experimental drugs and its small but productive research operation.

Extremely popular in international undertakings because of financial and political–legal constraints, joint ventures are a convenient way for corporations to work together without losing their independence. Disadvantages of joint ventures include loss of control, lower profits, probability of conflicts with partners, and the likely transfer of technological advantage to the partner. Joint ventures are often meant to be temporary, especially by some companies who may view them as a way to rectify a competitive weakness until they can achieve long-term dominance in the partnership. Partially for this reason, joint ventures have a high failure rate. Research does indicate, however, that joint ventures tend to be more successful when both partners have equal ownership in the venture and are mutually dependent on each other for results.

WHAT IS A LICENSING ARRANGEMENT?

A *licensing arrangement* is an agreement in which the licensing firm grants rights to another firm in another country or market to produce or sell a product. The licensee pays compensation to the licensing firm in return for technical expertise. Licensing is an especially useful strategy if the trademark or brand name is well known, but a company does not have sufficient funds to finance entering another country directly. Anheuser-Busch is using this strategy to produce and market Budweiser beer in the United Kingdom, Japan, Israel, Australia, Korea, and the Philippines. This strategy also becomes important if the country makes entry via investment either difficult or impossible. The danger always exists, however, that the licensee might develop its competence to the point that it becomes a competitor to the licensing firm. Therefore, a company should never license its distinctive competence, even for some short-run advantage.

WHAT IS A VALUE-CHAIN PARTNERSHIP?

The *value-chain partnership* is a strong and close alliance in which one company or unit forms a long-term arrangement with a key supplier or distributor for mutual advantage. Value-chain partnerships are becoming extremely popular as more companies and business units outsource activities that were previously done within the company or business unit. For example, DuPont contracts out project engineering and design to Morrison Knudsen; AT&T contracts out its credit card processing to Total System Services; Northern Telecom contracts out its electronic component manufacturing to Comptronix; and Eastman Kodak contracts out its computer support services to Businessland.

Another example of a value-chain partnership is the long-term relationship between a company or business unit with a supplier or distributor. To improve the quality of parts it purchases, companies in the U.S. auto industry, for example, have decided to work more closely with fewer suppliers and to involve them more in product design decisions. Such partnerships are also a way for a firm to acquire new technology to use in its own products. For example, Maytag Company was approached by one of its suppliers, Honeywell's Microswitch Division, which offered its expertise in fuzzy logic technology, a technology Maytag did not have at that time. The resulting partnership in product development resulted in Maytag's new IntelliSense™ dishwasher. Unlike previous dishwashers that the operator had to set, Maytag's fuzzy logic dishwasher automatically selected the proper cleaning cycle based on a series of factors such as the amount of dirt and presence of detergent.

IN CONCLUSION

When Sheri Poe founded Rykä, Inc., she knew that to succeed she had to follow a business strategy of focus differentiation. How else was her company to compete with Nike and Reebok? Poe explained:

> At that time (1987), women's athletic shoes were sized-down versions of men's; but a woman's body is obviously different, and when she's not wearing shoes designed for her physiology, the constant pounding of a workout will make her more likely to develop nagging injuries. . . . What Rykä developed was a fitness shoe built specifically for a woman, a patented design for better shock absorption and durability. . . .

> In any industry, the key is to have a strong niche; that way, if anyone copies the product, yours will still be viewed as the original. Staying a step ahead as the megabucks companies attempt to invade your niche is essential to long-term success in a crowded market. [10]

Discussion Questions

1. What industry forces might cause a propitious niche to disappear?
2. Is it possible for a company or business unit to follow a cost leadership strategy and a differentiation strategy simultaneously? Why or why not?
3. Is it possible for a company to have a sustainable competitive advantage when its industry becomes hypercompetitive?
4. What are the advantages and disadvantages of being a first mover in an industry? Give some examples of first mover and late mover firms. Were they successful?
5. Why are most strategic alliances temporary?

Key Terms (listed in order of appearance)

SWOT
SFAS table
propitious niche
TOWS matrix
SO, ST, WO, and WT strategies
business strategy
competitive strategy
lower-cost strategy
differentiation strategy
competitive scope
cost leadership
cost focus
differentiation focus

tactic
timing tactics
first mover
late mover
market location tactics
offensive tactics
defensive tactics
cooperative strategies
strategic alliances
mutual service consortium
joint venture
licensing agreement
value-chain partnership

Notes

1. W. H. Newman, "Shaping the Master Strategy of Your Firm," *California Management Review,* Vol. 9, No. 3 (1967): 77–88.
2. R. L. Simpson and O. Suris, "Alex Trotman's Goal: To Make Ford No. 1 in World Auto Sales," *Wall Street Journal* (July 18, 1995): A5.
3. M. E. Porter, *Competitive Strategy* (New York: The Free Press, 1980), pp. 34–41 as revised in M. E. Porter, The *Competitive Advantage of Nations* (New York: The Free Press, 1990), 37–40.
4. M. E. Porter, *Competitive Strategy* (New York: The Free Press, 1980), 35.
5. R. E. Caves, and P. Ghemawat, "Identifying Mobility Barriers," *Strategic Management Journal* (January 1992): 1–12.

6. R. A. D'Aveni, *Hypercompetition* (New York: Free Press, 1994), xiii–xiv.
7. Summarized from various articles by L. Fahey in *The Strategic Management Reader,* edited by L. Fahey (Englewood Cliffs, NJ: Prentice Hall, 1989), 178–205.
8. This information on defensive tactics is summarized from M. E. Porter, *Competitive Advantage* (New York: Free Press, 1985), 482–512
9. R. M. Kanter, "Collaborative Approach: The Art of Alliances," *Harvard Business Review* (July–August 1994): 96–108.
10. S. Poe, "To Compete with Giants, Choose Your Niche," *Nation's Business* (July 1992): 6.

CHAPTER 6

STRATEGY FORMULATION: CORPORATE STRATEGY

Deregulation and antitrust decisions by the U.S. federal government forced American Telephone and Telegraph (AT&T) to sell its local telephone business. This presented AT&T with some serious problems. For one thing, it no longer had any direct access to the individual households. It could no longer sell local service to its long-distance customers. The so-called "Baby Bells," such as US West and Bell South, controlled the telephone lines as well as the local phone business. Thanks to deregulation, upstarts like MCI and Sprint entered the long-distance business and began a price war to cut into AT&T's dominance of this market. As if this wasn't bad enough, the Baby Bells began talking about also entering the long-distance business. AT&T's market research revealed that consumers preferred to buy local and long-distance service from one source and get just one bill. The company had to either create a way to offer local phone service or watch its current long-distance customers be taken by competitors.

AT&T's top management established a new objective to obtain local access for its long-distance customers. How could it achieve this objective? One possibility, becoming a wholesaler by reselling local Bell service, didn't allow the company to control its costs or provide innovative services. The firm still needed its own local lines. It could buy a local phone system, such as Bell South, but for financial and antitrust reasons it could not purchase all of the Baby Bells. In a drastic change to the company's corporate strategy, AT&T chose to acquire the country's biggest cable operators, TCI and Media One, for $110 billion. With cable modems offering faster service than standard modems using phone lines, these acquisitions put AT&T directly into the booming internet business. This was a significant advantage of the strategy. Unfortunately, the cable companies only served about half of AT&T's long-distance customers. To achieve its corporate objective, should the company purchase more cable companies (very expensive), form strategic alliances with cable companies (many cable companies were not interested), or should it try something different?[1]

AT&T's solution was to offer the tens of millions of U.S. households not served by AT&T Cable Services with a new technology called "fixed wireless." This new technology would be able to beam both phone and internet service from existing AT&T

cell phone towers. This would enable the company to offer not only local and long-distance services, but also digital television, interactive TV, and high-speed Internet access. The hope was that this new strategy would provide AT&T with significant growth potential and sizable profits for many years to come.

This vignette illustrates the importance of corporate strategy to a firm's survival and success. *Corporate strategy* deals with three key issues facing the corporation as a whole:

1. The firm's overall orientation toward growth, stability, or retrenchment (directional strategy)
2. The industries or markets in which the firm competes through its products and business units (portfolio strategy)
3. The manner in which management coordinates activities and transfers resources and cultivates capabilities among product lines and business units (parenting strategy)

Corporate strategy is primarily about the choice of direction for the firm as a whole. This is true whether the firm is a small, one-product company or a large multinational corporation. In a large multibusiness company, however, corporate strategy is also about managing various product lines and business units for maximum value. In this instance, corporate headquarters must play the role of the organizational "parent" in that it must deal with various product and business unit "children." Even though each product line or business unit has its own competitive or cooperative strategy that it uses to obtain its own competitive advantage in the marketplace, the corporation must coordinate these different business strategies so that the corporation as a whole succeeds as a "family."

Corporate strategy, therefore, includes decisions regarding the flow of financial and other resources to and from a company's product lines and business units. Through a series of coordinating devices, a company transfers skills and capabilities developed in one unit to other units that need such resources. In this way, it attempts to obtain synergies among numerous product lines and business units so that the corporate whole is greater than the sum of its individual business unit parts. All corporations, from the smallest company offering one product in only one industry to the largest conglomerate operating in many industries with many products must, at one time or another, consider one or more of these issues.

To deal with each of the key issues, this chapter is organized into three parts that examine corporate strategy in terms of *directional strategy* (orientation toward growth), *portfolio analysis* (coordination of cash flow among units), and *corporate parenting* (building corporate synergies through resource sharing and development).

6.1 DIRECTIONAL STRATEGY

Just as every product or business unit must follow a business strategy to improve its competitive position, every corporation must decide its orientation toward growth by asking the following three questions:

- Should we expand, cut back, or continue our operations unchanged?
- Should we concentrate our activities within our current industry or should we diversify into other industries?

- If we want to grow and expand, should we do so through internal development or through external acquisitions, mergers, or joint ventures?

A corporation's *directional strategy* is composed of three general orientations toward growth (sometimes called grand strategies):

- *Growth strategies* expand the company's activities.
- *Stability strategies* make no change to the company's current activities.
- *Retrenchment strategies* reduce the company's level of activities.

Each of these orientations can be further categorized into more specific strategies as shown in Figure 6.1.

WHAT ARE GROWTH STRATEGIES?

By far the most widely pursued corporate strategies of business firms are those designed to achieve growth in sales, assets, profits, or some combination of these. There are two basic corporate growth strategies: *concentration* within one product line or industry and *diversification* into other products or industries. These can be achieved either internally by investing in new product development or externally through mergers, acquisitions, or strategic alliances.

A *merger* is a transaction involving two or more corporations in which stock is exchanged, but from which only one corporation survives. Mergers usually occur between firms of somewhat similar size and are usually "friendly." The resulting firm is likely to have a name derived from its composite firms. One example is the merging of Allied Corporation and Signal Companies to form Allied Signal.

An *acquisition* is the purchase of a company that is completely absorbed as an operating subsidiary or division of the acquiring corporation. Examples are Procter & Gamble's acquisition of Richardson-Vicks, known for its Oil of Olay and Vidal Sassoon brands, and Noxell Corporation, known for Noxema and Cover Girl. Acquisitions usually occur between firms of different sizes and can be either friendly or hostile. Hostile acquisitions are often called takeovers.

FIGURE 6.1 Corporate Directional Strategies

- GROWTH
  - Concentration
    - Vertical Growth
    - Horizontal Growth
  - Diversification
    - Concentric
    - Conglomerate

- STABILITY
  - Pause/Proceed with Caution
  - No Change
  - Profit

- RETRENCHMENT
  - Turnaround
  - Captive Company
  - Sell Out/Divestment
  - Bankruptcy/Liquidation

A *strategic alliance* (discussed in chapter 5) is a partnership of two or more corporations or business units to achieve strategically significant objectives that are mutually beneficial.

WHY USE CONCENTRATION STRATEGIES?

If a company's current product lines have real growth potential, concentration of resources on those product lines makes sense as a strategy for growth. There are two basic concentration strategies: vertical and horizontal integration.

Vertical Integration. Growth can be achieved via *vertical integration* by taking over a function previously provided by a supplier (*backward integration*) or by a distributor (*forward integration*). This is a logical strategy for a corporation or business unit with a strong competitive position in a highly attractive industry. To keep and even improve its competitive position through backward integration, the company may act to minimize resource acquisition costs and inefficient operations, as well as to gain more control over quality and product distribution through forward integration. The firm, in effect, builds on its distinctive competence to gain greater competitive advantage. The amount of vertical integration can range from *full integration,* in which a firm makes 100% of key supplies and distributors, to *taper integration,* in which the firm internally produces less than half of its key supplies, to *no integration,* in which the firm uses long-term contracts with other firms to provide key supplies and distribution. *Outsourcing,* the use of long-term contracts to reduce internal administrative costs, has become more popular as large corporations have worked to reduce costs and become more competitive by becoming less vertically integrated.

A firm can achieve vertical integration either internally or externally. Henry Ford, for example, used internal company resources to build his River Rouge Plant outside Detroit. The manufacturing process was integrated to the point that iron ore entered one end of the long plant and finished automobiles rolled out the other end into a huge parking lot. In contrast, DuPont, the huge chemical company, chose the external route to backward vertical integration by acquiring Conoco for oil needed in the production of DuPont's synthetic fabrics.

Although backward integration is usually more profitable than forward integration, it can reduce a corporation's strategic flexibility; by creating an encumbrance of expensive assets that might be hard to sell, it can thus create for the corporation an *exit barrier* to leaving that particular industry. With sales of its autos declining, General Motors, for example, has resorted to offering outside parts suppliers the use of its idle factories and workers.

Horizontal Integration. *Horizontal integration* is the degree to which a firm operates in multiple geographic locations at the same point in an industry's value chain. Growth can be achieved via horizontal integration by expanding the firm's products into other geographic locations or by increasing the range of products and services offered to current markets. A company can acquire market share, production facilities, distribution outlets, or specialized technology through internal development or externally through acquisitions or via joint ventures with another firm in the same industry. Horizontal integration for a firm may range from full to partial ownership to long-term contracts. For example, KLM, the Dutch airline, purchased a controlling stake (partial ownership) in Northwest Airlines to obtain access to American and Asian markets. KLM was unable to acquire all of Northwest's stock because of U.S. government regulations forbidding foreign ownership of a domestic airline (for defense reasons). Many small commuter airlines engage in long-term contracts with major airlines in order to offer a complete arrangement for travelers. For example, Mesa Airlines arranged a 5-year agreement with United Airlines to be listed on United's computer reservations as United Express through the Denver airport.

WHY USE DIVERSIFICATION STRATEGIES?

If a company's current product lines do not have much growth potential, management may choose to diversify. There are two basic diversification strategies: concentric and conglomerate.

Concentric (Related) Diversification. Growth through *concentric diversification* is expansion into a related industry. This may be an appropriate corporate strategy when a firm has a strong competitive position but industry attractiveness is low. By focusing on the characteristics that have given the company its distinctive competence, the company uses those very strengths as its means of diversification. The firm attempts to secure a strategic fit in a new industry where it can apply the firm's product knowledge, its manufacturing capabilities, and the marketing skills it used so effectively in the original industry can be put to good use. The corporation's products are related in some way; they possess some common thread. The search is for *synergy,* the concept that two businesses will generate more profits together than they could separately. The point of commonality may be similar technology, customer usage, distribution, managerial skills, or product similarity.

The firm may choose to diversify concentrically through either internal or external means. American Airlines, for example, has diversified both internally and externally out of the increasingly unprofitable airline business into a series of related businesses run by its parent company, AMR Corporation. Building on the expertise of its Sabre Travel Information Network, it built a computer reservations system for the French high-speed rail network and for the tunnel under the English Channel.

Conglomerate (Unrelated) Diversification. When management realizes that the current industry is unattractive and that the firm lacks outstanding abilities or skills it could easily transfer to related products or services in other industries, the most likely strategy is *conglomerate diversification*—diversifying into an industry unrelated to its current one. Rather than maintaining a common thread throughout their organization, managers who adopt this strategy are concerned primarily with financial considerations of cash flow or risk reduction.

The emphasis in conglomerate diversification is on financial considerations rather than on the product-market synergy common to concentric diversification. A cash-rich company with few opportunities for growth in its industry might, for example, move into another industry where opportunities are great but cash is hard to find. Another instance of conglomerate diversification might be when a company with a seasonal and therefore uneven cash flow purchases a firm in an unrelated industry with complementing seasonal sales that will level out the cash flow. The management of CSX Corporation (a railroad-dominated transportation company) considered the purchase of a natural gas transmission business (Texas Gas Resources) to be a good fit because most of the gas transmission revenue was realized in the winter months when railroads experience a seasonally lean period.

WHAT ARE STABILITY STRATEGIES?

A corporation may choose stability over growth by continuing its current activities without any significant change in direction. The stability family of corporate strategies can be appropriate for a successful corporation operating in a reasonably predictable environment. Stability strategies can be very useful in the short run but can be dangerous if followed for too long. Some of the more popular of these strategies are the pause and proceed with caution strategy, the no change strategy, and the profit strategy.

WHY USE A PAUSE AND PROCEED WITH CAUTION STRATEGY?

A *pause and proceed with caution strategy* is, in effect, a timeout; an opportunity to rest before continuing a growth or retrenchment strategy. It may be very appropriate as a temporary strategy to enable a company to consolidate its resources after prolonged rapid growth in an industry that faces an uncertain future. It is typically a temporary strategy to be used until the environment becomes more hospitable or to enable a company to consolidate its resources after prolonged rapid growth. This was the strategy Dell Computer Corporation followed in 1993 after its growth strategy had resulted in more growth than it could handle. Explained CEO Michael Dell, "We grew 285% in 2 years, and we're having some growing pains." Selling personal computers by mail enabled it to under price Compaq Computer and IBM, but it could not keep up with the needs of the $2 billion, 5600-employee company selling PCs in 95 countries. Dell was not giving up on its growth strategy but merely putting it temporarily in limbo until the company could hire new managers, improve the structure, and build new facilities.

WHY USE A NO CHANGE STRATEGY?

A *no change strategy* is a decision to do nothing new; a choice to continue current operations and policies for the foreseeable future. Rarely articulated as a definite strategy, a no change strategy's success depends on a lack of significant change in a corporation's situation. The relative stability created by the firm's modest competitive position in an industry facing little or no growth encourages the company to continue on its current course, making only small adjustments for inflation in its sales and profit objectives. The company faces no obvious opportunities or threats and has no significant strengths or weaknesses. Few aggressive new competitors are likely to enter such an industry. The corporation has probably found a reasonably profitable and stable niche for its products. Unless the industry is undergoing consolidation, the relative comfort that a company in this situation experiences is likely to cause management to follow a no change strategy in which the future is expected to continue as an extension of the present. Most small-town businesses probably follow this strategy before a Wal-Mart moves into their areas.

WHY USE A PROFIT STRATEGY?

A *profit strategy* is a decision to do nothing new in a worsening situation, but instead to act as though the company's problems are only temporary. The profit strategy is an attempt to artificially support profits when a company's sales are declining by reducing investment and short-term discretionary expenditures. Rather than announcing the company's poor position to stockholders and the investment community at large, top management may be tempted to follow this seductive strategy. Blaming the company's problems on a hostile environment (such as antibusiness government policies, unethical competitors, finicky customers, or greedy lenders), management defers investments or cuts expenses, such as R&D, maintenance, and advertising, to keep profits at a stable level during this period. It may even sell one of its product lines for the cash flow benefits. Obviously the profit strategy is useful only to help a company get through a temporary difficulty. Unfortunately the strategy is seductive and if continued long enough will lead to a serious deterioration in a corporation's competitive position. The profit strategy is thus usually a top management's passive, short-term, and often self-serving response to the situation.

WHAT ARE RETRENCHMENT STRATEGIES?

Management may pursue retrenchment strategies when the company has a weak competitive position in some or all of its product lines resulting in poor performance; when sales are down and profits are becoming losses. These strategies generate a great deal of pressure to improve performance. Like the coach of a losing football team, the CEO is typically under pressure to do something quickly or be fired. In an attempt to eliminate the weaknesses that are dragging the company down, management may follow one of several retrenchment strategies ranging from turnaround or becoming a captive company to selling out, bankruptcy, or liquidation.

WHY USE A TURNAROUND STRATEGY?

The *turnaround strategy* emphasizes the improvement of operational efficiency and is probably most appropriate when a corporation's problems are pervasive but not yet critical. Analogous to a diet, the two basic phases of a turnaround strategy include contraction and consolidation.

Contraction is the initial effort to quickly "stop the bleeding" with a general, across-the-board cutback in size and costs. The second phase, *consolidation,* is the implementation of a program to stabilize the now leaner corporation. To streamline the company, management develops plans to reduce unnecessary overhead and to justify the costs of functional activities. This is a crucial time for the organization. If the consolidation phase is not conducted in a positive manner, many of the company's best people will leave. If, however, all employees are encouraged to get involved in productivity improvements, the firm is likely to emerge from this strategic retrenchment period as a much stronger and better organized company. It has improved its competitive position and is able once again to expand the business.

WHY USE A CAPTIVE COMPANY STRATEGY?

A *captive company strategy* is becoming another company's sole supplier or distributor in exchange for a long-term commitment from that company. The firm, in effect, gives up independence in exchange for security. A company with a weak competitive position may offer to be a captive company to one of its larger customers in order to guarantee the company's continued existence with a long-term contract. In this way, the corporation may be able to reduce the scope of some of its functional activities, such as marketing, thus reducing costs significantly. For example, in order to become the sole supplier of an auto part to General Motors, Simpson Industries of Birmingham, Michigan, agreed to have its engine parts facilities and books inspected and its employees interviewed by a special team from GM. In return, nearly 80% of the company's production was sold to GM through long-term contracts.

WHY USE A SELL OUT OR DIVESTMENT STRATEGY?

If a corporation with a weak competitive position in this industry is unable either to pull itself up by its bootstraps or to find a customer to which it can become a captive company, it may have no choice but to sell out and leave the industry completely. In a *sell-out strategy* the entire company is sold. This makes sense if management can still obtain a good price for its shareholders by selling the entire company to another firm.

If the corporation has multiple business lines, it may choose *divestment,* which is selling a business unit. Monsanto is one example of a company using this strategy. Monsanto realized in 1997 that the very chemical business for which it had been known was hurting its growth as a corporation. The chemical division's performance had been overshadowed in the past 10 years by advances in biotechnology and agricultural products such as Roundup. Divestment seemed a viable decision.

WHY USE A BANKRUPTCY OR LIQUIDATION STRATEGY?

When a company finds itself in the worst possible situation with a poor competitive position in an industry with few prospects, management has only a limited number of alternatives, all of them distasteful. Because no one is interested in buying a weak company in an unattractive industry, the firm must pursue a bankruptcy or liquidation strategy. *Bankruptcy* involves giving up management of the firm to the courts in return for some settlement of the corporation's obligations. This is often called a Chapter Eleven reorganization. Top management hopes that after the court decides the claims on the company, the company will be stronger and better able to compete in a more attractive industry. Wang Laboratories, Inc., took this approach in 1992. Founded by An Wang, the company had been unable to make the transition from word processors to personal computers and finally collapsed after the death of its founder. The company emerged from bankruptcy in 1993 under a court-supervised reorganization plan that required the company to focus on office software.

In contrast to bankruptcy, which seeks to perpetuate the corporation, *liquidation* is piecemeal sale of all of the firm's assets. Because the industry is unattractive and the company is too weak to be sold as a going concern, management may choose to convert as many salable assets as possible to cash, which is then distributed to the stockholders after all obligations are paid. The benefit of liquidation over bankruptcy is that the board of directors, as representatives of the stockholders, together with top management make the decisions instead of turning them over to the court, which may choose to ignore stockholders completely.

6.2 PORTFOLIO ANALYSIS

Chapter 5 of this book deals with how individual product lines and business units can gain competitive advantage in the marketplace by using competitive and cooperative strategies. Companies with multiple product lines or business units must also ask themselves how these various products and business units should be managed to boost overall corporate performance.

- How much of our time and money should we spend on our best products and business units to ensure that they continue to be successful?
- How much of our time and money should we spend developing new costly products, most of which will never be successful?

One of the most popular aids to developing corporate strategy in a multibusiness corporation is portfolio analysis. Although its popularity has dropped since the 1970s and 1980s when over half of the largest business corporations used portfolio analysis, it is still used by 27% of Fortune 500 firms in corporate strategy formulation.[2] Portfolio analysis puts corporate headquarters into the role of an internal banker. In *portfolio analysis,* top management views its product lines and business units as a series of investments from which it expects a profitable return. The product lines and business units form a portfolio of investments that top management must constantly juggle to ensure the best return on the corporation's invested money. Two of the most popular approaches are the BCG Growth-Share Matrix and GE Business Screen.

WHY USE THE <u>BOSTON CONSULTING GROUP</u> GROWTH-SHARE MATRIX?

The *Boston Consulting Group* (BCG) *Growth-Share Matrix* depicted in Figure 6.2 is the simplest way to portray a corporation's portfolio of investments. Each of the corporation's product lines or business units is plotted on the matrix according to both the growth rate of the industry in which it competes and its relative market share. A unit's relative competitive position is defined as its market share in the industry divided by that of the largest other competitor. By this calculation, a relative market share above 1.0 belongs to the market leader. The business growth rate is the percentage of market growth, that is, the percentage by which sales of a particular business unit classification of products have increased. The matrix assumes that, other things being equal, a growing market is an attractive one.

The line separating areas of high and low relative competitive position is set at 1.5 times. A product line or business unit must have relative strengths of this magnitude to ensure that it will have the dominant position needed to be a "star" or "cash cow." On the other hand, a product line or unit having a relative competitive position less than 1.0 has "dog" status. Each product or unit is represented in Figure 6.2 by a circle, the area which represents the relative significance of each business unit or product line to the corporation in terms of assets used or sales generated.

The growth-share matrix has a lot in common with the product life cycle. As a product moves through its life cycle, it is categorized into one of four types for the purpose of funding decisions:

- **Question marks** (sometimes called "problem children" or "wildcats") are new products with the potential for success but that need a lot of cash for development. If one of these products is to gain enough market share to become a market leader and thus a star, money must be taken from more mature products and spent on a question mark.

FIGURE 6.2   BCG Growth Share Matrix

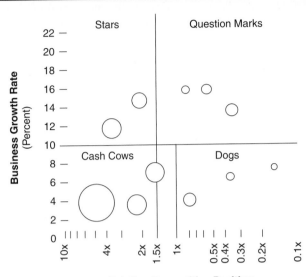

Source: Reprinted from *Long-Range Planning,* February 1977, B. Hedley, "Strategy and the Business Port-folio" p. 12. Copyright © 1977, with kind permission from Elsevier Science Ltd., The Boulevard, Langford Lane, Kidlington 0X5 1GB, UK.

- **Stars** are market leaders typically at the peak of their product life cycle and are usually able to generate enough cash to maintain their high share of the market. When their market growth rate slows, stars become cash cow products.
- **Cash cows** typically bring in far more money than is needed to maintain their market share. As these products move along the decline stage of their life cycle, they are "milked" for cash that will be invested in new question mark products. Question mark products that fail to obtain a dominant mar-ket share (and thus become a star) by the time the industry growth rate inevitably slows become "dogs."
- **Dogs** are those products with low market share that do not have the poten-tial (because they are in an unattractive industry) to bring in much cash. According to the BCG growth-share matrix, dogs should be either sold off or managed carefully for the small amount of cash they can generate.

Underlying the BCG growth-share matrix is the concept of the experience curve (discussed in chapter 4). The key to success is assumed to be market share. Firms with the highest market share tend to have a cost leadership position based on economies of scale, among other things. If a company uses the experience curve to its advantage, it should be able to manufacture and sell new products at a price low enough to gar-ner early market share leadership. When a product becomes a star, it is destined to be very profitable, considering its inevitable future as a cash cow.

After the current positions of a company's product lines or business units have been plotted on a matrix, a projection can be made of their future positions, assuming no change in strategy. Management can then use the present and projected matrixes to identify major strategic issues facing the organization. The goal of any company is to maintain a balanced portfolio so that the firm can be self-sufficient in cash and always working to harvest mature products in declining industries to support new ones in growing industries.

Research into the growth-share matrix generally supports its assumptions and recommendations except for the advice that dogs should be promptly harvested or liquidated. A product with a low share in a declining industry can be very profitable if the product has a niche in which market demand remains stable and predictable. Some firms may also keep a dog because its presence creates an entry barrier for potential competitors. All in all, the BCG growth-share matrix is a popular technique because it is quantifiable and easy to use.

Nevertheless, the growth-share matrix has been criticized for several reasons:

- The use of highs and lows to make just four categories is too simplistic.
- The link between market share and profitability is not necessarily strong. Low-share businesses can be profitable, too (and vice versa).
- Growth rate is only one aspect of industry attractiveness. High-growth markets may not always be the best for every business unit or product line.
- It considers the product line or business unit only in relation to one competitor: the market leader. It misses small competitors with fast-growing market shares.
- Market share is only one aspect of overall competitive position.

WHY USE THE GENERAL ELECTRIC BUSINESS SCREEN?

General Electric (GE) developed a more complicated matrix with the assistance of the McKinsey and Company consulting firm. As depicted in Figure 6.3, the *GE Business Screen* includes nine cells based on long-term industry attractiveness and business strength and competitive position. The GE Business Screen, in contrast to the BCG growth-share matrix, includes much more data in its two key factors than just business growth rate and comparable market share. For example, at GE, industry attractiveness includes market growth rate, industry profitability, size, and pricing practices, among other possible opportunities and threats. Business strength and competitive position includes market share as well as technological position, profitability, and size, among other possible strengths and weaknesses.

The individual product lines or business units are identified by a letter and are plotted as circles on the GE Business Screen. The area of each circle is in proportion to the size of the industry in terms of sales. The pie slices within the circles depict the market share of each product line or business unit.

To plot product lines or business units on the GE Business Screen, the following four steps are recommended:

Step 1. Select criteria to rate the industry for each product line or business unit. Assess overall industry attractiveness for each product line or business unit on a scale from 1 (very unattractive) to 5 (very attractive).

FIGURE 6.3   General Electric's Business Screen

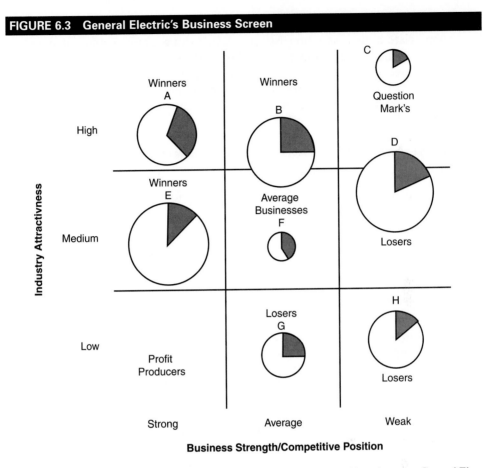

Source: Adapted from *Strategic Management in GE,* Corporate Planning and Development, General Electric Corporation. Reprinted with permission of General Electric Company.

Step 2. Select the key factors needed for success in each product line or business unit. Assess business strength and competitive position for each product line or business unit on a scale of 1 (very weak) to 5 (very strong).

Step 3. Plot each product line's or business unit's current position on a matrix like that depicted in Figure 6.3.

Step 4. Plot the firm's future portfolio, assuming that present corporate and business strategies remain unchanged. Is there a performance gap between projected and desired portfolios? If so, this gap should serve as a stimulus for them to seriously review the corporation's current mission, objectives, strategies, and policies.

Overall, the nine-cell GE Business Screen is an improvement over the BCG Growth-Share Matrix. The GE Business Screen considers many more variables and does not lead to such simplistic conclusions. It recognizes, for example, that the attractiveness of an industry can be assessed in many different ways (other than simply using growth rate), and thus it allows users to select whatever criteria they feel are most appropriate to their situation. Nevertheless, it can get quite complicated and cumbersome. The numerical estimates of industry attractiveness and business strength and competitive position give the appearance of objectivity but are in reality subjective judgments that may vary from one person to another. Another shortcoming of this portfolio matrix is that it cannot effectively depict the positions of new products or business units in developing industries.

WHAT ARE THE ADVANTAGES AND LIMITATIONS OF PORTFOLIO ANALYSIS?

Portfolio analysis is commonly used in strategy formulation because it offers certain advantages:

- It encourages top management to evaluate each of the corporation's businesses individually and to set objectives and allocate resources for each.
- It stimulates the use of externally oriented data to supplement management's judgment.
- It raises the issue of cash flow availability for use in expansion and growth.
- Its graphic depiction facilitates communication.

Portfolio analysis does, however, have some very real limitations that have caused some companies to reduce their use of the matrixes:

- It is not easy to define product and market segments.
- It suggests the use of standard strategies that can miss opportunities or be impractical.
- It provides an illusion of scientific rigor when in reality positions are based on subjective judgments.
- Its value-laden terms like cash cow and dog can lead to self-fulfilling prophecies.
- It is not always clear what makes an industry attractive or what stage a product is at in its life cycle.
- Naively following the prescriptions of a portfolio model may actually reduce corporate profits if they are used inappropriately. For example, General Mills' Chief Executive H. Brewster Atwater cites his company's Bisquick brand of flour as a product that would have been written off years ago based on portfolio analysis. "This product is 57 years old. By all rights it should have been overtaken by newer products. But with the proper research to improve the product and promotion to keep customers excited, it's doing very well."[3]

6.3 CORPORATE PARENTING

Campbell, Goold, and Alexander contend that corporate strategists must address two crucial questions:

- Which businesses should this company own and why?

- Which organizational structure, management processes, and philosophy will foster superior performance from the company's business units?[4]

Portfolio analysis attempts to answer these questions by examining the attractiveness of various industries and by managing business units for cash flow, that is, by using cash generated from mature units to build new product lines. Unfortunately portfolio analysis fails to deal with the question of what industries a corporation should enter or with how a corporation can attain synergy among its product lines and business units. As suggested by its name, portfolio analysis tends to primarily view matters financially, regarding business units and product lines as separate and independent investments.

Corporate parenting, in contrast, views the corporation in terms of resources and capabilities that can be used to build business unit value as well as generate synergies across business units. According to Campbell, Goold, and Alexander:

> Multibusiness companies create value by influencing—or parenting—the businesses they own. The best parent companies create more value than any of their rivals would if they owned the same businesses. Those companies have what we call parenting advantage.[5]

Corporate parenting generates corporate strategy by focusing on the core competencies of the parent corporation and on the value created from the relationship between the parent and its businesses. In the form of corporate headquarters, the parent has a great deal of power in this relationship. If there is a good fit between the parent's skills and resources and the needs and opportunities of the business units, the corporation is likely to create value. If, however, there is not a good fit, the corporation is likely to destroy value. This approach to corporate strategy is useful not only in deciding what new businesses to acquire, but also in choosing how each existing business unit should be best managed. The primary job of corporate headquarters is, therefore, to obtain synergy among the business units by providing needed resources to units, transferring skills and capabilities among the units, and by coordinating the activities of shared unit functions to attain economies of scope (as in centralized purchasing).

How to Develop a Corporate Parenting Strategy?

Campbell, Goold, and Alexander recommend that the search for appropriate corporate strategy involves three analytical steps.

1. Examine each business unit (or target firm in the case of acquisition) in terms of its critical success factors. *Critical success factors* are those elements of a company that determine its success or failure. They emphasize its distinctive competence to ensure competitive advantage. Like strategic factors, critical success factors will likely vary from company to company and from one business unit to another. People in the business units probably identified the critical success factors when they were generating business strategies for their units.

2. Examine each business unit (or target firm) in terms of areas in which performance can be improved. These are considered to be parenting opportunities. For example, two business units might be able to gain economies of scope by combining their sales forces. In another instance, a unit may have good, but not great, manufacturing and logistics skills. A parent company having world-class expertise in these areas can improve that unit's performance. The corporate parent could also transfer some people from one business unit having the desired skills to another unit in need of those skills. People at corporate headquarters may, because of their experience in many industries, spot areas where improvements are possible that even people in the business unit may not have noticed. Unless specific areas are significantly weaker than the competition, people in the business units may not even be aware that these areas could be improved, especially if each business unit only monitors its own particular industry.

3. Analyze how well the parent corporation fits with the business unit (or target firm). Corporate headquarters must be aware of its own strengths and weaknesses in terms of resources, skills, and capabilities. To do this, the corporate parent must ask if it has the characteristics that fit the parenting opportunities in each business unit. It must also ask if there is a misfit between the parent's characteristics and the strategic factors of each business unit.

CAN A PARENTING STRATEGY ALSO BE A COMPETITIVE STRATEGY?

Although competitive strategy was discussed in chapter 5 in terms of a company or a business unit operating only in one industry, competitive strategy can also be used across business units. A *horizontal strategy* is a corporate parenting strategy that cuts across business unit boundaries to build synergy across business units and to improve the competitive position of one or more business units. When used to build synergy, it acts like a parenting strategy. When used to improve the competitive position of one or more business units, it can be thought of as a corporate competitive strategy. Large multibusiness corporations often compete against other large multibusiness firms in a number of markets. These *multipoint competitors* are firms that compete with each other not only in one business unit, but also in a number of business units. At one time or another, a cash-rich competitor may choose to build its own market share in a particular market to the disadvantage of another corporation's business unit. Although each business unit has primary responsibility for its own business strategy, it may sometimes need some help from its corporate parent, especially if the competitor business unit is getting heavy financial support from its corporate parent. In this instance, corporate headquarters develops a horizontal strategy to coordinate the various goals and strategies of related business units.[6]

For example, Procter & Gamble, Kimberly-Clark, Scott Paper, and Johnson and Johnson compete with one another in varying combinations of consumer paper products, from disposable diapers to facial tissue. If (purely hypothetically) Johnson and Johnson had just developed a toilet tissue with which it chose to challenge Procter & Gamble's high-share Charmin brand in a particular district, it might charge a low price for its new brand to build sales quickly. Procter & Gamble might not choose to respond to this attack on its share by cutting prices on Charmin. Because of Charmin's high market share, Procter & Gamble would lose significantly more sales dollars in a price war than Johnson and Johnson would with its initially low-share brand. To retaliate, Procter & Gamble might thus challenge Johnson and Johnson's high-share baby shampoo with Procter & Gamble's own low-share brand of baby shampoo in a different district. Once Johnson and Johnson had perceived Procter & Gamble's response, it might choose to stop challenging Charmin so that Procter & Gamble would stop challenging Johnson and Johnson's baby shampoo.

IN CONCLUSION

KinderCare Learning Centers is a good example of a corporation that has experimented with many kinds of corporate strategy. The company had been founded to take advantage of the increasing numbers of dual-career couples who were turning to day care centers to watch their children while they were at work. In comparison to some centers that were nothing more than baby-sitting services providing only minimal attention to the needs of the children, KinderCare offered pleasant surroundings staffed by well-trained personnel. Soon, KinderCare had over 1000 centers in almost 40 states in the United States. Not satisfied with its success, however, KinderCare's top management decided to take advantage of its relationship with working parents to diversify into the somewhat related businesses of banking, insurance, and retailing. Financed through junk bonds, the strategy failed to bring in enough cash to pay for its implementation. After years of losses, the company was driven to bankruptcy in the late 1980s. It emerged from bankruptcy divested of its acquisitions. New management pledged to stay away from diversification. The new CEO initiated a concentration strategy with an emphasis on horizontal integration to take advantage of its distinctive competencies in childcare. KinderCare opened its first center catering expressly to commuters in a renovated supermarket near the Metro line to Chicago. It also offered to build child care centers for big employers or to run existing facilities for a fee. Management planned to open its first overseas center in Britain with eventual expansion into New Zealand and Australia.

Discussion Questions

1. How does horizontal integration differ from vertical integration? How does it differ from concentric diversification?
2. What are the tradeoffs between an internal and an external growth strategy?
3. Is stability really a strategy or is it just a term for no strategy?
4. Compare and contrast SWOT analysis with portfolio analysis.
5. Are critical success factors the same as distinctive competencies?

Key Terms (listed in order of appearance)

corporate strategy	backward integration
growth strategies	forward integration
directional strategy	outsourcing
merger	horizontal integration
acquisition	diversification
strategic alliance	concentric diversification
concentration	synergy
vertical integration	conglomerate diversification

stability strategies
pause and proceed with caution strategy
no change strategy
profit strategy
retrenchment strategies
turnaround strategy
contraction
consolidation
captive company strategy
divestment
selling out
bankruptcy

liquidation
portfolio analysis
BCG Growth Share Matrix
stars
question marks
cash cows
dogs
GE Business Screen
parenting strategy
critical success factors
horizontal strategy
multipoint competitors

Notes

1. J. Guyon, "AT&T's Big Bet Keeps Getting Dicier," *Fortune* (January 10, 2000): 126–129.
2. B. C. Reimann and A. Reichert, Portfolio Planning Methods for Strategic Capital Allocation: A Survey of Fortune 500 Firms," *International Journal of Management* (March 1996): 84–93.
3. J. J. Curran, "Companies That Rob the Future," *Fortune* (July 4, 1988): 84.
4. A. Campbell, M. Goold, and M. Alexander, *Corporate Level Strategy: Creating Value in the Multibusiness Company* (New York: John Wiley & Sons, 1994).
5. A. Campbell, M. Goold, and M. Alexander, "Corporate Strategy: the Quest for Parenting Advantage," *Harvard Business Review* (March–April 1995): 121.
6. M. E. Porter, *Competitive Advantage* (New York: Free Press, 1985), 317–382.

CHAPTER 7

STRATEGY FORMULATION: FUNCTIONAL STRATEGY AND STRATEGIC CHOICE

For almost 150 years, the Church & Dwight Company has been building market share on a brand name whose products are in 95% of all U.S. households. Yet if you asked the average person what products this company made, few would know. Although Church & Dwight may not be a household name, the company's ubiquitous orange box of Arm & Hammer brand baking soda is cherished throughout North America. Church & Dwight is a classic example of a marketing functional strategy called product development. Shortly after its introduction in 1878, Arm & Hammer baking soda became a fundamental item on the pantry shelf as people found many uses for sodium bicarbonate other than baking, such as cleaning, deodorizing, and tooth brushing. Hearing of the many uses people were finding for its product, the company advertised that its baking soda was not only good for baking, but also for deodorizing refrigerators simply by leaving an open box in the refrigerator. In a brilliant marketing move, the firm then suggested that consumers buy the product and throw it away: deodorize a kitchen sink by dumping Arm & Hammer baking soda down the drain! The company did not stop here. It looked for other uses of its sodium bicarbonate in new products. Church & Dwight has achieved consistent growth in sales and earnings through the use of *line extensions;* putting the Arm & Hammer brand first on baking soda, then on laundry detergents, toothpaste, and deodorants. By the mid-1990s, Church & Dwight had become a significant competitor in markets previously dominated only by giants like Procter & Gamble, Lever Brothers, and Colgate, using only one brand name. Was there a limit to this growth? Was there a point at which these continuous line extensions would begin to eat away at the integrity of the Arm & Hammer name? This is one example of the importance of a marketing functional strategy taking advantage of a company's well-marketed brand name and distinctive competence in calcium carbonate technology.

7.1 FUNCTIONAL STRATEGY

Functional strategy is the approach a functional area takes to achieve corporate and business unit objectives and strategies by maximizing resource productivity. It is concerned with developing and nurturing a distinctive competence to provide a company or business unit with a competitive advantage. For example, just as a multidivisional corporation has several business units, each with its own business strategy, each business unit has its own set of departments, each with its own functional strategy. The orientation of the functional strategy is dictated by its parent business unit's strategy. For example, a business unit following a competitive strategy of differentiation through high quality needs a manufacturing functional strategy that emphasizes expensive, quality-assurance processes over cheaper, high-volume production; a human resource functional strategy that emphasizes the hiring and training of a highly skilled, but costly, workforce; and a marketing functional strategy that emphasizes distribution channel "pull" using advertising to increase consumer demand over "push" using promotional allowances to retailers. If a business unit were to follow a low-cost competitive strategy, however, a different set of functional strategies would be needed to support the business strategy.

HOW ARE CORE COMPETENCIES DIFFERENT FROM DISTINCTIVE COMPETENCIES?

As stated in chapter 4 of this book, a *core competency* is something that a corporation can do exceedingly well. It is a key strength. It may also be called a *core capability* because it includes a number of constituent skills. When these competencies or capabilities are superior to those of the competition, they are called *distinctive competencies.* Although it is typically not an asset in the accounting sense, it is a very valuable capability; it does not "wear out." In general, the more core competencies are used, the more refined they get and the more valuable they become. To be considered a *distinctive competency,* the competency must meet three tests:

1. **Customer Value.** It must make a disproportionate contribution to customer perceived value.
2. **Competitor Unique.** It must be unique and superior to competitor capabilities.
3. **Extendibility.** It must be something that can be used to develop new products and services or enter new markets.[1]

Even though a distinctive competency is certainly considered a corporation's key strength, a key strength is not always considered to be a distinctive competency. As competitors attempt to imitate another company's competence in a particular functional area, what was once a distinctive competency becomes a minimum requirement to compete in the industry. Even though the competency may still be a core competency and thus a strength, it is no longer unique. For example, when Maytag Company alone had high-quality products, Maytag's ability to make exceedingly reliable and durable washing machines was a distinctive competency. As other appliance makers imitated its quality control and design processes, this continued to be a key strength (that is, a core competency and a strategic factor) of Maytag, but it was less and less a distinctive competency.

Where do these competencies come from? A corporation can gain access to a distinctive competency in four ways:

- It may be an asset endowment, such as a key patent, coming from the founding of the company: Xerox grew on the basis of its original copying patent.
- It may be acquired from someone else: Whirlpool bought a worldwide distribution system when it purchased Philips's appliance division.
- It may be shared with another business unit or alliance partner: Apple Computer worked with a design firm to create the special appeal of its Apple II and Mac computers.
- It may be carefully built and accumulated over time within the company: Honda carefully extended its expertise in small motor manufacturing from motorcycles to autos and lawnmowers.[2]

For a functional strategy to have the best chance of success, it should be built on a distinctive competency residing within that functional area. If a corporation does not have a distinctive competency in a particular functional area, even if it is still a core competency, that functional area could be a candidate for outsourcing.

WHAT IS THE ROLE OF OUTSOURCING?

Where should a function be housed? Should it be integrated within the organization or purchased from an outside contractor? *Outsourcing* is purchasing from someone else a product or service that had been previously provided internally. It is the opposite of vertical integration. Increasingly, outsourcing is considered to be an important part of strategic decision making. For example, DuPont contracts out project engineering and design to Morrison Knudsen, AT&T contracts its credit card processing to Total System Services, Northern Telecom contracts its electronic-component manufacturing to Comptronix, and Eastman Kodak contracts its computer support services to Businessland. Sophisticated strategists, according to Quinn, no longer think just of market share or vertical integration as the keys to strategic planning:

> Instead they concentrate on identifying those few core service activities where the company has or can develop: (1) a continuing strategic edge and (2) long-term streams of new products to satisfy future customer demands. They develop these competencies in greater depth than anyone else in the world. Then they seek to eliminate, minimize, or outsource activities where the company cannot be preeminent, unless those activities are essential to support or protect the chosen areas of strategic focus.[3]

The key to outsourcing is to purchase from outside only those activities that are not key to the company's distinctive competence. Otherwise, the company may give up the very core technologies or capabilities that made it successful in the first place, thus putting itself on the road to eventual decline as a "hollow corporation." Therefore, in deciding on functional strategy, the strategic manager must (1) identify the company's or business unit's core competencies, (2) ensure that the competencies are continually being strengthened, and (3) manage the competencies in such a way that best preserves the competitive advantage they create. An outsourcing decision depends on the fraction of total value added by the activity under consideration and by the amount of competitive advantage in that activity for the company or business unit. Only when the fraction of total value is small and the competitive advantage in the activity is low should a company or business unit outsource.

WHAT MARKETING STRATEGIES CAN BE EMPLOYED?

Marketing strategy deals with pricing, selling, and distributing a product. Using a *market development strategy,* a company or business unit can (1) capture a larger share of an existing market for current products through market saturation and market penetration or (2) develop new markets for current products. Consumer product giants such as Procter & Gamble, Colgate-Palmolive, and Unilever are experts at using advertising and promotion to implement a market saturation or penetration strategy in order to gain the dominant market share in a product category. As seeming masters of the product life cycle, these companies extend product life almost indefinitely through new and improved variations of product and packaging that appeal to most market niches. These companies also follow the second market development strategy by taking a successful product they market in one part of the world and marketing it elsewhere. Noting the success of their presoak detergents in Europe, both P&G and Colgate successfully introduced this type of laundry product to North America under the trade names of Biz and Axion.

Using the *product development strategy,* a company or unit can (1) develop new products for existing markets or (2) develop new products for new markets. Church & Dwight has had great success following the first product development strategy by developing new products to sell to its current customers. Acknowledging the widespread appeal of its Arm & Hammer brand baking soda, the company generated new uses for its sodium bicarbonate by reformulating it as toothpaste, deodorant, and detergent. The company has also successfully followed the second product development strategy by developing pollution reduction products (using sodium compounds) for sale to coal-fired electrical plants.

Numerous other marketing strategies exist. For advertising and promotion, for example, a company or business unit can choose between a "push" or a "pull" marketing strategy. Many large food and consumer product companies in the United States and Canada have followed a *push strategy* by spending a large amount of money on trade promotion in order to gain or hold shelf space in retail outlets. Trade promotion includes discounts, in-store special offers, and advertising allowances designed to push products through the distribution system. The Kellogg Company recently decided to change its emphasis from a push to a *pull strategy,* in which advertising pulls the products through the distribution channels. The company now spends more money on consumer advertising designed to build brand awareness so that shoppers will ask for the products.

Other marketing strategies deal with distribution and pricing. When pricing a new product, a company or business unit can follow one of two strategies. For new-product pioneers, *skim pricing* offers the opportunity to "skim the cream" from the top of the demand curve with a high price while the product is novel and competitors are few. *Penetration pricing,* in contrast, attempts to hasten market development and offers the pioneer the opportunity to use the experience curve to gain market share with a low price and dominate the industry. Depending on corporate and business unit objectives and strategies, either of these choices may be desirable to a particular company or unit. Penetration pricing is, however, more likely than skim pricing to raise a unit's operating profit in the long term.[4]

WHAT FINANCIAL STRATEGIES CAN BE EMPLOYED?

Financial strategy examines the financial implications of corporate and business-level strategic options and identifies the best financial course of action. It can also provide competitive advantage through a lower cost of funds and a flexible ability to raise capital to support a business strategy. Financial strategy usually attempts to maximize the financial value of the firm.

The desired level of debt versus equity versus internal long-term financing via cash flow is a key issue in financial strategy. Many small and medium-sized companies, such as Urschel Laboratories, try to avoid all external sources of funds in order to avoid outside entanglements and to keep control of the company within the family. Many companies are also experimenting with different types of stock offerings to balance risk. One approach to funding innovative products is to create a *tracking stock*. For example, when AT&T decided to use a new wireless technology to provide both phone and internet service from its cell phone towers (mentioned in chapter 6 of this book), it created a special stock offering for this wireless business. In this way, the highly risky new business was kept separate from existing businesses.

A popular financial strategy is the leveraged buyout (LBO). In a *leveraged buyout,* a company is acquired in a transaction financed largely by debt, usually obtained from a third party such as an insurance company. Ultimately the debt is paid with money generated from the acquired company's operations or by sales of its assets. The acquired company, in effect, pays for its own acquisition! Management of the LBO is then under tremendous pressure to keep the highly leveraged company profitable. Unfortunately the huge amount of debt on the acquired company's books may actually cause its eventual decline unless it goes public once again.

The management of dividends to stockholders is an important part of a corporation's financial strategy. Corporations in fast-growing industries, such as computers and computer software, often do not declare dividends. They use the money they might have spent on dividends to finance rapid growth. If the company is successful, its growth in sales and profits is reflected in a higher stock price, eventually resulting in a hefty capital gain when stockholders sell their common stock. Other corporations, such as electric utilities, that do not face rapid growth must support the value of their stock by offering generous and consistent dividends.

WHAT RESEARCH AND DEVELOPMENT STRATEGIES ARE AVAILABLE?

Research and Development (R&D) *strategy* deals with product and process innovation and improvement. One of the R&D choices is to be either a *technological leader* (pioneers an innovation) or a *technological follower* (imitates the products of competitors). Porter suggests that making the decision to become a technological leader or follower can be a way of achieving either overall low cost or differentiation. (See Table 7.1.)

TABLE 7.1 Research and Development Strategy and Competitive Advantage

	Technological Leadership	*Technological Followership*
Cost Advantage	Pioneer the lowest cost product design Be the first firm down the learning curve Create low-cost ways of performing value activites	Lower the cost of the product or value activities by learning from the leader's experience Avoid R&D costs through imitation
Differentiation	Pioneer a unique product that increases buyer value Innovate in other activities to increase buyer value	Adapt the product or delivery system more closely to buyer needs by learning from the leader's experience

Source: Reprinted with the permission of The Free Press, a division of Simon & Schuster, from *Competitive Advantage: Creating and Sustaining Superior Performance* by Michael E. Porter. Copyright (c) 1985 by Michael E. Porter.

One example of an effective use of the leader R&D functional strategy to achieve a differentiation competitive advantage is Nike, Inc. Nike spends more than most companies in the industry on R&D in order to differentiate its athletic shoes from its competitors in terms of performance. As a result, its products have become the favorite of the serious athlete.

WHAT OPERATIONS STRATEGIES MAY BE USED?

Operations strategy determines how and where a product or service is to be manufactured, the level of vertical integration, the deployment of physical resources, and relationships with suppliers. To begin with, a firm's manufacturing strategy is affected by the product or process life cycle. This concept describes the increase in production volume ranging from lot sizes as low as that in a *job shop* (one-of-a-kind production using skilled labor) through *connected line batch flow* (components are standardized; each machine functions like a job shop but is positioned in the same order as the parts are processed) to *flexible manufacturing systems* (parts are grouped into manufacturing families to produce a wide variety of mass-produced items), in which lot sizes as high as 100,000 or more per year are produced and *dedicated transfer lines* (highly automated assembly lines making one mass-produced product using little human labor). According to this concept, the product becomes standardized into a commodity over time in conjunction with increasing demand, as flexibility gives way to efficiency.

Operations strategy also should deal with the optimum level of technology the firm should use in its operations processes. The use of CAD/CAM, flexible manufacturing systems, computer numerically controlled systems, automatic-guided vehicles, robotics, manufacturing resource planning (MRP II), optimized production technology, and just-in-time delivery contribute to increased flexibility, quick response time, and higher productivity. Such investments also act to increase fixed costs and could cause significant problems if the company is unable to achieve economies of scale or scope.

Increasing competitive intensity in many industries has forced companies to switch from traditional mass production using dedicated transfer lines to a *continuous improvement* production strategy in which cross-functional work teams strive constantly to improve production processes. Because continuous improvement enables firms to use the same low-cost competitive strategy as mass production firms but at a significantly higher level of quality, it is rapidly replacing mass production as an operations strategy.

A number of companies are now experimenting with mass customization as an operations strategy. In contrast to continuous improvement, mass customization requires flexibility and quick responsiveness. Appropriate for an ever-changing environment, *mass customization* requires that people, processes, units, and technology reconfigure themselves to give customers exactly what they want, when they want it. The result is low-cost, high-quality, customized goods and services. An example of mass customization is the new "Personal Pair" system Levi Strauss introduced to combat the growing competition from private label jeans. The customer is measured at one of the company's Personal Pair outlets, the measurements are sent to Levi's by computer, and the made-to-order jeans arrive a few days later. The jeans cost about $10 more than an off-the-shelf pair.

WHAT HUMAN RESOURCE STRATEGIES CAN BE USED?

Human resource management (HRM) *strategy* attempts to find the best fit between people and the organization. It addresses the issue of whether a company or business unit should hire a large number of low-skilled employees who receive low pay, perform repetitive jobs, and most likely quit after a short time (the McDonald's restaurant strategy) or hire skilled employees who receive relatively high pay and are cross-trained to participate in self-managed work teams (appropriate in continuous improvement). To reduce costs and obtain increased flexibility, many companies are not only using increasing numbers of part-time and temporary employees, they are also experimenting with leasing employees from employee leasing companies. Companies are also finding that hiring a more diverse workforce (in terms of race, age, and nationality) can provide a competitive advantage. DuPont, for example, found that a group of African American employees were able to create promising new markets for its agricultural products by focusing on black farmers. In addition, DuPont's use of multinational teams has helped the company develop and market products internationally.

As work increases in complexity, the more suited it is for teams. An increasing number of corporations are using autonomous work teams. Research indicates that the use of work teams leads to increased quality and productivity.[5]

WHAT INFORMATION SYSTEMS STRATEGIES ARE AVAILABLE?

Corporations are increasingly adopting *information systems strategies* to use information technology to provide business units with competitive advantage. When Federal Express first provided its customers with PowerShip computer software to store addresses, print shipping labels, and track package location, its sales jumped significantly. UPS soon followed with its own MaxiShips software. Viewing its information system as a distinctive competency, Federal Express continued to push for further advantage against UPS by using its web site to enable customers to track their packages.

Many companies are also attempting to use information systems to form closer relationships with both their customers and suppliers and to improve efficiency through sophisticated intranets. For example, BMW and other automotive manufacturers have put their inventories on an Internet shared with suppliers. Suppliers now know the status of each part at each plant and are responsible for keeping inventories at a specified level.

7.2 STRATEGIES TO AVOID

Several strategies, which could be considered corporate, business, or functional, are very dangerous. Managers who have made a poor analysis or lack creativity may be trapped into considering them.

- **Follow the Leader.** Imitating the strategy of a leading competitor might seem a good idea, but it ignores a firm's particular strengths and weaknesses and the possibility that the leader may be wrong. Fujitsu Ltd., the world's second-largest computer maker, was driven since the 1960s by the sole ambition of catching up to IBM. Like IBM, Fujitsu competed primarily as a mainframe computer maker. It was so devoted to catching IBM, however, that it failed to notice that the mainframe business was reaching maturity and by 1993 was rapidly going into decline.
- **Hit Another Home Run.** If a company is successful because it pioneered an extremely successful product, it has a tendency to search for another super-product that will ensure growth and prosperity. Like betting on long shots at the horse races, the probability of finding a second winner is slight. Polaroid spent a lot of money developing an "instant" movie camera, but the public ignored it.
- **Arms Race.** Entering into a spirited battle with another firm for an increase in market share might increase sales revenue, but that increase will probably be more than offset by increases in advertising, promotion, R&D, and manufacturing costs. Since the deregulation of airlines, price wars and rate "specials" have contributed to the low profit margins or bankruptcy of many major airlines, such as Eastern and Continental.
- **Do Everything.** When faced with several interesting opportunities, management might tend to leap at all of them. At first, a corporation might have enough resources to develop each idea into a project, but money, time, and energy are soon exhausted as each of the many projects demand large infusions of resources.
- **Losing Hand.** A corporation might have invested so much in a particular strategy that top management is unwilling to accept the fact that the strategy is not successful. Believing that it has too much invested to quit, the corporation continues to throw "good money after bad." Pan American Airlines, for example, chose to sell its Pan Am Building and Intercontinental Hotels, the most profitable parts of the corporation, to keep its money-losing airline flying. Continuing to suffer losses, the company followed this strategy of shedding assets for cash until it had sold off everything and went bankrupt.

7.3 STRATEGIC CHOICE: SELECTION OF THE BEST STRATEGY

After the pros and cons of the potential strategic alternatives have been identified and evaluated, one must be selected for implementation. By now, many feasible alternatives probably will have emerged. How is the best strategy determined?

Perhaps the most important criterion is the ability of the proposed strategy to deal with the specific strategic factors developed earlier in the SWOT analysis. If the alternative doesn't take advantage of environmental opportunities and corporate strengths and lead away from environmental threats and corporate weaknesses, it will probably fail.

Another important consideration in the selection of a strategy is the ability of each alternative to satisfy agreed-on objectives with the least use of resources and with the fewest negative side effects. It is therefore important to develop a tentative implementation plan so that the difficulties that management is likely to face are addressed. This should be done in light of societal trends, the industry, and the company's situation based on the construction of scenarios.

HOW IS A CORPORATE SCENARIO CONSTRUCTED?

Corporate scenarios are pro forma balance sheets and income statements that forecast the effect that each alternative strategy and its various programs will likely have on division and corporate return on investment. Strategists in most large corporations use spreadsheet-based scenarios and various computer simulation models in strategic planning.

Corporate scenarios are simply extensions of the industry scenarios discussed in chapter 3 of this book. If, for example, industry scenarios suggest that a strong market demand is likely to emerge for certain products, a series of alternative strategy scenarios can be developed for a specific firm. The alternative of acquiring another company having these products can be compared with the alternative of developing the products internally. Using three sets of estimated sales figures (optimistic, pessimistic, and most likely) for the new products over the next 5 years, the two alternatives can be evaluated in terms of their effect on future company performance as reflected in its probable future financial statements. Pro forma (estimated future) balance sheets and income statements can be generated with spreadsheet software on a personal computer.

To construct a corporate scenario, follow these steps:

1. Use the *industry scenarios* discussed earlier in chapter 3 and develop a set of assumptions about the task environment. At 3M, for example, the general manager of each business unit is required annually to describe what his or her industry will look like in 15 years. *Optimistic, pessimistic,* and *most likely* assumptions should be listed for key economic factors such as the gross domestic product (GDP), consumer price index (CPI), prime interest rate, and for other key external strategic factors such as governmental regulation and industry trends. These same underlying assumptions should be listed for each of the alternative scenarios to be developed.

2. Develop *common-size financial statements* (discussed in chapter 11 of this book) for the company's or business unit's previous years. These common-size financial statements are the basis for the projections of pro forma financial statements. Use the historical common-size percentages to estimate the level of revenues, expenses, and other categories in estimated pro forma statements for future years. For each strategic alternative, develop a set of optimistic, pessimistic, and most likely assumptions about the impact of key variables on the company's future financial statements. Forecast three sets of sales and cost of goods sold figures for at least 5 years into the future. Look at historical data and make adjustments based on the environmental assumptions made. Do the same for other figures that can vary significantly. For the rest, assume that they will continue in their historical relationship to sales or some other key determining factor. Plug in expected inventory levels, accounts receivable, accounts payable, R&D expenses, advertising and promotion expenses, capital expenditures, and debt payments (assuming that debt is used to finance the strategy), among others. Consider not only historical trends, but also programs that might be needed to implement each alternative strategy (such as building a new manufacturing facility or expanding the sales force). Table 7.2 presents a form to use in developing pro forma financial statements using historical averages from common-size financial statements.

TABLE 7.2   Scenario Box for Use in Generating Financial Pro Forma Statements

				Projections[1]									
				20—			20—			20—			
Factor	*Last Year*	*Historical Average*	*Trend Analysis*	*O*	*P*	*ML*	*O*	*P*	*ML*	*O*	*P*	*ML*	*Comments*
GDP													
CPI													
Other													
Sales—units													
Sales—dollars													
COGS													
Advertising and marketing													
Interest expense													
Plant expansion													
Dividends													
Net profits													
EPS													
ROI													
ROE													
Other													

Note 1: O = Optimistic; P = Pessimistic; ML = Most Likely.

Source: T. L. Wheelen and J. D. Hunger, "Scenario Box for Use in Generating Financial Pro Forma Statements." Copyright © 1993 by Wheelen and Hunger Associates. Reprinted by permission.

3. Construct detailed *pro forma financial statements* for each strategic alternative. Using a spreadsheet program, list the actual figures from this year's financial statements in the left column. To the right of this column, list the optimistic figures for year 1, year 2, year 3, year 4, and year 5. Repeat this same process with the same strategic alternative but now list the pessimistic figures for the next 5 years. Do the same with the most likely figures. Then develop a similar set of optimistic (O), pessimistic (P), and most likely (ML) pro forma statements for the second strategic alternative. This process generates six different pro forma scenarios reflecting three different situations (O, P, and ML) for two strategic alternatives. Next, calculate financial ratios and common-size income statements and balance sheets to accompany the pro forma statements. To determine the feasibility of the scenarios, compare the assumptions underlying the scenarios with these financial statements and ratios. For example, if cost of goods sold drops from 70% to 50% of total sales revenue in the pro forma income statements, this drop should result from a change in the production process or a shift to cheaper raw materials or labor costs, rather than from a failure to keep the cost of goods sold in its usual percentage relationship to sales revenue when the predicted statement was developed.

The result of this detailed scenario construction should be anticipated net profits, cash flow, and net working capital for each of three versions of the two alternatives for 5 years into the future. A strategist might want to go further into the future if the strategy is expected to have a major impact on the company's financial statements beyond 5 years. The result of this work should provide sufficient information on which to base forecasts of the likely feasibility and probable profitability of each of the strategic alternatives.

Obviously these corporate scenarios can quickly become very complicated, especially if three sets of acquisition prices and development costs are calculated. Nevertheless, this sort of detailed "what if" analysis is needed in order to realistically compare the projected outcome of each reasonable alternative strategy and its attendant programs, budgets, and procedures. Regardless of the quantifiable pros and cons of each alternative, the actual decision probably will be influenced by several subjective factors like those described in the following sections.

WHY CONSIDER MANAGEMENT'S ATTITUDE TOWARD RISK?

The attractiveness of a particular strategic alternative is partially a function of the amount of risk it entails. *Risk* is composed not only of the probability that the strategy will be effective, but also of the amount of assets the corporation must allocate to that strategy and the length of time the assets will be unavailable for other uses. The greater the assets involved and the longer they are committed, the more likely top management is to demand a high probability of success. This demand might be one reason that innovations seem to occur more often in small firms than in large, established corporations. An entrepreneur managing a small firm is willing to accept greater risk than would professional managers running a large firm of diversified ownership. It is one thing to take a chance if you are the primary stockholder and are not concerned with periodic changes in the value of the company's common stock; it is something else if the corporation's stock is widely held and acquisition-hungry competitors or takeover artists surround the company like sharks every time the company's stock price falls below some external assessment of the firm's value!

WHAT PRESSURES FROM THE EXTERNAL ENVIRONMENT AFFECT DECISIONS?

The attractiveness of a strategic alternative is affected by its perceived compatibility with the key stakeholders in a corporation's task environment. Creditors want to be paid on time. Unions exert pressure for comparable wage and employment security. Governments and interest groups demand social responsibility. Stockholders want dividends. Management must consider all of these pressures in selecting the best alternative.

To assess the importance of stakeholder concerns in a particular decision, strategic managers should ask four questions: (1) Which stakeholders are most crucial for corporate success? (2) How much of what they want are they likely to get under this alternative? (3) What are they likely to do if they don't get what they want? (4) What is the probability that they will do it?

Strategy-makers should be better able to choose strategic alternatives that minimize external pressures and maximize stakeholder support. In addition, top management can propose a *political strategy* aimed at influencing key stakeholders. Some of the most commonly used political strategies are constituency building, political action committee (PAC) contributions, advocacy advertising, lobbying, and coalition building.

WHAT PRESSURES FROM THE CORPORATE CULTURE AFFECT STRATEGIC DECISIONS?

If a strategy is incompatible with the corporate culture, it probably will not succeed. Foot-dragging and even sabotage could result, as employees fight to resist a radical change in corporate philosophy. Precedents tend to restrict the kinds of objectives and strategies that management can seriously consider. The "aura" of the founders of a corporation can linger long past their lifetimes because they have imprinted their values on a corporation's members.

In considering a strategic alternative, strategy-makers must assess its compatibility with the corporate culture. If there is little fit, management must decide if it should (1) take a chance on ignoring the culture, (2) manage around the culture and change the implementation plan, (3) try to change the culture to fit the strategy, or (4) change the strategy to fit the culture. Further, a decision to proceed with a particular strategy without a commitment to change the culture or manage around the culture (both very tricky and time consuming) is dangerous. Nevertheless, restricting a corporation to only those strategies that are completely compatible with its culture might eliminate the most profitable alternatives from consideration. (See chapter 9, this book, for more information on managing corporate culture.)

HOW DO THE NEEDS AND DESIRES OF KEY MANAGERS AFFECT DECISIONS?

Even the most attractive alternative might not be selected if it is contrary to the needs and desires of important top managers. People's egos may be tied to a particular proposal to the extent that they strongly lobby against all other alternatives. Key executives in operating divisions, for example, might be able to influence other people in top management to favor a particular alternative and to ignore objections to it.

People tend to maintain the status quo, which means that decision makers continue with existing goals and plans beyond the point when an objective observer would recommend a change in course. People may ignore negative information about a particular course of action to which they are committed because they want to appear competent and consistent. It may take a crisis or an unlikely event to cause strategic decision makers to seriously consider an alternative they had previously ignored or discounted. For example, it wasn't until the CEO of ConAgra, a multinational food products company, had a heart attack that ConAgra started producing the Healthy Choice line of low-fat, low-cholesterol, low-sodium frozen-food entrees.

WHAT IS THE PROCESS OF STRATEGIC CHOICE?

There is an old story at General Motors about Alfred E. Sloan. At a meeting with his key executives, CEO and Chairman Sloan proposed a controversial strategic decision. When asked for comments, each executive responded with supportive comments and praise. After announcing that they were all in apparent agreement, Sloan stated that they were not going to proceed with the decision. He explained that either his executives didn't know enough to point out potential downsides of the decision, or they were agreeing to avoid upsetting the boss and disrupting the cohesion of the group. The decision was delayed until a real debate could occur over the pros and cons.[6]

Strategic choice is the evaluation of alternative strategies and the selection of the best alternative. There is mounting evidence that when an organization faces a dynamic environment, the best strategic decisions are not arrived at through consensus; they actually involve a certain amount of heated disagreement and even conflict. Because unmanaged conflict often carries a high emotional cost, authorities in decision making propose that strategic managers use programmed conflict to raise different opinions, regardless of the personal feelings of the people involved. One approach is to appoint someone as *devil's advocate,* a person or group assigned to identify potential pitfalls and problems with a proposed alternative. Another approach would be to appoint a person (or group) to present the advantages of a particular alternative and a second person (or group) to present the disadvantages of the same alternative in a debate.

7.4 DEVELOPMENT OF POLICIES

The selection of the best strategic alternative is not the end of strategy formulation. Management now must establish *policies* that define the ground rules for implementation. Flowing from the selected strategy, policies provide guidance for decision making and actions throughout the organization. At General Electric, for example, Chairman Welch insists that GE be Number One or Number Two wherever it competes. This policy gives clear guidance to managers throughout the organization. Another example is Casey's General Stores' policy, which states that a new service or product line may be added to its stores only when the product or service can be justified in terms of increasing store traffic.

Policies tend to be rather long-lived and can even outlast the particular strategy that created them. Interestingly, these general policies, such as "The customer is always right" or "Research and development should get first priority on all budget requests," can become, in time, part of a corporation's culture. Such policies can make the implementation of specific strategies easier, but they can also restrict top management's strategic options in the future. For this reason, a change in policies should quickly follow any change in strategy. Managing policy is one way to manage the corporate culture.

IN CONCLUSION

The board of directors of Intel Corporation met in 1991 to decide the future of the company. They were being asked to vote on a proposal to commit $5 billion to making the next generation of microprocessor chip, 5 times the amount previously needed for the 486 chip and 50 times that for the earlier 386 chip. By 1991, Intel was already the world's largest manufacturer of microprocessors, the brains of personal computers. Its latest chip, the 486, was just beginning to take off. Its successor, the Pentium, was still in design. Intel's CEO, Andy Grove, received the startling estimate of the capital spending needed to make the Pentium just before the start of the board meeting. Grove hastily drew the spending curve on graph paper as the directors looked on. The proposal committed the company to building new factories, something Intel had been slow to do during the 1980s. Based on Grove's presentation, the board decided to take the gamble. As a result, Intel's manufacturing expansion consumed $10 billion from 1991 through 1995. It was, however, timed perfectly for the boom in personal computer sales. Although rivals Motorola and IBM also began to add manufacturing capacity, none has been able to yet match the cash generated by Intel's 75% share of the microprocessor business. In this one crucial decision, Intel was able to turn the spiraling cost of competition into a competitive weapon.

Discussion Questions

1. How can a corporation identify its core competencies? Its distinctive competencies?
2. When should a corporation or business unit outsource a function or activity?
3. Why is penetration pricing more likely than skim pricing to raise a company's or a business unit's operating profit in the long run?
4. How does mass customization support a business unit's competitive strategy?
5. What is the relationship of policies to strategies?

Key Terms (listed in order of appearance)

functional strategy
core competency
core capability
distinctive competency
outsourcing
marketing strategies
market development strategy

product development strategy
push strategy
pull strategy
skim pricing
penetration pricing
financial strategy
leveraged buyout

R&D strategy
technological leader
technological follower
operations strategy
job shop
connected line batch flow
flexible manufacturing system
dedicated transfer lines
continuous improvement
mass customization

HRM strategy
information systems strategy
strategies to avoid
corporate scenarios
risk
political strategy
strategic choice
devil's advocate
policies

Notes

1. G. Hamel and S. K. Prahalad, *Competing for the Future* (Boston: Harvard Business School Press, 1994), 202–207.

2. P. J. Verdun and P. J. Williamson, "Core Competencies, Competitive Advantage, and Market Analysis: Forging the Links," in *Competence-Based Competition,* edited by G. Hamel and A. Heene (New York: John Wiley & Sons, 1994), 83–84.

3. J. B. Quinn, "The Intelligent Enterprise: A New Paradigm," *Academy of Management Executive* (November 1992): 48–63.

4. W. Redmond, "The Strategic Pricing of Innovative Products," in *Handbook of Business Strategy,* 1992/1993 Yearbook, edited by H. E. Glass and M. A. Hovde (Boston: Warren, Gorham & Lamont, 1992), 16.1–16.13.

5. R. D. Banker, J. M. Field, R. G. Schroder, and K. K. Sinha, "Impact of Work Teams on Manufacturing Performance: A Longitudinal Field Study," *Academy of Management Journal* (August 1996): 867–890.

6. R. A. Cosier, and C. R. Schwenk, "Agreement and Thinking Alike: Ingredients for Poor Decisions," *Academy of Management Executive* (February 1990): 69.

CHAPTER 8

STRATEGY IMPLEMENTATION: ORGANIZING FOR ACTION

PepsiCo, Inc., the maker of Pepsi Cola, was not pleased with only having 10 percent of the soft drink market in Brazil, the third largest soft-drink market in the world after the United States and Mexico. Coca-Cola, in contrast, controlled more than 50 percent of the market. Coke had successfully consolidated its many independent local bottlers into a set of regional bottlers that worked well together. The new regional Coke bottlers had close local connections, large capital budgets, and a solid distribution system. To combat Coke's entrenched position, PepsiCo formulated an ambitious growth strategy in 1994. It wanted to achieve at least 20 percent share of Brazil's main urban markets by selling more than 250 million cases annually. To manage this growth strategy, PepsiCo selected Charles Beach as its partner. After successfully building PepsiCo's market shares in both Puerto Rico and Argentina, Beach was offered the Brazilian franchise as well. Beach used his bottling company, Buenos Aires Embotelladora SA (known simply as Baesa) to expand soft drink production and market share. With PepsiCo's encouragement, Baesa built four Brazilian plants with a total capacity of 250 million cases of soft drinks—more than twice PepsiCo's highest amount of sales in Brazil. Rather than distributing its products via beer trucks (as did most of the soft-drink companies in Brazil), Baesa built its own distribution fleet by purchasing 700 new trucks. The company introduced four new flavors of its Kas line of juice-based sodas that PepsiCo had formulated especially for Brazil—offering them not just in the usual returnable bottles, but also in cans and plastic containers. To the amazement of analysts, Baesa and PepsiCo pledged to have the Brazilian operations running within a year.

Operating problems plagued the company from the start. The new bottling plants were often forced to close down lines because of rushed installation and insufficient employee training. Baesa found itself discarding 10 times as many bent or punctured cans as did its competitors. Management turnover was a serious problem. Many managers were unable to keep up with Baesa's fast pace and Beach's conflicting signals. At one point, Beach fired more than 20 executives who had been hired from other multinationals after they had been on the job only 3 months! Even though Baesa's debt had increased from $15.4 million in 1993 (before the Brazilian expansion) to $374 million in 1995, it planned to purchase two additional Brazilian bottling plants. By 1996, Baesa's debt reached $745 million.

In May 1996, PepsiCo announced that Beach had been relieved of operational responsibility and that it would assume control of Baesa's operations. In August, Baesa announced a quarterly loss of $250 million. The bottler defaulted on $34 million in debt payments. Sales had not met expectations. In addition to selling some of its franchises, Baesa closed one of its new plants and laid off more than 1,500 workers. PepsiCo's aggressive Brazilian growth strategy had failed. According to Craig Weatherup, PepsiCo's new head of global beverages, "I guess we got a little ahead of our headlights. We may have gone too fast."[1]

8.1 WHAT IS STRATEGY IMPLEMENTATION?

Strategy implementation is the sum total of the activities and choices required for the execution of a strategic plan. It is the process by which strategies and policies are put into action through the development of programs, budgets, and procedures. Although implementation is usually considered after strategy has been formulated, implementation is a key part of strategic management. Pepsi's attempted expansion into Brazil is one example of how a good strategy can result in a disaster through poor strategy implementation. Strategy formulation and strategy implementation should thus be considered as two sides of the same coin.

To begin the implementation process, strategy-makers must consider three questions:

- Who are the people who will carry out the strategic plan?
- What must be done?
- How are they going to do what is needed?

Management should have addressed these questions and similar ones initially when they analyzed the pros and cons of strategic alternatives, but the questions must be addressed again before management can make appropriate implementation plans. Unless top management can answer these basic questions satisfactorily, even the best-planned strategy is unlikely to provide the desired outcome.

A survey of 93 Fortune 500 firms revealed that over half of the corporations experienced the following 10 problems (listed in order of frequency) when they attempted to implement a strategic change:

1. Slower implementation than originally planned
2. Unanticipated major problems
3. Ineffective coordination of activities
4. Competing activities and crises that distracted attention away from implementation
5. Insufficient capabilities of the involved employees
6. Inadequate training and instruction of lower-level employees
7. Uncontrollable external environmental factors
8. Inadequate leadership and direction by departmental managers

9. Poor definition of key implementation tasks and activities
10. Inadequate monitoring of activities by the information system[2]

8.2 WHO IMPLEMENTS STRATEGY?

Depending on how the corporation is organized, those who implement strategy will probably be a much more diverse group of people than those who formulate it. In most large, multi-industry corporations, the implementers will be everyone in the organization. Vice-presidents of functional areas and directors of divisions or SBUs will work with their subordinates to put together large-scale implementation plans. Plant managers, project managers, and unit heads will put together plans for their specific plants, departments, and units. Therefore, every operational manager down to the first-line supervisor and every employee will be involved in some way in the implementing of corporate, business, and functional strategies.

Most of the people in the organization who are crucial to successful strategy implementation probably had little, if anything, to do with the development of the corporate and even business strategy. Therefore, they might be entirely ignorant of the vast amount of data and work that went into the formulation process. Unless changes in mission, objectives, strategies, and policies and their importance to the company are communicated clearly to all operational managers, resistance and foot-dragging can result. Managers might hope to convince top management to abandon its new plans and return to its old ways. This is one reason why involving middle managers in the formulation as well as in the implementation of strategy tends to result in better organizational performance.

8.3 WHAT MUST BE DONE?

The managers of divisions and functional areas work with their fellow managers to develop programs, budgets, and procedures for the implementation of strategy. They also work to achieve synergy among the divisions and functional areas in order to establish and maintain a company's distinctive competence.

HOW DEVELOP PROGRAMS, BUDGETS, AND PROCEDURES?

WHAT PROGRAMS MUST BE DEVELOPED?

A *program* is a statement of the activities or steps needed to accomplish a single-use plan. The purpose of a program is to make the strategy action-oriented. For example, assume Ajax Continental chose forward vertical integration as its best strategy for growth. It purchased existing retail outlets from another firm (Jones Surplus) instead of building its own. To integrate the new stores, the company would now have to develop various programs, such as restructuring Jones Surplus to be a part of Ajax Continental, a new advertising program, a training program for store managers, a program to modernize Jones Surplus stores, and a new reporting system for all the stores.

WHAT BUDGETS MUST BE DEVELOPED?

A *budget* is a statement of a corporation's programs in dollar terms. After programs are developed, the budget process begins. Planning a budget is the last real check a corporation has on the feasibility of its selected strategy. An ideal strategy might be found to be completely impractical only after specific implementation programs are costed in detail.

WHAT NEW PROCEDURES MUST BE DEVELOPED?

Procedures, sometimes termed standard operating procedures (SOP), are a system of sequential steps or techniques that describe in detail how a particular task or job is to be done. After program, divisional, and corporate budgets are approved, SOPs must be developed or revised. They typically detail the various activities that must be carried out to complete a corporation's programs. In the case of Ajax Corporation's acquisition of Jones Surplus' retail outlets, new operating procedures must be established for, among others, in-store promotions, inventory ordering, stock selection, customer relations, credits and collections, warehouse distribution, pricing, paycheck timing, grievance handling, and raises and promotions. These procedures ensure that the day-to-day store operations will be consistent over time (that is, next week's work activities will be the same as this week's) and consistent among stores (that is, each store will operate in the same manner as the others).

HOW DOES A COMPANY ACHIEVE SYNERGY?

One of the goals to be achieved in strategy implementation is synergy between and among functions and business units, which is why corporations commonly reorganize after an acquisition. The acquisition or development of additional product lines is often justified on the basis of achieving some advantages of scale in one or more of a company's functional areas. For example, when Ralston Purina acquired Union Carbide's Eveready and Energizer lines of batteries, Ralston's CEO argued that his company would earn better profit margins on batteries than Union Carbide would because of Ralston's expertise in developing and marketing branded consumer products. Ralston Purina felt it could lower the battery costs by taking advantage of synergies in advertising, promotion, and distribution.

8.4 HOW IS STRATEGY TO BE IMPLEMENTED?
ORGANIZING FOR ACTION

Before plans can lead to actual performance, top management must ensure that the corporation is appropriately organized, programs are adequately staffed, and activities are being directed toward the achievement of desired objectives. Organizing activities are reviewed briefly in this chapter. (Staffing, directing, and control activities are discussed in chapters 9 and 10.)

A change in corporate strategy will likely require some sort of change in organizational structure and in the skills needed in particular positions. Strategic managers must therefore closely examine how their company is structured to decide what, if any, changes should be made in the way work is accomplished. Should activities be grouped differently? Should the authority to make key decisions be centralized at headquarters or decentralized to managers in distant locations? Should the company be managed tightly with many rules and controls or loosely with few rules and controls? Should the corporation be organized into a tall structure with many layers of managers, each having a narrow span of control (that is, few employees to supervise) for better control of subordinates; or should it be organized into a flat structure with fewer layers of managers, each having a wide span of control (that is, more employees to supervise) to give more freedom to subordinates? For example, Ford used to have a fairly tall structure with 15 layers of managers, whereas Toyota had a relatively flat structure (for an automaker) of seven layers. Was Toyota's or Ford's structure "better"?

DOES STRUCTURE FOLLOW STRATEGY?

In a classic study of large U.S. corporations such as DuPont, General Motors, Sears, and Standard Oil, Alfred Chandler concluded that structure follows strategy, that is, changes in corporate strategy lead to changes in organizational structure.[3] He also concluded that organizations follow a pattern of development from one kind of structural arrangement to another as they expand. According to him, these structural changes occur because inefficiencies caused by the old structure have, by being pushed too far, become too obviously detrimental to live with. Chandler therefore proposed the following sequence of what occurs:

1. New strategy is created.
2. New administrative problems emerge.
3. Economic performance declines.
4. New appropriate structure is invented.
5. Profit returns to its previous level.

Chandler found that in their early years, corporations such as DuPont tend to have a centralized functional organizational structure that is well suited to producing and selling a limited range of products. As they add new product lines, purchase their own sources of supply, and create their own distribution networks, they become too complex for highly centralized structures. To remain successful, this type of organization needs to shift to a decentralized structure with several semiautonomous divisions (referred to in chapter 4 as the divisional structure).

Alfred P. Sloan, past CEO of General Motors, detailed how GM conducted such structural changes in the 1920s. He saw decentralization of structure as centralized policy determination coupled with decentralized operating management. After top management developed a strategy for the total corporation, the individual divisions, such as Chevrolet, Buick, and so on, were free to choose how to implement that strategy. Patterned after DuPont, GM found the decentralized multidivisional structure to be extremely effective in allowing the maximum amount of freedom for product development. Return on investment (ROI) was used as a financial control. (ROI is discussed in more detail in chapter 10.)

Research generally supports Chandler's proposition that structure follows strategy (as well as the reverse proposition that structure influences strategy). As mentioned earlier, changes in the environment tend to be reflected in changes in a corporation's strategy, thus leading to changes in a corporation's structure. Strategy, structure, and the environment need to be closely aligned; otherwise, organizational performance will likely suffer. For example, a business unit following a differentiation strategy needs more freedom from headquarters to be successful than does another unit following a low-cost strategy.[4]

Although it is agreed that organizational structure must vary with different environmental conditions, which, in turn, affect an organization's strategy, there is no agreement about an optimal organizational design. What was appropriate for DuPont and General Motors in the 1920s might not be appropriate today. Firms in the same industry do, however, tend to organize themselves in a similar manner. For example, automobile manufacturers tend to emulate General Motors' divisional concept, whereas consumer goods producers tend to emulate the brand management concept (a type of matrix structure) pioneered by Procter & Gamble Company. The general conclusion seems to be that firms following similar strategies in similar industries tend to adopt similar structures.

WHAT ARE THE STAGES OF CORPORATE DEVELOPMENT?

Successful corporations tend to follow a pattern of structural development, called *stages of development,* as they grow and expand. Beginning with the simple structure of the entrepreneurial firm (in which everybody does everything), they usually (if they are successful) get larger and organize along functional lines with marketing, production, and finance departments. With continuing success, the company adds new product lines in different industries and organizes itself into interconnected divisions. The differences among these three stages of corporate development in terms of typical problems, objectives, strategies, reward systems, and other characteristics are specified in detail in Table 8.1.

WHAT IS STAGE I? SIMPLE STRUCTURE

Stage I is completely centralized in the entrepreneur, who founds the company to promote an idea (product or service). The entrepreneur tends to make all the important decisions personally and is involved in every detail and phase of the organization. The Stage I company has little formal structure, which allows the entrepreneur to directly supervise the activities of every employee (see Figure 4.3, chapter 4, this book, for an illustration of the simple, functional, and divisional structures). Planning is usually short-range or reactive. The typical managerial functions of planning, organizing, directing, staffing, and controlling are usually performed to a very limited degree, if at all. The greatest strengths of a Stage I corporation are its flexibility and dynamism. The drive of the entrepreneur energizes the organization in its struggle for growth. Its greatest weakness is its extreme reliance on the entrepreneur to decide general strategies as well as detailed procedures. If the entrepreneur falters, the company usually flounders. This is often referred to as a *crisis of leadership.*[5]

Stage I describes Oracle Corporation, the computer software firm, under the management of its co-founder and CEO Lawrence Ellison. The company adopted a pioneering approach to retrieving data called structured query language (SQL). When IBM made SQL its standard, Oracle's success was assured. Unfortunately Ellison's technical wizardry was not sufficient to manage the company. Often working at home, he lost sight of details outside his technical interests. Although the company's sales were rapidly increasing, its financial controls were so weak that management had to restate an entire year's results to rectify irregularities. After the company recorded its first loss, Ellison hired a set of functional managers to run the company while he retreated to focus on new product development.

TABLE 8.1   Factors Differentiating Stage I, II, and III Companies

Function	Stage I	Stage II	Stage III
1. Sizing up: Major problems	Survival and growth dealing with short-term operating problems.	Growth, rationalization, and expansion of resources, providing for adequate attention to product problems.	Trustreeship in management and investment and control of large, increasing, and diversified resources. Also, important to diagnose and take action on problems at divison level.
2. Objectives	Personal and subjective.	Profits and meetings functionally oriented budgets and performance targets.	ROI, profits, earnings per share.
3. Strategy	Implicit and personal; exploitation of immediate opportunities seen by owner-manager.	Functionally oriented moves restricted to "one product" scope; exploitation of one basic product or service field.	Growth and product diversification; exploitation of general business opportunities.
4. Organization: Major characteristic of structure	One unit, "one-man show."	One unit, functionally specialized group.	Multiunit general staff office and decentralized operating divisions.
5. (a) Measurement and control	Personal, subjective control based on simple accounting system and daily communication and obsservation.	Control grows beyond one person; assessment of functional operations necessary; structured control systems evolve.	Complex formal system geared to comparative assessment of performance measures, indicating problems and opportunities and assessing management ability of division managers.
5. (b) Key performance indicators	Personal criteria, relationships with owner, operating efficiency, ability to solve operating problems.	Functional and internal criteria such as sales, performance compared to budget, size of empire, status in group, personal relationships, etc.	More impersonal applications of comparisons such as profits, ROI, P/E ratio, sales, market share, productivity, product leadership, personnel development, employee attitudes, public responsibility.
6. Reward–punishment system	Informal, personal, subjective; used to maintain control and divide small pool of resources to provide personal incentives for key performers.	More structures; usually based to a greater extent on agreed policies as opposed to personal opinion and relationships.	Allotment by "due process" of a wide variety of different rewards and punishments on a formal and systematic basis. Companywide policies usually apply to many different classes of managers and workers with few major exceptions for individual cases.

Source: D. H. Thain, "Stages of Corporate Development," *Business Quarterly* (Winter 1969). Reprinted with permission of *Business Quarterly,* published by the Western Business School, the University of Western Ontario, London, Canada.

WHAT IS STAGE II? FUNCTIONAL STRUCTURE

At *Stage II,* a team of managers who have functional specializations replaces the entrepreneur. The transition to this stage requires a substantial managerial style change for the chief officer of the company, especially if he or she was the Stage I entrepreneur. Otherwise, having additional staff members yields no benefits to the organization. Lawrence Ellison's retreat from top management at Oracle Corporation to new product development manager is one way that technically brilliant founders are able to get out of the way of the newly empowered functional managers. Once into Stage II, the corporate strategy favors protectionism through dominance of the industry, often through vertical or horizontal integration. The great strength of a Stage II corporation lies in its concentration and specialization in one industry. Its great weakness is that all of its eggs are in one basket.

By concentrating on one industry while that industry remains attractive, a Stage II company, like Oracle Corporation in computer software, can be very successful. Once a functionally structured firm diversifies into other products in different industries, however, the advantages of the functional structure break down. A *crisis of autonomy* can now develop, in which people managing diversified product lines need more decision-making freedom than top management is willing to delegate to them. The company needs to move to a different structure.

WHAT IS STAGE III? DIVISIONAL STRUCTURE

The *Stage III* corporation focuses on managing diverse product lines in numerous industries; it decentralizes the decision-making authority. These organizations grow by diversifying their product lines and expanding to cover wider geographic areas. They move to a divisional structure with a central headquarters and decentralized operating divisions; each division or business unit is a functionally organized Stage II company. They may also use a conglomerate structure if top management chooses to keep its collection of Stage II subsidiaries operating autonomously. Headquarters attempts to coordinate the activities of its operating divisions through performance- and results-oriented control and reporting systems, and by stressing corporate planning techniques. The divisions are not tightly controlled but are held responsible for their own performance results. Therefore, to be effective, the company has to have a decentralized decision process. The greatest strength of a Stage III corporation is its almost unlimited resources. Its most significant weakness is that it is usually so large and complex that it tends to become relatively inflexible. General Electric, DuPont, and General Motors are Stage III corporations.

WHAT ARE THE BLOCKS TO CHANGING STAGES?

Corporations often experience difficulty because they are blocked from moving into the next logical stage of development. Blocks to development may be internal, such as lack of resources, lack of ability, or a refusal of top management to delegate decision making to others, or they may be external, such as economic conditions, labor shortages, and lack of market growth. For example, Chandler noted in his study that the successful founder/CEO in one stage was rarely the person who created the new structure to fit the new strategy, and that, as a result, the transition from one stage to another was often painful. This was true of General Motors Corporation under the management of William Durant, Ford Motor Company under Henry Ford I, Polaroid

Corporation under Edwin Land, and Apple Computer under Steven Jobs. This difficulty in moving to a new stage is compounded by the founder's tendency to maneuver around the need to delegate by carefully hiring, training, and grooming his or her own team of managers. The team tends to maintain the founder's influence throughout the organization long after the founder is gone. This is what happened at Walt Disney Productions when the family continued to emphasize Walt's policies and plans long after he was dead. Although this may often be an organization's strength, it may also be a weakness. to the extent that the culture supports the status quo and blocks needed change.

IS THERE AN ORGANIZATIONAL LIFE CYCLE?

Instead of considering stages of development in terms of structure, the organizational life cycle approach places the primary emphasis on the dominant issue facing the corporation. Organizational structure is only a secondary concern. The *organizational life cycle* describes how organizations grow, develop, and eventually decline. It is the organizational equivalent of the product life cycle in marketing. The stages of the organizational life cycle are Birth (Stage I), Growth (Stage II), Maturity (Stage III), Decline (Stage IV), and Death (Stage V). The impact of these stages on corporate strategy and structure is summarized in Table 8.2. Note that the first three stages are similar to the three commonly accepted stages of corporate development. The only significant difference is the addition of decline and death stages to complete the cycle. Even though a company's strategy may still be sound, its aging structure, culture, and processes may be such that they prevent the strategy from being executed properly; thus, the company moves into decline.

Movement from growth to maturity to decline and finally to death is not, however, inevitable. A Revival phase may occur sometime during the maturity or decline stages. Managerial and product innovations can extend the corporation's life cycle. This often occurs during the implementation of a turnaround strategy.

Unless a company is able to resolve the critical issues facing it in the decline stage, it is likely to move into Stage V: corporate death, also known as bankruptcy. This is what happened to TWA, Macy's Department Stores, Baldwin-United, Eastern Airlines, Colt Manufacturing, Orion Pictures, and Wheeling-Pittsburgh Steel, as well as to many other firms. As in the cases of Johns Manville and International Harvester, both of

TABLE 8.2 Organizational Life Cycle					
	Stage I	*Stage II*	*Stage III*	*Stage IV*	*Stage V*
Dominant Issue	Birth	Growth	Maturity	Decline	Death
Popular Strategies	Concentration in a niche	Horizontal and vertical integration	Concentric and conglomerate diversification	Profit strategy followed by retrenchment	Liquidation or bankruptcy
Likely Structure	Entrepreneur-dominated	Functional management emphasized	Decentralization into profit or investment centers	Structural surgery	Dismemberment of structure

which went bankrupt in the 1980s, a corporation might nevertheless rise like a phoenix from its own ashes and live again (as Manville Corporation and Navistar International Corporation, respectively). The company may be reorganized or liquidated, depending on individual circumstances.

Few corporations move through these five stages in sequence. Some corporations, for example, might never move past Stage II. Others, like General Motors, might go directly from Stage I to Stage III. Many entrepreneurial ventures jump from Stage I into Stages IV and V. The key is for management to be able to identify when the firm is changing stages and to make the appropriate strategic and structural adjustments to maintain or even improve corporate performance.

WHAT ARE ADVANCED TYPES OF ORGANIZATIONAL STRUCTURES?

The basic structures (simple, functional, divisional, strategic business unit, and conglomerate) were discussed earlier in chapter 4. The previous sections described how a business corporation tends to grow and develop from a Stage I simple structure to a functional structure and finally to a Stage III divisional structure. Even with its evolution into strategic business units during the 1970s and 1980s, the divisional form is not the last word in organization structure. Under conditions of (1) increasing environmental uncertainty, (2) greater use of sophisticated technological production methods and information systems, (3) the increasing size and scope of worldwide business corporations, (4) a greater emphasis on multi-industry competitive strategy, and (5) a more educated cadre of managers and employees, new advanced forms of organizational structure have emerged and are continuing to emerge in recent decades. The *matrix* and the *network* are two possible candidates for a fourth stage in corporate development; a stage that not only emphasizes horizontal over vertical connections between people and groups, but also organizes work around temporary projects in which sophisticated information systems support collaborative activities.

WHAT IS A MATRIX STRUCTURE?

Most organizations find that organizing around either functions (in the functional structure) or around products and geography (in the divisional structure) provides an appropriate organizational structure. The strategic business unit form is simply a more advanced version of the divisional structure pioneered by General Motors and DuPont. SBUs provide horizontal links for related product divisions so that the organization as a whole can better address changing product-market issues. The matrix structure, in contrast, may be very appropriate when organizations conclude that neither functional nor divisional forms, even when combined with horizontal linking mechanisms, are right for their situations. In the *matrix structure,* functional and product forms are combined simultaneously at the same level of the organization. (See Figure 8.1.) Employees have two superiors, a product or project manager and a functional manager. The "home" department—engineering, manufacturing, or sales—is usually functional and is reasonably permanent. People from these functional units are often assigned on a temporary basis to one or more product units or projects. The product units or projects are usually temporary and act like divisions in that they are differentiated on a product-market basis.

FIGURE 8.1   Matrix and Network Structures

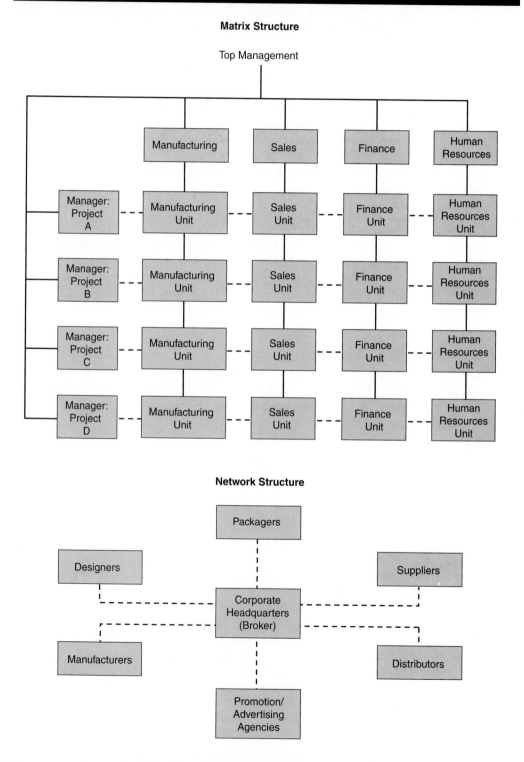

The matrix structure is likely to be used in an organization or within an SBU when the following three conditions exist:

- Cross-fertilization of ideas across projects or products is needed.
- Resources are scarce.
- The abilities to process information and to make decisions need improvement.[6]

Although a corporation may not organize itself as a full-blown matrix organization, it is becoming common to use some of the horizontal connections common to a matrix structure. It may use cross-functional work teams (like Chrysler Corporation in product development) or brand management (like Procter & Gamble and other consumer products companies).

WHAT IS A NETWORK STRUCTURE?

Perhaps the newest and most radical organizational design, the *network structure* (see Figure 8.1), is an example of what could be termed a non-structure because it virtually eliminates in-house business functions and replaces them with long-term contracts with suppliers and distributors. Sometimes called a "virtual organization," the network structure becomes most useful when the firm's environment is unstable and is expected to remain so. Under such conditions, the need for innovation and quick response usually is strong. The company draws up long-term contracts with suppliers and distributors to replace services that it could provide for itself through vertical integration. Electronic markets and sophisticated information systems reduce the transaction costs of the marketplace, thus justifying a buy over a make decision. Rather than being located in a single building or area, an organization's business functions are scattered worldwide. The organization is, in effect, only a shell, with a small headquarters acting as a "broker," electronically connected to some completely owned divisions, partially owned subsidiaries, and other independent companies. In its ultimate form, the network organization is a series of independent firms or business units linked by computers in an information system that designs, produces, and markets a product or service.

An example of a complete network organization is Just Toys. The New York City company licenses characters like Disney's Little Mermaid, Hanna-Barbera's Flintstones, and Marvel Entertainment's Spiderman to make bendable polyvinyl chloride figures called Bend-Ems. The company contracts out the manufacturing and administrative work for Bend-Ems and employs only 30 people. If a toy isn't selling well, production can be reduced and shipments stopped almost immediately. It would take Mattel and Hasbro months to react in a similar situation. Other companies like Nike, Reebok, and Benetton use the network structure in their operations function by subcontracting manufacturing to other companies in low-cost locations around the world.

The network organization structure gives a company the increased flexibility and adaptability it needs to cope with rapidly changing technology and shifting patterns of international trade and competition. It allows a company to concentrate on its distinctive competencies while gathering efficiencies from other firms that are concentrating their efforts in their areas of expertise. The network does, however, have disadvantages. The availability of numerous potential partners can be a potential source of trouble. If a particular firm overspecializes, it runs the risk of becoming a *hollow corporation*: a firm without a clearly defined essential contribution to its product or service.

WHY IS REENGINEERING IMPORTANT TO STRATEGY IMPLEMENTATION?

Reengineering is the radical redesign of business processes to achieve major gains in cost, service, or time. It is not in itself a type of structure, but it is an effective way to implement a turnaround strategy. Reengineering strives to break away from the old rules and procedures that develop and become ingrained in every organization over the years. These may be a combination of policies, rules, and procedures that have never been seriously questioned since they were established years earlier. These may range from "Credit decisions are made by the credit department" to "Local inventory is needed for good customer service." These rules of organization and work design were based on assumptions about technology, people, and organizational goals that may no longer be relevant. Rather than attempting to fix existing problems through minor adjustments and fine-tuning existing processes, the key to reengineering is to ask "If this were a new company, how would we run this place?"

Michael Hammer, who popularized the concept, suggests the following principles for reengineering:

- Organize around outcomes, not tasks. Design a person's or a department's job around an objective or outcome instead of a single task or series of tasks.
- Have those who use the output of the process perform the process. With computer-based information systems, processes can now be reengineered so that the people who need the result of the process can do it themselves.
- Subsume information-processing work into the real work that produces the information. People or departments that produce information can also process it for use instead of just sending raw data to others in the organization to interpret.
- Treat geographically dispersed resources as though they were centralized. With modern information systems, companies can provide flexible service locally while keeping the actual resources in a centralized location for coordination purposes.
- Link parallel activities instead of integrating their results. Instead of having separate units perform different activities that must eventually come together, have them communicate while they work so that they can do the integrating.
- Put the decision point where the work is performed and build control into the process. The people who do the work should make the decisions and be self-controlling.
- Capture information once and at the source. Instead of each unit developing its own database and information processing activities, the information can be put on a network so all can have access to the data.[7]

Several companies have had success with reengineering. Union Carbide, for example, used the concept to reduce fixed costs by $400 million over 3 years. Nevertheless, because reengineering is almost always accompanied by a significant amount of pain, between 50 and 70 percent of reengineering efforts fail to achieve their goals.[8]

How Design Jobs to Implement Strategy?

Organizing a company's activities and people to implement strategy involves more than simply redesigning a corporation's overall structure; it also involves redesigning the way jobs are done. With the increasing emphasis on reengineering, many companies are beginning to rethink their work processes with an eye toward phasing unnecessary people and activities out of the process. Process steps that had traditionally been performed sequentially can be improved by performing them concurrently using cross-functional work teams. Harley-Davidson, for example, reduced total plant employment by 25 percent while reducing the time needed to build a motorcycle by 50 percent. Restructuring through fewer people requires broadening the scope of jobs and encouraging teamwork. The design of jobs and subsequent job performance are therefore increasingly being considered as sources of competitive advantage.

Job design is the rethinking of individual tasks in order to make them more relevant to the company and to the employee(s). In an effort to minimize some of the adverse consequences of task specialization, corporations have turned to new job design techniques: *job enlargement* (combining tasks to give a worker more of the same type of duties to perform), *job rotation* (moving workers through several jobs to increase variety), and *job enrichment* (altering jobs by giving the worker more autonomy and control over activities). Although each of these methods has its adherents, none of them seems to work in all situations.

The *job characteristics model* is an advanced approach to job enrichment based on the belief that tasks can be described in terms of certain objective characteristics and that these characteristics affect employee motivation. For the job to be motivating, (1) the worker needs to feel a sense of responsibility, feel the task to be meaningful, and receive useful feedback on performance, and (2) the job has to satisfy needs that are important to the worker. The model proposes that managers follow five principles for redesigning work:

1. Combine tasks to increase task variety and enable workers to identify with what they are doing.
2. Form natural work units to make a worker more responsible and accountable for the performance of the job.
3. Establish client relationships so the worker will know what performance is required and why.
4. Vertically load the job by giving workers increased authority and responsibility over their activities.
5. Open feedback channels by providing workers information on how they are performing.[9]

Although several other approaches to job design exist besides the job characteristics model, practicing managers increasingly seem to follow the prescriptions of the model as a way of improving productivity and product quality. For example, Corning, Inc., the glass manufacturer, introduced team-based production in its Blacksburg, Virginia, plant. With union approval, Corning reduced job classifications from 47 to 4 to enable production workers to rotate jobs after learning new skills. The workers were divided into 14-member teams that, in effect, managed themselves. The plant had only two levels of management: Plant Manager Robert Hoover and two line leaders who only advised the teams. Employees worked demanding 12.5 hour shifts, alternating three-day and four-day weeks. The teams made managerial decisions, imposed discipline on fellow workers, and were required to learn three "skill modules" within 2 years or else lose their jobs. As a result of this new job design, a Blacksburg team, made up of workers with interchangeable skills, can retool a line to produce a different type of filter in only 10 minutes—six times faster than workers in a traditionally designed filter plant. The Blacksburg plant earned a $2 million profit in its first 8 months of production, instead of losing the $2.3 million projected for the start-up period. The plant performed so well that Corning's top management acted to convert the company's 27 other factories to team-based production.[10]

8.5 INTERNATIONAL ISSUES IN STRATEGY IMPLEMENTATION

Strategic alliances, such as joint ventures and licensing agreements, between a multinational company (MNC) and a local partner in a host country are becoming an increasingly popular means for an MNC to gain entry into other countries, especially less developed countries. The key to the successful implementation of these strategies is the selection of the local partner. Each party needs to assess not only the strategic fit of each company's project strategy, but also the fit of each company's respective resources. A successful joint venture may require as many as 2 years of prior contacts between both parties.

A company's level of involvement in international activities and the types of industries engaged in by the company strongly influence the design of an organization's structure. The issue of centralization versus decentralization becomes especially important for a multinational corporation operating in both multidomestic and global industries.

A basic dilemma facing the multinational corporation is how to organize authority centrally so that it operates as a vast interlocking system that achieves synergy and at the same time decentralize authority so that local managers can make the decisions necessary to meet the demands of the local market or host government. To deal with this problem, MNCs tend to structure themselves either along product groups or geographic areas. They may even combine both in a matrix structure, the design chosen by 3M Corporation. One side of 3M's matrix represents the company's product divisions; the other side includes the company's international country and regional subsidiaries.

Two examples of the usual international structures are Nestlé and American Cyanamid. Nestlé's structure is one in which significant power and authority have been decentralized to geographic entities. This structure is similar to that depicted in Figure 8.2, in which each geographic set of operating companies has a different group of products. In contrast, American Cyanamid has a series of product groups with worldwide responsibilities. To depict Cyanamid's structure, the geographical entities in Figure 8.2 would have to be replaced by product groups or strategic business units.

The product-group structure enables the company to introduce and manage a similar line of products around the world. This enables the corporation to centralize decision making along product lines. The geographic-area structure, in contrast, allows a

FIGURE 8.2   Geographic Area Structure for a Multinational Corporation

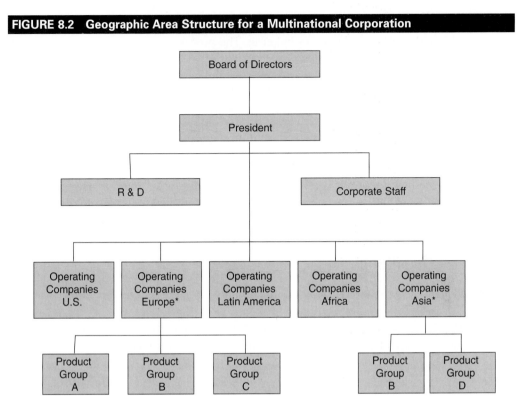

*Note: Because of space limitations, product groups for only Europe and Asia are shown here.

company to tailor products to regional differences and to achieve regional coordination. This decentralizes decision making to the local subsidiaries.

Simultaneous pressures for decentralization to be locally responsive and centralization to be maximally efficient are causing interesting structural adjustments in most large corporations. This is what is meant by the phrase "Think globally, act locally." Companies are attempting to decentralize those operations closest to the customers: manufacturing and marketing. At the same time, the companies are consolidating centrally less visible internal functions, such as research and development, finance, and information systems, to achieve significant economies of scale.

IN CONCLUSION

When the Nabisco Biscuit Company decided to introduce a new line of fat-free cookies, no one in management had any idea that it would cause the company so many problems. SnackWell's Devil's Food Cookie Cakes were introduced as a very special type of cookie. The cookie center was covered completely with marshmallow, then drenched with chocolate icing, followed by a chocolate glaze. Because each cookie was completely covered, it would stick to a conveyor belt, and thus could not be baked using conventional methods. These devil's food cookies could only be made on equipment available only in one of Nabisco's bakeries. The process took 4 hours compared to 30 minutes for chocolate chip cookies.

The devil's food cookies were an immediate hit with consumers. SnackWell's had the authentic-tasting chocolate that most fat-free cookies lacked, and the marshmallow center kept the cookies moist. Unfortunately the company couldn't produce the cookies fast enough. More than a year after the introduction of the cookie, Nabisco was still unable to meet demand. Management had three production lines running overtime at the bakery and was adding a fourth. Meanwhile, the company was introducing a new SnackWell's Double Fudge Cookie Cake containing two layers of cake with fat-free fudge in the middle. This was a much easier cookie to make, but management wasn't taking any chances this time. Until Nabisco could accurately judge market demand for the new product, it was being sold only in the northeastern United States. Admitted a company spokesperson: "We've learned our lesson."[11]

Discussion Questions

1. How should a corporation attempt to achieve synergy among functions and business units?
2. What are the advantages and disadvantages of the network structure?
3. How should an owner-manager prepare a company for its movement from Stage I to Stage II?
4. How can a corporation keep from sliding into the decline part of the organizational life cycle?
5. Is reengineering just another management fad or does it offer something of lasting value?

Key Terms (listed in order of appearance)

strategy implementation
program
budget
procedures
structure follows strategy
stages of corporate development
Stages I—III
organizational life cycle
matrix structure

network structure
reengineering
job design
job enlargement
job rotation
job enrichment
job characteristics model
product-group structure
geographic-area structure

Notes

1. R. Frank, and J. Friedland, "How Pepsi's Charge Into Brazil Fell Short of Its Ambitious Goals," *Wall Street Journal* (August 30, 1996): A1, A6.
2. L. D. Alexander, "Strategy Implementation: Nature of the Problem," in *International Review of Strategic Management,* Vol. 2, No.

1, edited by D. E. Hussey (New York: John Wiley & Sons, 1991), 73–113.
3. A.D. Chandler, *Strategy and Structure* (Cambridge, MA: MIT Press, 1962).
4. A. K. Gupta, "SBU Strategies, Corporate-SBU Relations, and SBU Effectiveness in Strategy Implementation," *Academy of*

Management Journal (September 1987): 477–500.

5. L. E. Greiner, "Evolution and Revolution as Organizations Grow," *Harvard Business Review* (July–August 1972): 37–46.

6. L. G. Hrebiniak, and W. F. Joyce, *Implementing Strategy* (New York: Macmillan, 1984), 85–86.

7. Summarized from M. Hammer, "Reengineering Work: Don't Automate, Obliterate," *Harvard Business Review* (July–August 1990), 104–112.

8. T. A. Stewart, "Reengineering: The Hot New Managing Tool," *Fortune* (August 23, 1993): 41–42.

9. J. R. Hackman, and G. R. Oldham, *Work Redesign* (Reading, MA: Addison-Wesley, 1980), 135–141.

10. J. Hoerr, "Sharpening Minds for a Competitive Edge," *Business Week* (December 17, 1990):72–78.

11. K. Deveny, "Man Walked on the Moon but Man Can't Make Enough Devil's Food Cookie Cakes," *Wall Street Journal* (September 28, 1993): B1, B12.

CHAPTER 9

STRATEGY IMPLEMENTATION: STAFFING AND LEADING

Have you heard of Enterprise Rent-A-Car? You won't find it at the airport with Hertz, Avis, or National car rental operations. Yet Enterprise owns more cars and operates in more locations than Hertz. The company accounts for over 20 percent of the $15 billion per year U.S. car rental market compared to 17 percent for Hertz and 12 percent for Avis. In ignoring the highly competitive airport market, Enterprise has chosen a differentiation competitive strategy by marketing to people in need of a spare car. Instead of locating many cars at a few high-priced locations at airports, Enterprise sets up inexpensive offices throughout metropolitan areas. As a result, cars are rented for 30 percent less than they cost at airports. As soon as one branch office grows to about 150 cars, the company opens another rental office a few miles away. People are increasingly renting from Enterprise even when their current car works fine. According to CEO Andy Taylor, "We call it a 'virtual car.' Small-business people who have to pick up clients call us when they want something better than their own car." Why is Enterprise able to follow this competitive strategy so successfully without attracting Hertz and Avis into its market?

The secret to Enterprise's success is its well-executed strategy implementation. Clearly laid out programs, budgets, and procedures support the company's competitive strategy by making Enterprise stand out in the mind of the consumer. When a new rental office opens, employees spend time developing relationships with the service managers of every auto dealership and body shop in the area. Enterprise employees bring pizza and doughnuts to workers at the auto garages across the country. Enterprise forms agreements with dealers to provide replacements for cars brought in for service. At major accounts, the company actually staffs an office at the dealership and has cars parked outside so customers don't have to go to an Enterprise office to complete paperwork.

One key to implementation at Enterprise is staffing, through hiring and promoting a certain kind of person. Virtually every Enterprise employee is a college graduate, usually from the bottom half of the class. According to COO Donald Ross, "We hire from the half of the college class that makes the upper half possible. We want athletes, fraternity types—especially fraternity presidents and social directors. People people." These new employees begin as management trainees in the $20,000–$25,000 salary range. Instead of regular raises, their pay is tied to branch office profits.

Another key to implementation at Enterprise is leading, through specifying clear performance objectives and promoting a team-oriented corporate culture. The company stresses promotion from within. Every Enterprise employee, including top executives, starts at the bottom. As a result, a bond of shared experience connects all employees and managers. To reinforce a cohesive culture of camaraderie, senior executives routinely do "grunt work" at branch offices. Even Andy Taylor, the CEO, joins the work. "We were visiting an office in Berkeley and it was mobbed, so I started cleaning cars," says Taylor. "As it was happening, I wondered if it was a good use of my time, but the effect on morale was tremendous." Because the financial results of every branch office and every region are available to all, the collegial culture stimulates good-natured competition. "We're this close to beating out Middlesex," grins Woody Erhardt, an area manager in New Jersey. "I want to pound them into the ground. If they lose, they have to throw a party for us, and we get to decide what they wear."[1]

This example from Enterprise Rent-A-Car illustrates how a competitive strategy must be implemented with carefully considered programs in order to succeed. This chapter discusses strategy implementation in terms of staffing and leading.

9.1 STAFFING

Staffing focuses on the selection and utilization of employees. The implementation of new strategies and policies often calls for new human resource management priorities and a different utilization of personnel. This may mean hiring new people with new skills, firing people with inappropriate or substandard skills, and/or training existing employees to learn new skills.

If a corporation plans to implement growth strategies, new people may need to be hired and trained. Experienced people with the necessary skills need to be promoted to newly created managerial positions. If the corporation adopts a retrenchment strategy, however, a large number of people may need to be laid off or fired, and top management and divisional managers need to specify the criteria to be used in making these personnel decisions. Should employees be fired on the basis of low seniority or on the basis of poor performance? Sometimes corporations find it easier to close an entire division than to choose which individuals to fire.

DOES STAFFING FOLLOW STRATEGY?

As in the case of structure, staffing requirements are also likely to follow a change in strategy.

HOW DO HIRING AND TRAINING REQUIREMENTS CHANGE?

Once a new strategy is formulated, either different kinds of people may be needed or the current employees may need to be retrained to implement the new strategy. Consider the introduction of team-based production at Corning's filter plant mentioned earlier in chapter 8. Employee selection and training were crucial to the success of the new manufacturing strategy. Plant Manager Robert Hoover sorted through 8000 job applications before hiring 150 people with the best problem-solving ability and a willingness to work in a team setting. Those selected received extensive training in technical and interpersonal skills. During the first year of production, 25 percent of all hours worked were devoted to training at a cost of $750,000.

Training and development is one way to implement a company's corporate or business strategy. It is very important for a differentiation strategy that emphasizes quality or customer service. For example, Motorola, with annual sales of $13.3 billion, spends $120 million on employee education. The company is especially concerned with attaining the highest quality possible in all its operations. The company estimates that every $1 it spends on training delivers $30 in productivity gains within three years.

Training is also important when implementing a retrenchment strategy. As suggested earlier, successful downsizing means that the company has to invest in its remaining employees. General Electric's Aircraft Engine Group used training to maintain its share of the market even though it had cut its workforce from 42,000 to 33,000 between 1991 and 1993.[2]

How Does a Company Match the Manager to the Strategy?

The most appropriate type of general manager needed to effectively implement a new corporate or business strategy depends on the strategic direction that firm or business unit desires. An *executive type* is a classification of managers with particular mixes of skills and experiences. A certain type may be paired with a specific corporate strategy for best results. For example, a corporation following a concentration strategy that emphasizes vertical or horizontal integration would probably want an aggressive new chief executive with a great deal of experience in that particular industry—a *dynamic industry expert.* A diversification strategy, in contrast, might call for someone with an analytical mind who is highly knowledgeable in other industries and can manage diverse product lines—an *analytical portfolio manager.* A corporation choosing to follow a stability strategy would probably want as its CEO a person with a conservative style, a production or engineering background, and experience with controlling budgets, capital expenditures, inventories, and standardization procedures—a *cautious profit planner.* Weak companies in a relatively attractive industry tend to turn to a challenge-oriented executive to save the company—a *turnaround specialist.* If a company cannot be saved, a *professional liquidator* might be called on by a bankruptcy court to close the firm and liquidate its assets.

This approach is in agreement with Chandler who proposed (in chapter 8) that the most appropriate CEO of a company changes as a firm moves from one stage of development to another. Because priorities certainly change over an organization's life, successful corporations need to select managers who have skills and characteristics appropriate to the organization's particular stage of development and position in its life cycle.

Nevertheless, one study of 173 firms over a 25-year period revealed that CEOs in these companies tended to have the same functional specialization as the former CEO, especially when the past CEO's strategy continued to be successful. This may be a pattern for successful corporations.[3] In particular, it explains why so many prosperous companies tend to recruit their top executives from one particular background. At

Procter & Gamble, for example, the route to the CEO's position has always been through brand management. In other firms, the route may be through manufacturing, marketing, accounting, or finance, depending on what the corporation has always considered its principal area of expertise.

How Important Are Selection and Management Development?

Selection and development are important not only to ensure that people with the right mix of skills and experiences are hired initially, but also to help them grow on the job and be prepared for future promotions.

Executive Succession: Should a CEO Come from Inside the Company?

Executive succession is the process of replacing a key top manager. Given that the typical large U.S. corporation changes its chief executive every 8 years, firms need to plan for this eventuality.[4] Particularly companies that usually promote from within must prepare their current managers for promotion. Prosperous firms tend to look outside for CEO candidates only if they have no obvious internal candidates. Firms in trouble, however, tend to choose outsiders to lead them. Boards realize that the best way to move to a new strategy and to ensure its implementation is to hire a new CEO with no connections to the current strategy.

How Can Abilities Be Identified and Potential Developed?

A company can identify and prepare its people for important positions in several ways. One approach is to establish a sound *performance appraisal system,* which not only evaluates a person's performance, but also identifies promotion potential. A survey of 34 corporate planners and human resource executives from 24 large U.S. corporations revealed that approximately 80 percent made some attempt to identify managers' talents and behavioral tendencies, so that they could match a manager as closely as possible with a given competitive strategy.[5]

Many large organizations are using *assessment centers,* a method of evaluating a person's suitability for an advanced position. Corporations such as AT&T, Standard Oil, IBM, Sears, and GE have successfully used assessment centers. Because each is specifically tailored to its corporation, these assessment centers are unique. They use special interviews, management games, in-basket exercises, leaderless group discussions, case analyses, decision-making exercises, and oral presentations to assess the potential of employees for specific positions. Promotions into these positions are based on performance levels in the assessment center. Many assessment centers have proved to be highly predictive of subsequent job performance.

Many large corporations use job rotation, moving people from one job to another, to ensure that employees are gaining the appropriate mix of experiences to prepare them for future responsibilities. For example, companies that pursue related diversification strategies through internal development make greater use of interdivisional transfers of people than do companies that grow through unrelated acquisitions. Following a parenting corporate strategy, the companies that grow internally attempt to transfer important knowledge and skills throughout the corporation in order to achieve synergy.[6]

DOES RETRENCHMENT CREATE PROBLEMS?

Downsizing refers to the planned elimination of positions or jobs. Companies commonly use this program to implement retrenchment strategies. Because the financial community is likely to react favorably to announcements of downsizing from a company in difficulty, such a program may provide some short-term benefits such as raising the company's stock price. If not done properly, however, downsizing may result in less rather than in more productivity. One study of downsizing revealed that at 20 out of 30 automobile-related U.S. industrial companies, either the wrong jobs were eliminated or blanket offers of early retirement prompted managers, even those considered invaluable, to leave. After the layoffs, the employees who were left had to do not only their work, but also the work of the people who had gone. Because the survivors often didn't know how to do the work of those who had left, morale and productivity plummeted.[7] In addition, cost-conscious executives tend to defer maintenance, skimp on training, delay new product introductions, and avoid risky new businesses—all of which decrease sales and eventually profits. A situation can thus develop in which retrenchment feeds on itself and acts to further weaken the company instead of strengthening it.

Following are some proposed guidelines for successful downsizing:

- **Eliminate Unnecessary Work Instead of Making Across-the-Board Cuts.** Spend the time to research where money is going and eliminate the task, not the workers, if it doesn't add value to what the firm is producing.
- **Contract Out Work That Others Can Do Cheaper.** For example, Bankers Trust of New York contracts out to a division of Xerox its mail room and printing services and some of its payroll and accounts payable activities.
- **Plan for Long-Run Efficiencies.** Don't simply eliminate all postponable expenses, such as maintenance, R&D, and advertising, in the unjustifiable hope that the environment will become more supportive.
- **Communicate the Reasons for Actions.** Tell employees not only why the company is downsizing, but also what the company is trying to achieve.
- **Invest in the Remaining Employees.** Because most "survivors" in a corporate downsizing probably will be doing different tasks after the change, firms need to draft new job specifications, performance standards, appraisal techniques, and compensation packages. Additional training will be needed to ensure that everyone has the proper skills to deal with expanded jobs and responsibilities.
- **Develop Value-Added Jobs to Balance Out Job Elimination.** When no other jobs are currently available within the organization to transfer employees, management must consider some other staffing alternatives. Harley-Davidson, for example, worked with the company's unions to find other work for surplus employees by moving work previously done by suppliers into Harley plants.

WHAT ARE INTERNATIONAL ISSUES IN STAFFING?

Because of cultural differences, managerial style and human resource practices must be tailored in other countries to fit particular situations. Most multinational corporations (MNCs) attempt to fill managerial positions in their subsidiaries with well-qualified citizens of the host countries. Unilever and IBM take this approach. This policy serves to placate nationalistic governments and to better attune management practices to the host country's culture. The danger in using primarily foreign nationals to staff managerial positions in subsidiaries is the increased likelihood of suboptimization (the local subsidiary ignores the needs of the larger parent corporation). This makes it difficult for an MNC to meet its long-term, worldwide objectives. To a local national in an MNC subsidiary, the corporation as a whole is an abstraction. Communication and coordination across subsidiaries become more difficult. As it becomes harder to coordinate the activities of several international subsidiaries, an MNC will have serious problems operating in a global industry.

Another approach to staffing the managerial positions of MNCs is to use people with an international orientation, regardless of their country of origin or host country assignment. This is a widespread practice among European firms. For example, A.B. Electrolux, a Swedish firm, had a French director in its Singapore factory. This approach to using third-country nationals allows for more opportunities for promotion than does Unilever's policy of hiring local people, but it can result in a greater number of misunderstandings and conflicts with the local employees and with the host country's government.

To improve their chances of success using expatriates, multinational corporations are now emphasizing intercultural training for managers being assigned to a foreign country. This training is one of the commonly cited reasons for the lower expatriate failure rates—6 percent or less—for European and Japanese MNCs, which have emphasized cross-cultural experiences, compared with 35 percent for U.S.-based MNCs.[8]

9.2 LEADING

Implementation also involves *leading: motivating people to use their abilities and skills most effectively and efficiently to achieve organizational objectives.* Without direction, people tend to do their work according to their personal view of what tasks should be done, how, and in what order. They may approach their work as they have in the past or emphasize those tasks that they most enjoy, regardless of the corporation's priorities. Leading may take the form of management leadership, communicated norms of behavior from the corporate culture, or agreements among workers in autonomous work groups. It may also be accomplished more formally through action planning or through programs such as Management By Objectives (MBO) and Total Quality Management (TQM).

How Can a Company Manage Corporate Culture?

Because an organization's culture can exert a powerful influence on the behavior of all employees, it can strongly affect a company's ability to shift its strategic direction. A problem for a strong culture is that a change in mission, objectives, strategies, or policies is not likely to be successful if it is in opposition to the accepted culture of the company. Corporate culture has a strong tendency to resist change because its very reason for existence often rests on preserving stable relationships and patterns of behavior.

There is no best corporate culture. An optimal culture is one that best supports the mission and strategy of the company of which it is a part. This means that, like structure and staffing, corporate culture should follow strategy. Unless the strategy is in complete agreement with the culture, a significant change in strategy should thus be followed by a modification of the organization's culture. Although corporate culture can be changed, it may often take a long time and require much effort. A key job of management is therefore to evaluate (1) what a particular strategy change will mean to the corporate culture, (2) whether a change in culture will be needed, and (3) whether an attempt to change the culture will be worth the likely costs.

HOW CAN ONE ASSESS STRATEGY–CULTURE COMPATIBILITY?

When implementing a new strategy, management should consider the following questions regarding the corporation's *strategy-culture compatibility:* the fit between the new strategy and the existing culture.

1. Is the planned strategy compatible with the company's current culture? *If yes,* then proceed full-steam ahead. Tie organizational changes into the company's culture by identifying how the new strategy will achieve the mission better than the current strategy does. *If no,* ask the following question.

2. Can the culture be easily modified to make it more compatible with the new strategy? *If yes,* move forward carefully by introducing a set of culture-changing activities, such as minor structural modifications, training and development activities, or hiring new managers who are more compatible with the new strategy. When Procter & Gamble's top management decided to implement a strategy aimed at reducing costs, for example, it changed how some things were done but did not eliminate its brand management system. The culture was able to adapt to these modifications over a couple of years and productivity increased. *If no . . .*

3. Is management willing and able to make major organizational changes and accept probable delays and a likely increase in costs? *If yes,* manage around the culture by establishing a new structural unit to implement the new strategy. At General Motors, for example, top management realized that in order to be more competitive, the company had to make some radical changes. Because the current structure, culture, and procedures were very inflexible, management decided to establish a completely new division (GM's first new division since 1918), Saturn, to build its new auto. In cooperation with the United Auto Workers, an entirely new labor agreement was developed based on decisions reached by consensus. Carefully selected employees received from 100 to 750 hours of training, and a whole new culture was built piece by piece. *If no . . .*

4. Is management still committed to implementing the strategy? *If yes,* find a joint-venture partner or contract with another company to carry out the strategy. *If no,* formulate a different strategy.

HOW CAN COMMUNICATION BE USED TO MANAGE CULTURE?

Communication is crucial to effectively managing change. The rationale for strategic changes should be communicated to workers not only in newsletters and speeches but also in training and development programs. Companies in which major cultural changes have successfully taken place had the following characteristics in common:

- The CEO and other top managers had a strategic vision of what the company could become and communicated this vision to employees at all levels. The current performance of the company was compared to that of its competition and constantly updated.
- The vision was translated into the key elements necessary to accomplish that vision. For example, if the vision called for the company to become a leader in quality or service, aspects of quality and service were pinpointed for improvement and appropriate measurement systems were developed to monitor them. These measures were communicated widely through contests, formal and informal recognition, and monetary rewards, among other devices.[9]

HOW CAN DIVERSE CULTURES BE MANAGED IN AN ACQUISITION GROWTH STRATEGY?

When merging with or acquiring another company, top management must consider a potential clash of cultures. To assume that the firms can simply be integrated into the same reporting structure is dangerous. The greater the gap between the cultures of acquired and acquiring firms, the faster executives in the acquired firms quit their jobs and valuable talent is lost.

The four general methods of managing two different cultures are integration, assimilation, separation, and deculturation. (See Figure 9.1.) The choice of which method to use should be based on (1) the degree to which members of the acquired firm value the preservation of their own culture, and (2) their perception of the attractiveness of the acquirer.[10]

Integration involves a relatively balanced give-and-take of cultural and managerial practices between the merger partners and no strong imposition of cultural change on either company. It allows the two cultures to merge while preserving the separate cultures of both firms in the resulting culture. This is what occurred when the Seaboard and Chesapeake & Ohio railroads merged to form CSX Corporation. The top executives were so concerned that both cultures be equally respected that they kept referring to the company as a "partnership of equals."

Assimilation involves the domination of one organization by another. The domination is not forced but is welcomed by members of the acquired firm, who may feel for many reasons that their culture and managerial practices have not produced success. The acquired firm surrenders its culture and adopts the culture of the acquiring company. When Admiral was acquired by Maytag, Admiral employees were happy to adopt the quality-oriented culture of Maytag. After being managed by a series of firms who had no interest in major appliances, Admiral's employees had very low morale and a deteriorating culture.

Separation is characterized by a separation of the two companies' cultures. In the case of the Shearson–American Express merger, both parties agreed to keep the fast-paced Shearson completely separate from the planning-oriented American Express.

Deculturation involves the disintegration of one company's culture resulting from unwanted and extreme pressure from the other to impose its culture and practices. A great deal of confusion, conflict, resentment, and stress often accompanies this method. Such a merger typically results in poor performance by the acquired company and its

FIGURE 9.1 Methods of Managing the Culture of an Acquired Firm

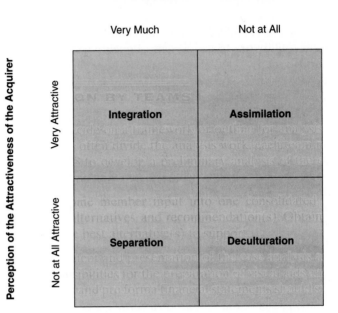

How Much Members of the Acquired Firm Value Preservation of Their Own Culture

	Very Much	Not at All
Very Attractive	Integration	Assimilation
Not at All Attractive	Separation	Deculturation

(vertical axis: Perception of the Attractiveness of the Acquirer)

Source: A. Nahavandi and A. R. Malekzadeh, "Acculturation in Mergers and Acquisitions," *Academy of Management Review* (January 1988), p. 83. Copyright © 1988 by the Academy of Management. Reprinted by permission.

eventual divestment. This is what happened when Exxon purchased a series of high-tech firms, each with a strong entrepreneurial culture. Exxon's insistence on following formal policies and procedures drove away the most creative employees from the acquired firms. Losing their entrepreneurial culture, the firms went into decline and were eventually sold.

WHAT IS ACTION PLANNING?

Activities can be directed toward accomplishing strategic goals through action planning. At a minimum, an *action plan* states what actions are going to be taken, by whom, during what timeframe, and with what expected results. Having selected a program to implement a particular strategy, the company should develop an action plan to put the program in place.

Take the example of a company that chose forward vertical integration through the acquisition of a retailing chain as its growth strategy. Now that it owns its own retail outlets, it must integrate them into the company. One of the many programs it would have to develop is a new advertising program for the stores. The resulting action plan to develop a new advertising program should include the following elements:

1. **Specific actions to be taken to make the program operational.** One action might be to contact three reputable advertising agencies and ask them to prepare a proposal for a new radio and newspaper ad campaign based on the theme "Jones Surplus is now a part of Ajax Continental. Prices are lower. Selection is better."

2. **Dates to begin and end each action.** Time would have to be allotted not only to select and contact three agencies, but to allow them sufficient time to prepare a detailed proposal. For example, allow 1 week to select and contact the agencies and 3 months for them to prepare detailed proposals to present to the company's marketing director. Also allow some time to make a decision on which proposal to accept.

3. **Person (identified by name and title) responsible for carrying out each action.** List someone, such as Jan Lewis, advertising manager, who can be put in charge of the program.

4. **Person responsible for monitoring the timeliness and effectiveness of each action.** Indicate that Jan Lewis is responsible for ensuring that the proposals are of good quality and are priced within the planned program budget. She is the primary company contact for the ad agencies and is expected to report on the progress of the program once a week to the company's marketing director.

5. **Expected financial and physical consequences of each action.** Estimate when a completed ad campaign will be ready to show top management and how long it will take after approval to begin to air the ads. Estimate also the expected increase in store sales over the 6-month period after the ads are first aired. Indicate if "recall" measures will be used to help assess the ad campaign's effectiveness and how, when, and by whom the recall data will be collected and analyzed.

6. **Contingency plans.** Indicate how long it will take to get another acceptable ad campaign ready to show top management if none of the initial proposals is acceptable.

Action plans are important for several reasons. *First,* they serve as a link between strategy formulation and evaluation and control. *Second,* the action plan specifies what needs to be done differently from the way operations are currently carried out. *Third,* during the evaluation and control process that comes later, an action plan helps appraise performance and identify any remedial actions, as needed. *Fourth,* the explicit assignment of responsibilities for implementing and monitoring the programs may improve motivation.

WHAT IS MANAGEMENT BY OBJECTIVES (MBO)?

Management by objectives (MBO) is an organization-wide approach to help assure purposeful action toward desired objectives by linking organizational objectives with individual behavior. Because it is a system that links plans with performance, MBO is a powerful implementation technique.

The MBO process involves:

1. Establishing and communicating organizational objectives.
2. Setting individual objectives (through superior–subordinate interaction) that help implement organizational ones.

3. Developing an action plan of activities needed to achieve the objectives.
4. Periodically (at least quarterly) reviewing performance as it relates to the objectives and including the results in the annual performance appraisal.

Management by objectives provides an opportunity for the corporation to connect the objectives of people at each level to those at the next higher level. Therefore, MBO ties together corporate, business, and functional objectives and the strategies developed to achieve them.

One of the real benefits of MBO is that it can reduce the amount of internal politics operating within a large corporation. Political actions can cause conflict and divide the very people and groups who should be working together to implement strategy. People are less likely to jockey for position if the company's mission and objectives are clear and they know that the reward system is based not on game playing, but on achieving clearly communicated, measurable objectives.

WHAT IS TOTAL QUALITY MANAGEMENT?

Total quality management (TQM) is an operational philosophy that stresses commitment to customer satisfaction and continuous improvement. Total quality management is committed to quality and excellence and to being the best in all functions. It has four objectives:

1. Better, less-variable quality of the product and service
2. Quicker, less-variable response in processes to customer needs
3. Greater flexibility in adjusting to customers' shifting requirements
4. Lower cost through quality improvement and elimination of nonvalue-adding work[11]

Because TQM aims to reduce costs as well as to improve quality, it can be used as a program to implement both an overall low cost or a differentiation business strategy.

According to TQM, faulty processes, not poorly motivated employees, cause defects in quality. To succeed in a company, the program usually involves a significant change in corporate culture, requiring strong leadership from top management, employee training, empowerment of lower level employees (giving people more control over their work), and teamwork. The emphasis in TQM is on prevention, not correction. Inspection for quality still takes place, but the emphasis is on improving the process to prevent errors and deficiencies. Thus *quality circles* (quality improvement teams) are formed to identify problems and suggest how to improve the processes that may be causing the problems.

The essential ingredients of TQM are:

- **An intense focus on customer satisfaction.** Everyone (not just people in the sales and marketing departments) understands that their jobs exist only because of customer needs. Thus all employees must approach their jobs in terms of how their work will affect customer satisfaction.
- **Customers are internal as well as external.** An employee in the shipping department may be the internal customer of another employee who completes the assembly of a product, just as a person who buys the product is a customer of the entire company. An employee must be just as concerned with pleasing the internal customer as with pleasing the external customer.

- **Accurate measurement of every critical variable in a company's operations.** Employees have to be trained in what to measure, how to measure, and how to interpret the data. A rule of TQM is "you only improve what you measure."
- **Continuous improvement of products and services.** Everyone realizes that operations need to be continuously monitored to find ways to improve products and services.
- **New work relationships based on trust and teamwork.** A key is the idea of *empowerment:* giving employees wide latitude in how they go about in achieving the company's goals.

WHAT ARE INTERNATIONAL CONSIDERATIONS IN LEADING?

In a study of 53 different national cultures, Hofstede found that each nation's unique culture could be identified using five dimensions. The *dimensions of national culture* are *power distance* (the extent to which a society accepts an unequal distribution of power in organizations), *uncertainty avoidance* (the extent to which a society feels threatened by uncertain and ambiguous situations), *individualism–collectivism* (the extent to which a society values individual freedom and independence of action compared with a tight social framework and loyalty to the group), *masculinity–femininity* (the extent to which society is oriented toward money and things or toward people), and *long-term orientation* (the extent to which society is oriented toward the long- versus the short-term).

Hofstede found that national culture is so influential that it tends to overwhelm even a strong corporate culture. In measuring the differences among these dimensions of national culture from country to country, he was able to explain why a certain management practice might be successful in one nation, but not in another.[12]

These dimensions of national culture may help to explain why some management practices work well in some countries but not in others. For example, MBO, which originated in the United States, has succeeded in Germany, according to Hofstede, because the idea of replacing the arbitrary authority of the boss with the impersonal authority of mutually agreed-upon objectives fits the small power distance and strong uncertainty avoidance that are dimensions of the German culture. It has failed in France, however, because the French are used to large power distances, to accepting orders from a highly personalized authority. Some of the difficulties experienced by U.S. companies in using Japanese-style quality circles may stem from the extremely high value U.S. culture places on individualism.

Multinational corporations must pay attention to the many differences in cultural dimensions around the world and appropriately adjust their management practices. Cultural differences can easily go unrecognized by a headquarters staff that may interpret these differences as personality defects, whether the people in the subsidiaries are locals or expatriates.

IN CONCLUSION

Shirley Young, a Vice-President of Marketing at General Motors, was instrumental in helping GM negotiate a $1 billion joint venture with Shanghai Automotive to build a Buick plant in China. Uniquely qualified for this assignment, Young had been born in

Shanghai, had relatives in China, and was fluent in Chinese. Her father, a hero in China, had been that country's Consul General to the Philippines during World War II. When GM wanted to establish links with China in 1992, it asked Young to help its people become acquainted with influential people in China's government and industrial circles. Young and other Chinese Americans formed a committee to advise GM on relations with China. Although just a part of a larger team of GM employees working on the joint venture, Young coached GM employees on Chinese customs and traditions. Rather than eating together after transacting business, for example, she suggested that GM follow the Chinese practice of dining first. "These are little things that are just differences in the way each one looks at the world," says Ms. Young. "My being Chinese helps in that regard."[13]

Discussion Questions

1. What skills should a person have for managing a business unit following a differentiation strategy? Why? What should a company do if no one is available internally and the company has a policy of promotion from within?

2. When should someone from outside the company be hired to manage the company of one of its business units?

3. What are some ways to implement a retrenchment strategy without creating a lot of resentment and conflict with labor unions?

4. How can corporate culture be changed?

5. What value does total quality management have in implementing strategy?

Key Terms (listed in order of appearance)

staffing
executive type
executive succession
performance appraisal system
assessment centers
downsizing
leading

strategy–culture compatibility
action plan
management by objectives (MBO)
total quality management (TQM)
quality circles
dimensions of national culture

Notes

1. B. O'Reilly, "The Rent-A-Car Jocks Who Made Enterprise #1," *Fortune* (October 28, 1996): 125–128.

2. R. Henkoff, "Companies That Train Best," *Fortune* (March 22, 1993): 62–75.

3. M. Smith, and M. C. White, "Strategy, CEO Specialization, and Succession," *Administrative Science Quarterly* (June 1987): 263–280.

4. R. F. Vancil, *Passing the Baton* (Boston: Harvard Business School Press, 1987).

5. P. Lorange, and D. Murphy, "Bringing Human Resources into Strategic Planning: System Design Characteristics," in *Strategic Human Resource Management,* edited by C. J. Fombrun, N. M. Tichy, and M. A. Devanna (New York: John Wiley & Sons, 1984), 281–283.

6. R. A. Pitts, "Strategies and Structures for Diversification," *Academy of Management Journal* (June 1977): 197–208.

7. B. O'Reilly, "Is Your Company Asking Too Much?" *Fortune* (March 12, 1990): 41.

8. R. L. Tung, *The New Expatriates* (Cambridge, MA: Ballinger, 1988); J. S. Black,

M. Mendenhall, and G. Oddou, "Toward a Comprehensive Model of International Adjustment: An Integration of Multiple Theoretical Perspectives," *Academy of Management Review* (April 1991): 291–317.

9. G. G. Gordon, "The Relationship of Corporate Culture to Industry Sector and Corporate Performance," in *Gaining Control of the Corporate Culture*, edited by R. H. Kilmann, M. J. Saxton, R. Serpa, and Associates (San Francisco: Jossey-Bass, 1985), 123.

10. A. R. Malekzadeh, and A. Nahavandi, "Making Mergers Work by Managing Cultures," *Journal of Business Strategy* (May–June 1990): 53–57; A. Nahavandi, and A. R. Malekzadeh, "Acculturation in Mergers and Acquisitions," *Academy of Management Review* (January 1988): 79–90.

11. R. J. Schonberger, "Total Quality Management Cuts a Broad Swath—Through Manufacturing and Beyond," *Organizational Dynamics* (Spring 1992): 16–28.

12. G. Hofstede, *Cultures and Organizations: Software of the Mind* (London: McGraw-Hill, 1991); G. Hofstede, and M. H. Bond, "The Confucius Connection: From Cultural Roots to Economic Growth," *Organizational Dynamics* (Spring 1988): 5–21; R. Hodgetts, "A Conversation with Geert Hofstede," *Organizational Dynamics* (Spring 1993): 53–61.

13. G. Stern, "GM Executive's Ties to Native Country Help Auto Maker Clinch Deal in China," *Wall Street Journal* (November 2, 1995): B7.

CHAPTER 10

EVALUATION AND CONTROL

During the spring of 1992, Jim Cannavino, the manager in charge of IBM's personal computer business, insisted that his was the most profitable PC business in the world. Unfortunately his comment was based on the very strange way in which IBM allocated its costs to products. For example, IBM's system of accounting allocated all of a particular technology's R&D spending to the first group that used the technology; other IBM units then were able to use that technology free. As IBM found itself facing declining profits, it changed its cost allocation system to a more realistic one. In the fall of 1992, IBM disclosed that its PC business was actually unprofitable. IBM's competitors commented that the business had probably been losing money on and off for years, IBM just didn't know it!

Evaluation and control is the process by which corporate activities and performance results are monitored so that actual performance can be compared with desired performance. The process provides the feedback necessary for management to evaluate the results and take corrective action, as needed. This process can be viewed as a 5-step feedback model, as depicted in Figure 10.1.

1. **Determine what to measure.** Top managers and operational managers must specify implementation processes and results to be monitored and evaluated. The processes and results must be measurable in a reasonably objective and consistent manner. The focus should be on the most significant elements in a process, the ones that account for the highest proportion of expense or the greatest number of problems. Measurements must be found for all important areas regardless of difficulty.

2. **Establish standards of performance.** Standards used to measure performance are detailed expressions of strategic objectives. They are measures of acceptable performance results. Each standard usually includes a tolerance range, which defines any acceptable deviations. Standards can be set not only for final output, but also for intermediate stages of production output.

3. **Measure actual performance.** Measurements must be made at predetermined times.

4. **Compare actual performance with the standard.** If the actual performance results are within the desired tolerance range, the measurement process stops here.

5. **Take corrective action.** If the actual results fall outside the desired tolerance range, action must be taken to correct the deviation. The action must not only correct the deviation, but also prevent its recurrence. The following issues must be resolved:

   (a) Is the deviation only a chance fluctuation?
   (b) Are the processes being carried out incorrectly?
   (c) Are the processes appropriate for achieving the desired standard?

Top management is often better at the first two steps of the control model than they are in the last three follow-through steps. The tendency to establish a control system and then delegate the implementation to others can have unfortunate results.

10.1 EVALUATION AND CONTROL IN STRATEGIC MANAGEMENT

Evaluation and control information consists of performance data and activity reports (gathered in Step 3 of Figure 10.1). Operational managers must know about any inappropriate use of strategic management processes that causes undesired performance so that they can correct the employee activity. Top management need not be involved. If, however, the processes themselves cause the undesired performance, both top managers and operational managers must know about it so that they can develop new implementation programs or procedures.

Evaluation and control information must be relevant to what is being monitored. The IBM example demonstrates how the use of inappropriate data clouded the perceptions of the head of IBM's PC unit and may have led to poor strategic decision making. Evaluation and control is not an easy process. One of the obstacles to effective control is the difficulty in developing appropriate measures of important activities and outputs.

10.2 MEASURING PERFORMANCE

Performance is the end result of activity. Which measures to select to assess performance depends on the organizational unit to be appraised and the objectives to be

FIGURE 10.1   Evaluation and Control Process

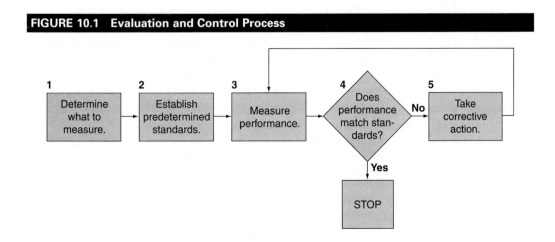

achieved. The objectives that were established earlier in the strategy formulation part of the strategic management process (dealing with profitability, market share, and cost reduction, among others) should certainly be used to measure corporate performance once the strategies have been implemented.

WHEN SHOULD MEASURES BE USED?

Some measures, such as *return on investment* (ROI), are appropriate for evaluating the corporation's or division's ability to achieve a profitability objective. This type of measure, however, is inadequate for evaluating additional corporate objectives such as social responsibility or employee development. Even though profitability is a corporation's major objective, ROI can be computed only after profits are totaled for a period. It tells what happened after the fact, not what is happening or what will happen. A firm, therefore, needs to develop measures that predict likely profitability. These are referred to as *steering controls* because they measure variables that influence future profitability. One example of this type of control is the use of control charts in statistical process control (SPC). In SPC, workers and managers maintain charts and graphs detailing quality and productivity on a daily basis. They are thus able to adjust the system before it gets out of control.

HOW DO BEHAVIOR AND OUTPUT CONTROLS DIFFER?

Controls can be established to focus either on actual performance results (output) or on the activities that generate the performance (behavior). *Behavior controls* specify how something is to be done through policies, rules, standard operating procedures, and orders from a superior. *Output controls* specify what is to be accomplished by focusing on the end result of the behaviors through the use of objectives and performance targets or milestones. Behavior and output controls are not interchangeable. Behavior controls (such as following company procedures, making sales calls to potential customers, and getting to work on time) are most appropriate when performance results are hard to measure and a clear cause–effect connection exists between activities and results. Output controls (such as sales quotas, specific cost reduction or profit objectives, and surveys of customer satisfaction) are most appropriate when specific output measures are agreed upon and no clear cause–effect connection exists between activities and results.

One example of an increasingly popular behavior control is the ISO 9000 series on quality management and assurance developed by the International Standards Association of Geneva, Switzerland. The ISO 9000 Standards Series (composed of five sections from 9000 to 9004) is a way of objectively documenting a company's high level of quality operations. Many corporations view ISO 9000 certification as assurance that a supplier sells quality products. Firms such as DuPont, Hewlett-Packard, and 3M have facilities registered to ISO standards. Companies in over 60 countries, including Canada, Mexico, Japan, the United States (including the entire U.S. auto industry), as well as in the European Union, are requiring ISO 9000 certification of their suppliers. In one survey of manufacturing executives, 51 percent of the executives found that certification increased their international competitiveness. Other executives noted that it signaled their commitment to quality and gave them a strategic advantage over non-certified competitors.[1]

WHAT IS THE VALUE OF ACTIVITY-BASED COSTING?

Activity-based costing (ABC) is a new accounting method for allocating indirect and fixed costs to individual products or product lines based on the value-added activities going into that product.[2] This accounting method is thus very useful in doing a value-chain analysis of a firm's activities for making outsourcing decisions. Traditional cost accounting, in contrast, focuses on valuing a company's inventory for financial reporting purposes. To obtain a unit's cost, cost accountants typically add direct labor to the cost of materials. Then they compute overhead from rent to R&D expenses, based on the number of direct labor hours it takes to make a product. To obtain unit cost, they divide the total by the number of items made during the period under consideration.

ABC accounting allows accountants to charge costs more accurately than the traditional method because it allocates overhead far more precisely. Activity-based costing can be used in many types of industries. For example, a bakery may use standard costs to allocate costs to products and to price customers' orders. Under the traditional standard cost system, overhead costs such as selling, advertising, warehousing, shipping, and administration are allocated to products and spread over the entire customer base. Under a traditional standard cost system, a bakery would allocate order-handling charges on a percentage of sales basis. When this is done, profitable accounts tend to subsidize unprofitable ones without anyone's knowledge. What is ignored is that the amount of time and expense spent processing an order is usually the same, regardless of whether the order is for 200 or 2000 donuts. The cost driver is not the number of cases ordered but the number of separate sales orders that must be processed. By assigning costs based on the number of orders that have to be processed, instead of by the dollar value of the order, the bakery can calculate a much more accurate cost for processing each customer's order. This information is crucial if management is to assess the profitability of different customers and to make strategic decisions regarding growth or retrenchment.[3]

WHAT ARE THE PRIMARY MEASURES OF CORPORATE PERFORMANCE?

The most commonly used measure of corporate performance (in terms of profits) is ROI. It is simply the result of dividing net income before taxes by total assets. Return on investment has several advantages. It is a single comprehensive figure that is influenced by everything that happens. It measures how well a division manager uses the division's assets to generate profits. It is a common denominator that can be compared with other companies and business units. It provides an incentive to use existing assets efficiently and to buy new ones only when it would increase profits. Nevertheless, ROI also has several distinct limitations. Although ROI gives the impression of objectivity and precision, it can be easily manipulated. For example, ROI is very sensitive to depreciation policy and to book value of assets, both of which can be manipulated by self-serving managers. A given amount of profits provides a greater ROI figure if the book value of the assets is low than if it is high. Further, it is difficult to set a *transfer price*, the price at which one division sells its product to another division. A more powerful division could force a less powerful division to sell its product at a lower price than it would get on the open market, thus reducing the selling division's ROI and increasing that of the purchasing division. Since ROI can be calculated for the short-run as well as for the long-run, there is a tendency to use it primarily for short-run purposes, such as quarterly or annual bonuses, thus driving out long-term strategic planning in favor of short-run tactical maneuvers.

Earnings per share (EPS), dividing net earnings by the amount of common stock, also has the advantage of being used as one overall measure of corporate performance. Nevertheless, it has several deficiencies as an evaluation of past and future performance. First, because alternative accounting principles are available, EPS can have several different but equally acceptable values, depending on the principle selected for its computation. Second, because EPS is based on accrual income, the conversion of income to cash can be near term or delayed. Therefore, EPS does not consider the present value of money. *Return on equity* (ROE), dividing net income by total equity, is another popular performance measure. It has its share of limitations because it is also derived from accounting-based data. In addition, EPS and ROE are often unrelated to a company's stock price. Because of these and other limitations, ROI, EPS, and ROE by themselves are not adequate measures of corporate performance.

WHAT ARE STAKEHOLDER MEASURES?

Each stakeholder has its own set of criteria to determine how well the corporation is performing. These criteria typically deal with the direct and indirect impact of corporate activities on stakeholder interests. Top management should establish one or more simple measures for each stakeholder category so that it can keep track of stakeholder concerns. For example, sales and sales growth are good measures to use with customers; costs and delivery time with suppliers; stock price and number of "buy lists" with the financial community; turnover and grievances with employees; number of pieces of negative legislation and amount of financial incentives with government; hostile encounters and legal actions with consumer and environmental advocates.

WHAT IS SHAREHOLDER VALUE?

Because of the belief that accounting-based numbers such as return on investment, return on equity, and earnings per share are not reliable indicators of a corporation's economic value, many corporations are using shareholder value as a better measure of corporate performance and strategic management effectiveness. *Shareholder value* is defined as the present value of the anticipated future stream of cash flows from the business plus the value of the company if liquidated. Arguing that the purpose of a company is to increase shareholder wealth, shareholder value analysis concentrates on cash flow as the key measure of performance. The value of a corporation is thus the value of its cash flows discounted back to their present value, using the business's cost of capital as the discount rate. As long as the returns from a business exceed its cost of capital, the business will create value and be worth more than the capital invested in it.

Economic value added (EVA) is after-tax operating profit minus the total annual cost of capital. It measures the difference between the pre-strategy and post-strategy value of the business. If the difference, discounted by the cost of capital, is positive, the strategy is generating value for the shareholders. Among the many companies using the new measure instead of ROI are Coca-Cola, AT&T, Quaker Oats, Briggs & Stratton, and CSX. Explained by Roberto Goizueta, when he was CEO of Coca-Cola, "We raise capital to make concentrate, and sell it at an operating profit. Then we pay the cost of that capital. Shareholders pocket the difference."[4] Unlike ROI, one of EVA's most powerful properties is its strong relationship to stock price. Managers can improve their company's or business unit's EVA by (1) earning more profit without using more capital, (2) using less capital, and (3) investing capital in high-return projects. The EVA approach can be further extended to an additional measure: *Market value added* (MVA) measures the stock market's estimate of the net present value of a firm's past and expected capital investment projects.[5]

HOW IS TOP MANAGEMENT EVALUATED?

Through its strategy, audit, and compensation committees, a board of directors closely evaluates the job performance of the CEO and the top management team. Of course, the board is concerned primarily with overall profitability as measured quantitatively by return on investment, return on equity, earnings per share, and shareholder value. The absence of short-run profitability is certainly a factor contributing to the firing of any CEO, but the board is also concerned with other factors.

Members of the compensation committees of today's boards of directors generally agree that measuring a CEO's ability to establish strategic direction, build a management team, and provide leadership is more critical in the long run than are a few quantitative measures. The board should evaluate top management not only on the typical output-oriented quantitative measures, but also on behavioral measures, factors relating to its strategic management practices.

The specific measures that a board uses to evaluate its top management should be based on the objectives agreed on earlier by both the board and top management. If better relations with the local community and improved safety practices in work areas were selected as objectives for the year (or for 5 years), these items should be included in the evaluation. In addition, other factors that tend to lead to profitability might be included, such as market share, product quality, or investment intensity.

WHAT IS THE VALUE OF A MANAGEMENT AUDIT?

Used by various consulting firms as a way to measure performance, audits of corporate activities are frequently suggested for use by boards of directors and by others in managerial positions. *Management audits* (in-depth analyses of organizational activities) have been developed to evaluate activities such as corporate social responsibility, functional areas such as the marketing department, and divisions such as the international division, as well as the corporation itself in a strategic audit. (See Appendix 11.C for an example of a strategic audit.)

WHAT ARE THE PRIMARY MEASURES OF DIVISIONAL AND FUNCTIONAL PERFORMANCE?

Companies use a variety of techniques to evaluate and control performance in divisions, strategic business units (SBUs), and functional areas. If a corporation is composed of SBUs or divisions, it will use many of the same performance measures (ROI or EVA, for instance) that it uses to assess overall corporation performance. To the extent that it can isolate specific functional units, such as R&D, the corporation may develop responsibility centers. It will also use typical functional measures such as market share and sales per employee (marketing), unit costs and percentage of defects (operations), percentage of sales from new products and number of patents (R&D), and turnover and job satisfaction (HRM).

During strategy formulation and implementation, top management approves a series of programs and supporting operating budgets from its business units. *Operating budgets* list the costs and expenses for each proposed program in dollar terms. During evaluation and control, management contrasts actual expenses with planned expenditures and assesses the degree of variance, typically on a monthly basis. In addition, top management probably will require *periodic statistical reports,* which summarize data on key factors such as the number of new customer contracts, volume of received orders, and productivity figures.

WHAT ARE RESPONSIBILITY CENTERS?

Control systems can be established to monitor specific functions, projects, or divisions. For example, budgets typically are used to control the financial indicators of performance. Responsibility centers are used to isolate a unit so that it can be evaluated separately from the rest of the corporation. A *responsibility center* has its own budget, is evaluated on its use of budgeted resources, and is headed by a manager who is responsible for its performance. The center uses resources (measured in terms of costs or expenses) to produce a service or a product (measured in terms of volume or revenues). The way in which the corporation's control system measures these resources and services or products determines which of the five major types of responsibility centers is used.

- **Standard cost centers.** Primarily used in manufacturing facilities, standard (or expected) costs are computed for each operation on the basis of historical data. In evaluating the center's performance, its total standard costs are multiplied by the units produced; the result is the expected cost of production, which is then compared to the actual cost of production.
- **Revenue centers.** Production, usually in terms of unit or dollar sales, is measured without considering resource costs (e.g., salaries). The center is thus judged in terms of effectiveness rather than efficiency. The effectiveness of a sales region, for example, is determined by comparing its actual sales to its projected or previous year's sales. Profits are not considered because sales departments have limited influence over the cost of the products they sell.
- **Expense centers.** Resources are measured in dollars without considering service or product costs. Thus budgets are prepared for engineered expenses (costs that can be calculated) and for discretionary expenses (costs that can be only estimated). Typical expense centers are administrative, service, and research departments. They cost an organization money, but they contribute only indirectly to revenues.
- **Profit centers.** Performance is measured in terms of the difference between revenues (which measure production) and expenditures (which measure resources). A profit center is typically established whenever an organizational unit controls both its resources and its products or services. By having such centers, a company can be organized into divisions of separate product lines. The manager of each division is given autonomy to the extent that she

or he is able to keep profits at a satisfactory (or better) level. Some organizational units that are not usually considered potentially autonomous can, for the purpose of profit-center evaluations, be made so by using transfer pricing.

- **Investment centers.** Because many divisions in large manufacturing corporations use significant assets to make their products, their asset base should be factored into their performance evaluation. Thus to focus only on profits, as in the case of profit centers, is insufficient. An investment center's performance is measured in terms of the difference between its resources and its services or products. For example, two divisions in a corporation made identical profits, but one division owns a $3 million plant, whereas the other owns a $1 million plant. Both make the same profits, but one is obviously more efficient: the smaller plant provides the shareholders with a better return on their investment. The most widely used measure of investment center performance is return on investment (ROI).

Most single-business corporations, such as Apple Computer, tend to use a combination of cost, expense, and revenue centers. In these corporations, most managers are functional specialists and manage against a budget. Total profitability is integrated at the corporate level. Multidivisional corporations with one dominating product line, such as Anheuser-Busch, which have diversified into a few small businesses but which still depend on a single product line (such as beer) for most of their revenue and income, generally use a combination of cost, expense, revenue, and profit centers. Multidivisional corporations, such as General Electric, tend to emphasize investment centers, although in various units throughout the corporation other types of responsibility centers will also be used. One problem with using responsibility centers, however, is that the separation needed to measure and evaluate a division's performance can make it difficult to achieve the level of cooperation among divisions needed to attain synergy for the corporation as a whole.

How Is Benchmarking Used to Evaluate Performance?

According to Xerox Corporation, the company that pioneered this concept in the United States, *benchmarking* is the continual process of measuring products, services, and practices against the toughest competitors or those companies recognized as industry leaders.[6] Benchmarking, an increasingly popular program, is based on the concept that to reinvent something that someone else is already using makes no sense. It involves openly learning how other companies do something better and not only imitating but perhaps even improving on their techniques. The benchmarking process usually involves the following steps:

1. Identify the area or process to be examined: It should be an activity which has the potential to determine a business unit's competitive advantage.

2. Find behavioral and output measures of the area or process and obtain measurements.

3. Select an accessible set of competitors and best-in-class companies against which to benchmark: These may very often be companies that are in completely different industries but perform similar activities. For example, when Xerox wanted to improve its order fulfillment, it went to L. L. Bean, the successful mail order firm, to learn how they achieved excellence in this area.

4. Calculate the differences among the company's performance measurements and those of the best-in-class: Determine why the differences exist.

5. Develop tactical programs for closing performance gaps.

6. Implement the programs and then compare the resulting new measurements with those of the best-in-class companies.

Manco, Inc., a small Cleveland-area producer of duct tape, regularly benchmarks itself against Wal-Mart, Rubbermaid, and PepsiCo to enable it to better compete with giant 3M. The American Productivity & Quality Center, a Houston research group, manages a "best practices database" of 600 leading techniques from 250 companies.[7]

WHAT ARE INTERNATIONAL MEASUREMENT ISSUES?

The three most widely used techniques for international performance evaluation are ROI, budget analysis, and historical comparisons. Even though ROI is the single most used measure of international operations, it has serious limitations. Because of foreign currencies, different rates of inflation, different tax laws, and the use of transfer pricing, both the net income figure and the investment base may be seriously distorted. Transfer pricing is used heavily in multinational corporations (MNC) not only to calculate the ROI for responsibility centers in various countries, but also to minimize taxes. For example, parts made in a subsidiary of an MNC in a low-tax country like Singapore can be shipped to its subsidiary in a high-tax country like the U.S. at such a high price that the U.S. subsidiary reports very little profit (and thus pays few taxes), while the Singapore subsidiary reports a very high profit (but also pays few taxes because of the lower tax rate). The MNC can, therefore, earn more profit worldwide by reporting less profit in high-tax countries and more profit in low-tax countries (assuming governments in high-tax countries do not retaliate with tariff barriers and lawsuits).

The control and reward systems used by a global MNC should be different from those used by a *multidomestic MNC*. The multidomestic MNC should use loose controls on its foreign units. The management of each geographic unit should be given considerable operational latitude, but it should be expected to meet some performance targets. Multiple measures should be used to differentiate between the worth of the subsidiary and the performance of its management. The *global MNC,* in contrast, needs tight controls over its many units. To reduce costs and gain competitive advantage, it is trying to spread the manufacturing and marketing operations of a few fairly uniform products around the world. Therefore, its key operational decisions must be centralized. Foreign units are thus evaluated more as cost centers, revenue centers, or expense centers than as investment or profit centers because MNCs operating in a global industry do not often make the entire product in the country in which it is sold.

10.3 STRATEGIC INFORMATION SYSTEMS

Before performance measures can have any impact on strategic management, they must first be communicated to the people responsible for formulating and implementing strategic plans. Strategic information systems—computer-based or manual, formal or informal—can perform this function. One of the main reasons given for the bankruptcy of International Harvester was the inability of the corporation's top management to precisely determine its income by major classes of similar products. Because of this inability, management kept trying to fix ailing businesses and was unable to respond flexibly to major changes and unexpected events. In contrast, one of the main reasons for the success of Toys 'R' Us has been management's use of the company's sophisticated information system to control purchasing decisions. Cash registers in the more than 300 U.S. Toys 'R' Us stores transmit information daily to computers at the company's headquarters. Consequently managers know every morning exactly how many of each item were sold the day before, how many have been sold so far in the year, and how this year's sales compare to last year's. The information system allows automatic reordering by computer without managerial input. It also allows the company to experiment with new toys without committing to big orders in advance. In effect, the system allows the customers to decide through their purchases what gets reordered.

At the divisional or SBU level of a corporation, the information system should be used to support, reinforce, or enlarge its business-level strategy through its decision support system. An SBU pursuing a strategy of overall cost leadership could use its information system to reduce costs by either improving labor productivity or using other resources such as inventory or machinery. For example, Merrill Lynch developed PRISM software to provide its 500 U.S. retail offices quick access to financial information in order to boost the efficiency of its brokers. Another SBU, in contrast, might wish to pursue a differentiation strategy. It could use its information system to add uniqueness to the product or service and contribute to quality, service, or image through the functional areas. Federal Express wanted to use superior service to gain a competitive advantage. It invested heavily in several types of information systems to measure and track the performance of its delivery service. Together, these information systems gave Federal Express the fastest error-response time in the overnight delivery business.

Multinational corporations are adopting enterprise resource planning (ERP) software, such as R/3 from the German company SAP A.G. The R/3 software system integrates and automates order taking, credit checking, payment verification, and book balancing. Because of R/3's ability to use a common information system throughout a company's many operations around the world, it is becoming the global standard of business information systems. Microsoft, for example, is using R/3 to replace a tangle of 33 financial tracking systems in 26 subsidiaries. Even though it cost the company $25 million and took 10 months to install, R/3 annually saves Microsoft $18 million. R/3 is, nevertheless, not for every company. The system is extremely complicated and demands a high level of standardization throughout a corporation. Its demanding nature often forces companies to change the way they do business. Over the 2-year period of installing R/3, Owens-Corning had to completely overhaul its operations.

10.4 GUIDELINES FOR PROPER CONTROL

Measuring performance is a crucial part of evaluation and control. The lack of quantifiable objectives or performance standards and the inability of the information system to provide timely, valid information are two obvious control problems. Without objective and timely measurements, making operational, let alone strategic, decisions would be extremely difficult. Nevertheless, the use of timely, quantifiable standards does not guarantee good performance. The very act of monitoring and measuring performance can cause side effects that interfere with overall corporate performance. Inappropriate controls can result in managers manipulating the measures for personal advantage to the detriment of the company.

In designing a control system, top management should remember that *controls should follow strategy.* Unless controls ensure the use of the proper strategy to achieve objectives, dysfunctional side effects are likely to completely undermine the implementation of the objectives. The following guidelines are recommended:

1. Controls should involve only the minimum amount of information needed to give a reliable picture of events. Too many controls create confusion. Focus on the *critical success factors:* the 20 percent of the factors that determine 80 percent of the results.

2. Controls should monitor only meaningful activities and results, regardless of measurement difficulty. If cooperation between divisions is important to corporate performance, some form of qualitative or quantitative measure should be established to monitor cooperation.

3. Controls should be timely. Corrective action must be taken before it is too late. Steering controls, controls that monitor or measure the factors influencing performance, should be stressed so that advance notice of problems is given.

4. Controls should be long-term and short-term. If only short-term measures are emphasized, a short-term managerial orientation is likely.

5. Controls should pinpoint exceptions. Only those activities or results that fall outside a predetermined tolerance range should call for action.

6. Controls should be used to reward meeting or exceeding standards rather than to punish failure to meet standards. Heavy punishment of failure typically results in goal displacement. Managers will "fudge" reports and lobby for lower standards.

To the extent that the culture complements and reinforces the strategic orientation of the firm, there is less need for an extensive formal control system. In their book *In Search of Excellence,* Peters and Waterman state that "the stronger the culture and the more it was directed toward the marketplace, the less need was there for policy manuals, organization charts, or detailed procedures and rules. In these companies, people way down the line know what they are supposed to do in most situations because the handful of guiding values is crystal clear."[8]

10.5 STRATEGIC INCENTIVE MANAGEMENT

To ensure congruence between the needs of the corporation as a whole and the needs of the employees as individuals, management and the board of directors should develop an incentive program that rewards desired performance. Incentive plans should be linked in some way to corporate and divisional strategy. For example, a survey of 600 business units indicates that the pay mix associated with a growth strategy emphasizes bonuses and other incentives over salary and benefits, whereas the pay mix associated with a stability strategy has the reverse emphasis.[9]

The following three approaches are tailored to help match measurements and rewards with explicit strategic objectives and timeframes.[10]

- **Weighted-factor method.** This method is particularly appropriate for measuring and rewarding the performance of top SBU managers and group-level executives when performance factors and their importance vary from one SBU to another. The measurements that one corporation uses might contain the following variations: The performance of high-growth SBUs is measured in terms of market share, sales growth, designated future payoff, and progress on several future-oriented strategic projects; the performance of low-growth SBUs, in contrast, is measured in terms of ROI and cash generation; and the performance of medium-growth SBUs is measured for a combination of these factors. (See Table 10.1.)
- **Long-term evaluation method.** This method compensates managers for achieving objectives set over a multiyear period. An executive is promised some company stock or "performance units" (convertible into money) in amounts to be based on long-term performance. An executive committee, for example, might set a particular objective in terms of growth in earnings per share during a 5-year period. Awards would be contingent on the corporation's meeting that objective within the designated time. Any executive who leaves the corporation before the objective is met receives nothing. The typical emphasis on stock price makes this approach more applicable to top management than to business unit managers.

TABLE 10.1   Weighted-Factor Approach to Strategic Incentive Management

Strategic Business Unit Category	Factor	Weight
High Growth	Return on assests	10%
	Cash flow	0%
	Strategic-funds programs (developmental expenses)	45%
	Market-share increase	45%
		100%
Medium Growth	Return on assests	25%
	Cash flow	25%
	Strategic-funds programs (developmental expenses)	25%
	Market-share increase	25%
		100%
Low Growth	Return on assests	50%
	Cash flow	50%
	Strategic-funds programs (developmental expenses)	0%
	Market-share increase	0%
		100%

Source: Reprinted by permission of the publisher from "The Performance Measurement and Reward System: Critical to Strategic Management," by Paul J. Stonich, from *Organizational Dynamics* (Winter 1984), p. 51. Copyright (c) 1984 by American Management Association, New York. All rights reserved.

- **Strategic-funds method.** This method encourages executives to look at developmental expenses as being different from those expenses required for current operations. The accounting statement for a corporate unit enters strategic funds as a separate entry below the current ROI. It is therefore possible to distinguish between those expense dollars consumed in the generation of current revenues and those invested in the future of the business. Therefore, the manager can be evaluated on both a short- and a long-term basis and has an incentive to invest strategic funds in the future. (See Table 10.2.)

An effective way to achieve the desired strategic results through a reward system is to combine the three approaches in the following manner:

1. Segregate strategic funds from short-term funds, as is done in the strategic-funds method.
2. Develop a weighted-factor chart for each SBU.
3. Measure performance on three bases: The pretax profit indicated by the strategic-funds approach, the weighted factors, and the long-term evaluation of SBU and corporate performance.

IN CONCLUSION

Mary Baechler, founder and president of Racing Strollers, Inc., became concerned that her company was not properly implementing its high-quality competitive strategy. The company's control system was not sufficient to track and to guarantee total customer satisfaction. She implemented a new delivery program with an innovative method of guaranteeing quality customer service:

> Anyone in our company can stop production if he thinks there's a flaw. Any employee can send a stroller that's on order via Federal Express (at $87 a pop!) if he feels we have not met our delivery commitments. Beyond our lifetime guarantee for frames and one-year guarantee on wheels, our customer service people can do whatever it takes, up to $300 per customer, to

TABLE 10.2 Strategic-Funds Approach to an SBU's Profit-and-Loss Statement

Sales	$12,300,000
Cost of sales	–6,900,000
Gross margin	$ 5,400,000
General and administrative expenses	–3,700,000
Operating profit (return on sales)	$ 1,700,000
Strategic funds (development expenses)	–1,000,000
Pretax profit	$ 700,000

Source: Reprinted by permission of the publisher from "The Performance Measurement and Reward System: Critical to Strategic Management," by Paul J. Stonich, from *Organizational Dynamics* (Winter 1984), p. 51. Copyright (c) 1984 by American Management Association, New York. All rights reserved.

make things right for the customer (we track costs religiously so that we can keep this up). We stay in contact after each repair, and the customer gets a postcard to send that comes directly to me and lets me know if we took care of matters to the customer's satisfaction. And we keep trying, until that customer is doing great. Those postcards are an immediate report card and the best part of my day.[11]

Discussion Questions

1. Is Figure 10.1 a realistic model of the evaluation and control process?
2. What are some examples of behavior controls? Output controls?
3. Is EVA really an improvement over ROI, ROE, or EPS?
4. How much faith can a manager place in a transfer price as a substitute for a market price in measuring a profit center's performance?
5. Is the evaluation and control process appropriate for a corporation that emphasizes creativity? Are control and creativity compatible?

Key Terms (listed in order of appearance)

evaluation and control process
performance
steering controls
behavior controls
output controls
ISO 9000 standard series
activity-based-costing
return on investment
transfer price
earnings per share
return on equity (ROE)
shareholder value

economic value added
market value added
management audits
operating budgets
periodic statistical reports
responsibility centers
benchmarking
critical success factors
weighted-factor method
long-term evaluation method
strategic-funds method

Notes

1. A. M. Hormozi, "Understanding and Implementing ISO 9000: A Manager's Guide," *SAM Advanced Management Journal* (autumn 1995): 4–11.
2. J. K. Shank and V. Govindarajan, *Strategic Cost Management* (New York: Free Press, 1993).
3. T. R. V. Davis, and B. L. Darling, "ABC in a Virtual Corporation," *Management Accounting* (October 1996): 18–26.
4. S. Tully, "The Real Key to Creating Wealth," *Fortune* (September 20, 1993): 38.

5. A. B. Fisher, "Creating Stockholder Wealth: Market Value Added," *Fortune* (December 11, 1995): 105–116.
6. H. Rothman, "You Need Not Be Big to Benchmark," *Nation's Business* (December 1992): 64.
7. G. Fuchsberg, "Here's Help in Finding Corporate Role Models," *Wall Street Journal* (June 1, 1993): B1.
8. T. J. Peters, and R. H. Waterman, *In Search of Excellence* (New York: HarperCollins, 1982), 75–76.

9. D. B. Balkin, and L. R. Gomez-Mejia, "Matching Compensation and Organizational Strategies," *Strategic Management Journal* (February 1990): 153–169.

10. P. J. Stonich, "The Performance Measurement and Reward System: Critical to Strategic Management," *Organizational Dynamics* (winter 1984): 45–57.

11. M. Baechler, "Tom Peters Ruined My Life," *The Wall Street Journal* (October 25, 1993): A18.

CHAPTER 11

SUGGESTIONS
FOR CASE ANALYSIS

An analysis of a corporation's strategic management calls for a comprehensive view of the organization. The case method of analysis provides the opportunity to move from a narrow, specialized view that emphasizes technical skills to a broader, less precise analysis of the overall corporation that emphasizes conceptual skills. Concentrating on strategic management processes forces you to develop a better understanding of the political, social, and economic environment of business, and to appreciate the interactions of the functional specialties required for corporate success.

11.1 THE CASE METHOD

The analysis and discussion of case problems has been the most popular method of teaching strategy and policy for many years. Cases present actual business situations and enable you to examine both successful and unsuccessful corporations. In case analysis, you might be asked to critically analyze a situation in which a manager had to make a decision of long-term corporate importance. This approach gives you a feel for what it is like to be faced with making and implementing strategic decisions.

11.2 FRAMEWORKS FOR CASE ANALYSIS

There is no one best way to analyze or present a case report. Each instructor has personal preferences for format and approach. Nevertheless, we suggest an approach for both written and oral reports in Appendix 11.A, which provides a systematic method for successfully attacking a case.

Case discussion focuses on critical analysis and logical development of thought. A solution is satisfactory if it resolves important problems and is likely to be implemented successfully. How the corporation actually dealt with the case problems has no real bearing on the analysis because management might have analyzed its problems incorrectly or implemented a series of flawed solutions.

The presentation of a case analysis can be organized on the basis of several frameworks. One framework is SWOT analysis, followed by a discussion of strategic alternatives and a recommendation. Another is the *strategic audit* as shown in Appendix 11.C. Regardless of the framework chosen, be especially careful to include a complete analysis of key environmental variables, especially industry trends, the competition, and international developments.

11.3 LIBRARY AND INTERNET RESEARCH

Depending on your instructor, you should undertake outside research into the environmental setting of the case. Find out the date when the case situation occurred and then screen the business periodicals for that time period. Use the computerized company and industry information services such as COMPUSTAT, Compact Disclosure, and CD/International, which are available on CD-ROM or on-line at the library. On the World Wide Web, Hoover's On Line Corporate Directory (http://www.hoovers.com) provides access to corporate reports via the SEC's Edgar database.

This background will give you an appreciation for the situation as the participants in the case experienced it. A company's annual report and 10-K form from that year can be very helpful. An understanding of the economy during that period will help you avoid making a serious error in your analysis; for example, suggesting a sale of stock when the stock market is at an all-time low or taking on more debt when the prime interest rate is over 15 percent. Information on the industry will provide insights on its competitive activities. Some resources available for research into the economy and a corporation's industry are suggested in Appendix 11.B.

11.4 FINANCIAL ANALYSIS: A PLACE TO BEGIN

Ratio analysis is the calculating of ratios from data in a company's financial statements. It is done to identify possible financial strengths or weaknesses. Thus it is a valuable part of SWOT analysis. A review of key financial ratios can help you assess the company's overall situation and pinpoint some problem areas. Ratios control for firm size and enable you to compare a company's ratios with industry averages. Table 11.1 lists some of the most important financial ratios: (1) liquidity ratios, (2) profitability ratios, (3) activity ratios, and (4) leverage ratios.

HOW ARE FINANCIAL STATEMENTS ANALYZED?

In your analysis do not simply make an exhibit including all the ratios but select and discuss only those ratios that have an impact on the company's problems. For instance, accounts receivable and inventory may provide a source of funds. If receivables and inventories are double the industry average, reducing them may provide needed cash. In this situation, the case report should include not only sources of funds, but also the number of dollars freed for use. Compare these ratios with industry averages to discover if the company is out of line with others in the industry. If industry averages are not available, use those of a successful competitor.

TABLE 11.1   Financial Ratio Analysis

	Formula	*How Expressed*	*Meaning*
1. Liquidity Ratios			
Current Ratio	$\dfrac{\text{Current assets}}{\text{Current liabilities}}$	Decimal	A short-term indicator of the company's ability to pay its short-term liabilities from short-term assets; how much of current assets are available to cover each dollar of current liabilities.
Quick (acid-test) ratio	$\dfrac{\text{Current assets} - \text{Inventory}}{\text{Current liabilities}}$	Decimal	Measures the company's ability to pay off its short-term obligations from current assets, excluding inventories.
Inventory to net working capital	$\dfrac{\text{Inventory}}{\text{Current assets} - \text{Current liabilities}}$	Decimal	A measure of inventory balance; measures the extent to which the cushion of excess current assets over current liabilities may be threatened by unfavorable changes in inventory.
Cash ratio	$\dfrac{\text{Cash} + \text{Cash equivalents}}{\text{Current liabilities}}$	Decimal	Measures the extent to which the company's capital is in cash or cash equivalents; shows how much of the current obligations can be paid from cash or near-cash assets.
2. Profitability Ratios			
Net profit margin	$\dfrac{\text{Net profit after taxes}}{\text{Net sales}}$	Percentage	Shows how much after-tax profits are generated by each dollar of sales.
Gross profit margin	$\dfrac{\text{Sales} - \text{Cost of goods sold}}{\text{Net sales}}$	Percentage	Indicates the total margin available to cover other expenses beyond cost of goods sold, and still yield a profit.
Return on investment (ROI)	$\dfrac{\text{Net profit after taxes}}{\text{Total assets}}$	Percentage	Measures the rate of return on the total assets utilized in the company; a measure of management's efficiency, it shows the return on all the assets under its control regardless of source of financing.
Return on equity (ROE)	$\dfrac{\text{Net profit after taxes}}{\text{Shareholders' equity}}$	Percentage	Measures the rate of return on the book value of shareholders' total investment in the company.

TABLE 11.1 Continued

	Formula	*How Expressed*	*Meaning*
Earnings per share (EPS)	$\dfrac{\text{Net profit after taxes} - \text{Preferred stock dividends}}{\text{Average number of common shares}}$	Dollars per share	Shows the after-tax earnings generated for each share of common stock.
3. Activity Ratios			
Inventory turnover	$\dfrac{\text{Net sales}}{\text{Inventory}}$	Decimal	Measures the number of times that average inventory of finished goods was turned over or sold during a period of time, usually a year.
Days of inventory	$\dfrac{\text{Inventory}}{\text{Cost of goods sold} \div 365}$	Days	Measures the number of one day's worth of inventory that a company has on hand at any given time.
Net working capital turnover	$\dfrac{\text{Net sales}}{\text{Net working capital}}$	Decimal	Measures how effectively the net working capital is used to generate sales.
Asset turnover	$\dfrac{\text{Sales}}{\text{Total assets}}$	Decimal	Measures the utilization of all the company's assets; measures how many sales are generated by each dollar of assets.
Fixed asset turnover	$\dfrac{\text{Sales}}{\text{Fixed assets}}$	Decimal	Measures the utilization of the company's fixed assets (i.e. plant and equipment); measures how many sales are generated by each dollar of fixed assets.
Average collection period	$\dfrac{\text{Accounts receivable}}{\text{Sales for year} \div 365}$	Days	Indicates the average length of time in days that a company must wait to collect a sale after making it; may be compared to the credit terms offered by the company to its customers.
Accounts receivable turnover	$\dfrac{\text{Annual credit sales}}{\text{Accounts receivable}}$	Decimal	Indicates the number of times that accounts receivable are cycled during the period (usually a year).
Accounts payable	$\dfrac{\text{Accounts payable}}{\text{Purchases for year} \div 365}$	Days	Indicates the average length of time in days that the company takes to pay its credit purchases.
Days of cash	$\dfrac{\text{Cash}}{\text{Net sales for year} \div 365}$	Days	Indicates the number of days of cash on hand, at present sales levels.

	Formula	How Expressed	Meaning
TABLE 11.1 Continued			
4. Leverage Ratios			
Debt to asset ratio	$\dfrac{\text{Total debt}}{\text{Total assets}}$	Percentage	Measures the extent to which borrowed funds have been used to finance the company's assets.
Debt to equity ratio	$\dfrac{\text{Total debt}}{\text{Shareholders' equity}}$	Percentage	Measures the funds provided by creditors versus the funds provided by owners.
Long-term debt to capital structure	$\dfrac{\text{Long-term debt}}{\text{Shareholders' equity}}$	Percentage	Measures the long-term component of capital structure.
Times interest earned	$\dfrac{\text{Profit before taxes} + \text{Interest charges}}{\text{Interest charges}}$	Decimal	Indicates the ability of the company to meet its annual interest costs.
Coverage of fixed charges	$\dfrac{\text{Profit before taxes} + \text{Interest charges} + \text{Lease charges}}{\text{Interest charges} + \text{Lease obligations}}$	Decimal	A measure of the company's ability to meet all of its fixed charge obligations.
Current liabilities to equity	$\dfrac{\text{Current liabilities}}{\text{Shareholders' equity}}$	Percentage	Measures the short-term financing portion versus that provided by owners.
5. Other Ratios			
Price/earnings ratio	$\dfrac{\text{Market price per share}}{\text{Earnings per share}}$	Decimal	Shows the current market's evaluation of a stock, based on its earnings; shows how much the investor is willing to pay for each dollar of earnings.
Dividend payout ratio	$\dfrac{\text{Annual dividends per share}}{\text{Annual earnings per share}}$	Percentage	Indicates the percentage of profit that is paid out as dividends.
Dividend yield on common stock	$\dfrac{\text{Annual dividends per share}}{\text{Current market price per share}}$	Percentage	Indicates the dividend rate of return to common shareholders at the current market price.

Note:
In using ratios for analysis, calculate ratios for the corporation and compare them to the average and quartile ratios for the particular industry. Refer to Standard and Poor's and Robert Morris Associates for average industry data. Special thanks to Dr. Moustafa H. Abdelsamad, Dean, Business School, Texas A&M University–Corpus Christi, Texas, for his definitions of these ratios.

A typical financial analysis of a firm would include a study of the operating statements for 5 or so years, including a trend analysis of sales, profits, earnings per share, debt-to-equity ratio, return on investment, and so on, plus a ratio study comparing the firm under study with industry standards or with a successful competitor. To begin, scrutinize historical income statements and balance sheets. These two basic statements provide most of the data needed for analysis. Statements of cash flow may also be useful. Compare the statements over time if a series of statements is available. Calculate changes that occur in individual categories from year to year and the cumulative total change. Determine the change as a percentage as well as an absolute amount. You may also need to adjust for inflation if that was a significant factor. Examination of this information may reveal developing trends. Compare trends in one category with trends in related categories. For example, an increase in sales of 15 percent over 3 years may appear to be satisfactory until you note an increase of 20 percent in the cost of goods sold during the same period. The outcome of this comparison might suggest that further investigation into the manufacturing process is necessary.

WHAT ARE COMMON-SIZE STATEMENTS?

Common-size statements are income statements and balance sheets in which the dollar figures have been converted into percentages. For the income statement, net sales represent 100 percent: calculate the percentage of each category so that the categories sum to the net sales percentage (100 percent). For the balance sheet, give the total assets a value of 100 percent and calculate other asset and liability categories as percentages of the total assets. (Individual asset and liability items, such as accounts receivable and accounts payable, can also be calculated as a percentage of net sales.)

When you convert statements to this form, it is relatively easy to note the percentage that each category represents of the total. Look for trends in specific items, such as cost of goods sold, when compared to the company's historical figures. To get a proper picture, however, compare these data with industry data, if available, to see if fluctuations merely reflect industry-wide trends. If a firm's trends are generally in line with those of the rest of the industry, the likelihood of problems is less than if the firm's trends are worse than industry averages. These statements are especially helpful in developing scenarios and pro forma statements because they provide a series of historical relationships (for example, cost of goods sold to sales, interest to sales, and inventories as a percentage of assets).

WHAT OTHER FINANCIAL CALCULATIONS ARE USEFUL IN ANALYSIS?

If the corporation being studied appears to be in poor financial condition, use *Altman's Bankruptcy Formula* to calculate its Z-value. The Z-value formula indicates how close a company is to bankruptcy. It combines 5 ratios by weighting them according to their importance to a corporation's financial strength. The formula is:

$$Z = 1.2x_1 + 1.4x_2 + 3.3x_3 + 0.6x_4 + 1.0x_5$$

where:

x_1 = Working capital/Total assets (%)
x_2 = Retained earnings/Total assets (%)

x_3 = Earnings before interest and taxes/Total assets (%)
x_4 = Market value of equity/Total liabilities (%)
x_5 = Sales/Total assets (number of times)

Scores below 1.81 indicate significant credit problems, whereas scores above 3.0 indicate a healthy firm. Scores between 1.81 and 3.0 indicate question marks.[1]

The *index of sustainable growth* is useful to learn if a company embarking on a growth strategy will need to take on debt to fund this growth. The index indicates how much of the growth rate of sales can be sustained by internally generated funds.

The formula is:

$$g^* = [P(1 - D)(1 + L)] / [T - P(1 - D)(1 + L)]$$

where:

P = (Net profit before tax/Net sales) × 100
D = Target dividends/Profit after tax
L = Total liabilities/Net worth
T = (Total assets/Net sales) × 100

If the planned growth rate calls for a growth rate higher than its g^*, external capital will be needed to fund the growth unless management is able to find efficiencies, decrease dividends, increase the debt-equity ratio, or reduce assets by renting or leasing arrangements. [2]

Takeover artists and leveraged buyout (LBO) specialists look at a corporation's financial statements for *operating cash flow:* the amount of money a company generates before the cost of financing and taxes. This is the company's net income plus depreciation plus depletion, amortization, interest expense, and income tax expense. Leveraged buyout specialists take on as much debt as the company's operating cash flow can support. Although operating cash flow is a broad measure of a company's funds, some takeover artists look at a much narrower *free cash flow:* the amount of money a new owner can take out of the firm without harming the business. This is net income plus depreciation, depletion, and amortization less capital expenditures and dividends.[3]

HOW SHOULD INFLATION, INTEREST RATES, AND GDP BE USED?

If you are analyzing a company over many years, you may want to adjust sales and net income for inflation to arrive at "true" financial performance in constant dollars. Constant dollars are dollars adjusted for inflation to make them comparable over various years. In the U.S., the *consumer price index* (CPI) is an easy way to adjust for inflation. (See Table 11.2.) Dividing sales and net income by the CPI factor for that year changes the figures to 1982–1984 constant dollars.

Another helpful analytical aid is *prime interest rate* (PIR), the rate of interest banks charge on their lowest risk loans. To better assess strategic decisions, note the level of the prime interest rate at the time of the case. (See Table 11.2.) A decision to borrow money to build a new plant would have been a good one in 1992, but more costly in 1995.

In preparing a scenario for your pro forma financial statements, you may want to use the *gross domestic product* (GDP) from Table 11.2. The GDP is used worldwide and measures the total output of goods and services within a country's borders.

TABLE 11.2   U.S. Economic Indicators: Gross Domestic Product (GDP) in Billions of Dollars; Consumer Price Index for All Items (CPI) (1982–84 = 1.0); Prime Interest Rate (PIR)

Year	GDP	CPI	PIR
1983	3,514.5	.996	10.79
1984	3,902.4	1.039	12.04
1985	4,180.7	1.076	9.93
1986	4,422.2	1.096	8.33
1987	4,693.3	1.136	8.21
1988	5,049.6	1.183	9.32
1989	5,483.7	1.240	10.87
1990	5,743.8	1.307	10.01
1991	5,916.7	1.362	8.46
1992	6,244.4	1.403	6.25
1993	6,553.0	1.445	6.00
1994	6,935.7	1.482	7.15
1995	7,253.8	1.524	8.83
1996	7,661.6	1.569	8.27
1997	8,110.9	1.605	8.44
1998	8,759.9	1.630	8.35
1999	9,248.4	1.666	8.00

Sources:

1. Gross Domestic Product from *Survey of Current Business* (February 2000), Vol. 80, No. 2, Table 1.1, p. D-3.

2. Consumer Price Index from U.S. Department of Commerce, *1997 Statistical Abstract of the United States,* 117th edition, Chart no. 752, p. 487; U.S. Bureau of Labor Statistics, *Monthly Labor Review* (October 1998), Chart no. 28, p. 74; *Survey of Current Business* (February 2000), Vol. 80, No. 2, Table D.1, p. D-41.

3. Prime Interest Rates from D. S. Benton, "Banking and Financial Information," Table 1-2, p. 3, in *Thorndike Encyclopedia of Banking and Financial Tables,* 3rd ed., 1998 Yearbook (Boston: Warren, Gorham and Lamont, 1998); *Survey of Current Business* (February 2000), Vol. 80, No. 2, Table D.1, p. D-41.

11.5 USING THE STRATEGIC AUDIT IN CASE ANALYSIS

Appendix 10.C is an example of a strategic audit proposed for use not only in strategic decision making, but also as a framework for the analysis of complex business policy cases. The questions in the audit parallel the eight steps depicted in Figure 1.3 (chapter 1, this book), the strategic decision making process. The *strategic audit* provides a checklist of questions, by area or issue, that enables you to make a systematic analysis of various corporate activities. It is extremely useful as a diagnostic tool to pinpoint problem areas and to highlight strengths and weaknesses. It is not an all-inclusive list, but it presents many of the critical questions that need to be addressed in the strategic analysis of any business corporation. Some questions or even some areas might be inappropriate for a particular case; in other cases, the questions may be insufficient for a complete analysis. However, each question in a particular area of the strategic audit can be broken down into an additional series of subquestions. It is up to you to develop these subquestions when they are needed.

You may also find the audit helpful in organizing a case for written or oral presentation and in seeing that all areas have been considered. The strategic audit can thus maximize your efficiency, both in analyzing why a certain area is creating problems for a corporation and in considering solutions to the problems.

IN CONCLUSION

Case study is one of the best ways to understand and remember the strategic management process. By applying the concepts and techniques you have learned to cases, you will be able to remember them long past the time when you have forgotten other memorized bits of information. The use of cases to examine actual situations brings alive the field of strategic management and helps build your analytic and decision-making skills.

Discussion Questions

1. Why should you begin a case analysis with a financial analysis? When are other approaches appropriate?
2. What are common-size financial statements? What is their value to case analysis? How are they calculated?
3. When should you go to the library to gather information outside the case?
4. When is inflation an important issue in conducting case analysis?
5. How can you learn the date on which a case took place?

Key Terms (listed in order of appearance)

ratio analysis
common-size statements
Z-value
index of sustainable growth
operating cash flow
free cash flow

constant dollars
consumer price index
prime interest rate
gross domestic product
strategic audit

Notes

1. M. S. Fridson, *Financial Statement Analysis* (New York: John Wiley & Sons, 1991), 192–194.

2. D. H. Bangs, *Managing by the Numbers* (Dover, N.H.: Upstart Publications, 1992): 106–107.

3. J. M. Laderman, "Earnings, Schmernings— Look at the Cash," *Business Week* (July 24, 1989): 56–57.

A P P E N D I X   1 1 . A

Suggested Techniques
for Case Analysis and Presentation

A. CASE ANALYSIS

1. Read the case to get an overview of the nature of the corporation and its environment. Note the date on which the case was written so that you can put it into proper context.

2. Read the case a second time, and give it a detailed examination according to the strategic audit (see Appendix 11.C) or some other framework of analysis. Regardless of the framework used, you should end up with a list of the salient issues and problems in the case. Perform a financial analysis.

3. Undertake outside research, when appropriate, to uncover economic and industrial information. Appendix 11.B suggests possible sources for outside research. These data should provide the environmental setting for the corporation. Conduct an in-depth analysis of the industry. Analyze the important *competitors*. Consider the bargaining power of both *suppliers* and *buyers* that might affect the firm's situation. Consider also the possible threats of *new entrants* in the industry and the likelihood of new or different products or services that might be *substitutes* for the company's present ones. Consider *other stakeholders* who might affect strategic decision making in the industry.

4. Compile facts and evidence to support selected issues and problems. Develop a framework or outline to organize the analysis. Consider using one of the following methods of organization:

    (a) The strategic decision making process or the strategic audit.

    (b) The key individual(s) in the case.

    (c) The corporation's functional areas: production, management, finance, marketing, and R&D.

    (d) SWOT analysis.

5. Clearly identify and state the central problem(s) as supported by the information in the case. Use the SWOT format to sum up the *strategic factors* facing the corporation: strengths and weaknesses of the company; opportunities and threats in the environment. Use the External (EFAS) and Internal (IFAS) Factor Analysis Summary Tables as well as the Strategic Factor Analysis Summary (SFAS) Table. . (See Table 3.3 in chapter 3 for the EFAS Table, Table 4.2 in chapter 4 for the IFAS Table, and Figure 5.1 in chapter 5 for the SFAS Table.)

6. Develop a logical series of mutually exclusive alternatives that evolve from the analysis to resolve the problem(s) or issue(s) in the case. One of the alternatives should be to continue the company's current strategy. Develop at least two other strategy alternatives. However, don't present three alternatives and then recommend that all three be adopted; that's one alternative presented in three parts!

7. Evaluate each of the alternatives in light of the company's environment (both external and internal), mission, objectives, strategies, and policies. Discuss pros and cons. For each alternative, consider both the possible obstacles to its implementation and its financial implications.

8. Make recommendations assuming that action must be taken regardless of whether needed information is available. The individuals in the case may have had the same or even less information than is given in the case.

(a) Base your recommendations on a total analysis of the case.

(b) Provide the evidence gathered earlier in step A4 to justify suggested changes.

(c) List the recommendations in order of priority.

(d) Show clearly how your recommendations deal with each of the *strategic factors* that were mentioned earlier in step A5. How do they build on corporate *strengths* to take advantage of environmental *opportunities*? How do they deal with environmental *threats* and corporate *weaknesses*?

(e) Explain how each recommendation will be implemented. How will the plan(s) deal with anticipated resistance?

(f) Suggest feedback and control systems to ensure that the recommendations are carried out as planned and to give advance warning of needed adjustments.

B. WRITTEN REPORT

1. Use the outline from step A4 to write the first draft of the case analysis. Follow steps A5 through A8.

(a) Don't rehash the case material; rather, supply the salient evidence and data to support your analysis and recommendation.

(b) Develop exhibits on financial ratios and other data, such as strategic factors summary, for inclusion in your report. The exhibits should provide meaningful information. Reference key elements of an exhibit in the text of the written analysis. If you include a ratio analysis as an exhibit, explain the implications of the ratios in the text and cite the critical ones in your analysis.

2. Review your written case analysis for content and grammar. Compare the outline (step A4) with the final product. Make sure you've presented sufficient data or evidence to support your problem analysis and recommendations. If the final product requires rewriting, do so. Keep in mind that the written report is going to be judged not only on what is said, but also on the manner in which it is said. Style, grammar, and spelling are just as important as the content in a written case analysis.

3. If your written report requires pro forma statements, you may wish to develop a scenario for each year in your forecast. A well-constructed corporate scenario helps improve the accuracy of your forecast. (See chapter 7 for corporate scenario construction.)

C. ORAL PRESENTATION BY TEAMS

1. The team should first decide on a framework or outline for analysis, as mentioned in step A4. Although teams often divide the analysis work, each team member should follow steps A5 through A8 to develop a preliminary analysis of the entire case and share it with team members.

2. The team should combine member input into one consolidated team analysis, including SWOT analysis, alternatives, and recommendation(s). Obtain agreement on the strategic factors and the best alternative(s) to support.

3. Divide further development and presentation of the case analysis and recommendation(s). Agree on responsibilities for the preparation of visual aids and handouts. As in written reports, scenarios and pro forma financial statements should support any recommendation.

4. Modify the team outline, if necessary, and have one or two rehearsals of the presentation. If exhibits are used, make sure to allow sufficient time to explain them. Check to ensure that any visual aids can be easily seen from the back of the room. Critique one another's presentations and make the necessary modifications to the analysis. Again, style, grammar, and delivery are just as important in an oral presentation as is content.

5. Begin your presentation by handing out a copy of the agenda specifying not only the topics to be covered, but also who will deal with each topic area. Introduce yourselves. Dress appropriately. If a presenter misses a key fact during the class presentation, deal with it in the summary speech.

6. Encourage questions from both the instructor and classmates. Begin the questioning period by calling on someone you consider a friend who can be expected to ask a question you can easily field to get you off to a good start. You may want to have one person act as a moderator who refers questions to the appropriate team member.

APPENDIX 11.B

Resources for Case Library Research

A. COMPANY INFORMATION

1. Annual Reports (prepared by individual corporations).
2. *Moody's Manuals on Investment* (a listing of companies within certain industries that contains a brief history and a 5-year financial statement of each company).
3. Securities and Exchange Commission Annual Report Form 10-K (annually) and Report Form 10-Q (quarterly).
4. Standard and Poor's *Register of Corporations, Directors, and Executives.*
5. *Value Line Investment Survey.*
6. *Findex: The Directory of Market Research Reports, Studies and Surveys* (a listing by Find/SVP of over 11,000 studies conducted by leading research firms).
7. COMPUSTAT, *Compact Disclosure, CD/International, Hoover's Online Corporate Directory,* and *SEC's Edgar database* (computerized operating and financial information on thousands of publicly held corporations).
8. Shareholder meeting notices.
9. Internet address of the company, such as maytag.com, caseys.com, and ge.com.

B. ECONOMIC INFORMATION

1. Regional statistics and local forecasts from large banks.
2. *Business Cycle Development* (Department of Commerce).
3. Chase Econometric Associates' publications.
4. U.S. Census Bureau publications on population, transportation, and housing.
5. *Current Business Reports* (U.S. Department of Commerce).
6. *Economic Indicators* (U.S. Joint Economic Committee).
7. Economic Report of the President to Congress (U.S.)
8. *Long-Term Economic Growth* (U.S. Department of Commerce).
9. *Monthly Labor Review* (U.S. Department of Labor).
10. *Monthly Bulletin of Statistics* (United Nations).
11. *Statistical Abstract of the United States* (U.S. Department of Commerce).
12. *Statistical Yearbook* (United Nations).
13. *Survey of Current Business* (U.S. Department of Commerce).
14. *U.S. Industrial Outlook* (U.S. Department of Defense).
15. *World Trade Annual* (United Nations).
16. *Overseas Business Reports* (by country, published by U.S. Department of Commerce).

C. INDUSTRY INFORMATION

1. Analyses of companies and industries by investment brokerage firms.
2. *Business Week* (provides weekly economic and business information, and quarterly profit and sales rankings of corporations).
3. *Fortune* (each April publishes listings of financial information on corporations within certain industries).
4. *Industry Survey* (published quarterly by Standard and Poor's Corporation).
5. *Industry Week* (late March/early April issue provides information on 14 industry groups).
6. *Forbes* (mid-January issue provides performance data on firms in various industries).
7. *Inc.* (May and December issues give information on entrepreneurial companies).

D. DIRECTORY AND INDEX INFORMATION ON COMPANIES AND INDUSTRIES

1. *Business Periodical Index* (on computer in many libraries).
2. *Directory of National Trade Associations.*
3. *Encyclopedia of Associations.*
4. Funk and Scott's *Index of Corporations and Industries.*
5. Thomas' *Register of American Manufacturers.*
6. *Wall Street Journal Index.*

E. RATIO ANALYSIS INFORMATION

1. *Almanac of Business and Industrial Financial Ratios* (Prentice Hall).
2. *Annual Statement Studies* (Robert Morris Associates).
3. *Dun's Review* (Dun and Bradstreet; published annually in September–December issues).
4. *Industry Norms and Key Business Ratios* (Dun and Bradstreet).
5. Value Line *Investment Survey* for company and industy ratios.

F. ON-LINE INFORMATION

1. *Hoover's Online.* Financial statements and profiles of public companies (http://www.hoovers.com)
2. *U.S. Securities & Exchange Commission.* Official filings of public companies in Edgar database (http://www.sec.gov/edgar.htm)
3. *Kompass International.* Statistics for 1.5 million corporations in 70 countries (http://www.kompass.com)
4. *Dun & Bradstreet's Online.* Short reports on 10 million public and private U.S. companies (http://www.dnb.com)

5. *Ecola's 24-Hour Newsstand.* Links to web sites of 2,000 newspapers, journals, and magazines (http://www.ecola.com/news)
6. *Competitive Intelligence Guide.* Information on company resources (http://www.fuld.com)
7. *The Economist.* Provides international information and surveys (http://www.economist.com)
8. *Web 100.* Information on 100 largest U.S. and international companies (http://www.w100.com)
9. *ZDNet Company Finder.* Information on computer and internet-industry companies (http://www.companyfinder.com)
10. *Bloomberg.* Information on interest rates, stock prices, currency conversion rates, and other general financial information(http://www.bloomberg.com)
11. *CorpTech Database of Technology Companies.* Information on 50,000 private and public technology companies (http://www.corptech.com)

A P P E N D I X 1 1 . C

Strategic Audit of a Corporation

I. Current Situation

A. Current Performance

How did the corporation perform the past year overall in terms of return on investment, market share, and profitability?

B. Strategic Posture

What are the corporation's current mission, objectives, strategies, and policies?

1. Are they clearly stated or are they merely implied from performance?

2. **Mission**: What business(es) is the corporation in? Why?

3. **Objectives**: What are the corporate, business, and functional objectives? Are they consistent with each other, with the mission, and with the internal and external environments?

4. **Strategies**: What strategy or mix of strategies is the corporation following? Are they consistent with each other, with the mission and objectives, and with the internal and external environments?

5. **Policies**: What are they? Are they consistent with each other, with the mission, objectives, and strategies, and with the internal and external environments?

6. Do the current mission, objectives, strategies, and policies reflect the corporation's international operations, whether global or multidomestic?

II. Corporate Governance

A. Board of Directors

1. Who are they? Are they internal or external?

2. Do they own significant shares of stock?

3. Is the stock privately held or publicly traded? Are there different classes of stock with different voting rights?

4. What do they contribute to the corporation in terms of knowledge, skills, background, and connections? If the corporation has international operations, do board members have international experience?

Source: T. L. Wheelen and J. D. Hunger, *Strategic Audit of a Corporation,* Copyright © 1982 by Wheelen and Hunger Associates. Reprinted by permission. Revised 1988, 1991, 1994, 1997, and 2000.

5. How long have they served on the board?

6. What is their level of involvement in strategic management? Do they merely rubber-stamp top management's proposals or do they actively participate and suggest future directions?

B. Top Management

1. What person or group constitutes top management?

2. What are top management's chief characteristics in terms of knowledge, skills, background, and style? If the corporation has international operations, does top management have international experience? Are executives from acquired companies considered part of the top management team?

3. Has top management been responsible for the corporation's performance over the past few years? How many managers have been in their current position for less than 3 years? Were they internal promotions or external hires?

4. Has it established a systematic approach to strategic management?

5. What is its level of involvement in the strategic management process?

6. How well does top management interact with lower level managers and with the board of directors?

7. Are strategic decisions made ethically in a socially responsible manner?

8. Is top management sufficiently skilled to cope with likely future challenges?

III. External Environment: Opportunities and Threats (SWOT)

A. Societal Environment

1. What general environmental forces are currently affecting both the corporation and the industries in which it competes? Which present current or future threats? Opportunities?

   (a) Economic

   (b) Technological

   (c) Political–legal

   (d) Sociocultural

2. Are these forces different in other regions of the world?

B. Task Environment

1. What forces drive industry competition? Are these forces the same globally or do they vary from country to country?

   (a) Threat of new entrants

   (b) Bargaining power of buyers

   (c) Threat of substitute products or services

(d) Bargaining power of suppliers

(e) Rivalry among competing firms

(f) Relative power of unions, governments, special interest groups, etc.

2. What key factors in the immediate environment (that is, customers, competitors, suppliers, creditors, labor unions, governments, trade associations, interest groups, local communities, and shareholders) are currently affecting the corporation? Which are current or future threats? Opportunities?

C. Summary of External Factors (EFAS Table)

Which of these forces and factors are the most important to the corporation and to the industries in which it competes at the present time? Which will be important in the future?

IV. Internal Environment: Strengths and Weaknesses (<u>S</u><u>W</u>OT)

A. Corporate Structure

1. How is the corporation structured at present?

   (a) Is the decision-making authority centralized around one group or decentralized to many units?

   (b) Is it organized on the basis of functions, projects, geography, or some combination of these?

2. Is the structure clearly understood by everyone in the corporation?

3. Is the present structure consistent with current corporate objectives, strategies, policies, and programs, as well as with the firm's international operations?

4. In what ways does this structure compare with those of similar corporations?

B. Corporate Culture

1. Is there a well-defined or emerging culture composed of shared beliefs, expectations, and values?

2. Is the culture consistent with the current objectives, strategies, policies, and programs?

3. What is the culture's position on important issues facing the corporation (that is, on productivity, quality of performance, adaptability to changing conditions, and internationalization)?

4 Is the culture compatible with the employees' diversity of backgrounds?

5. Does the company take into consideration the values of each nation's culture in which the firm operates?

C. Corporate Resources

1. Marketing

   (a) What are the corporation's current marketing objectives, strategies, policies, and programs?

    (i) Are they clearly stated, or merely implied from performance and/or budgets?

    (ii) Are they consistent with the corporation's mission, objectives, strategies, policies, and with internal and external environments?

(b) How well is the corporation performing in terms of analysis of market position and marketing mix (that is, product, price, place, and promotion) in both domestic and international markets? What percentage of sales comes from foreign operations?

    (i) What trends emerge from this analysis?

    (ii) What impact have these trends had on past performance, and how might these trends affect future performance?

    (iii) Does this analysis support the corporation's past and pending strategic decisions?

    (iv) Does marketing provide the company with a competitive advantage?

(c) How well does this corporation's marketing performance compare with that of similar corporations?

(d) Are marketing managers using accepted marketing concepts and techniques to evaluate and improve product performance? (Consider product life cycle, market segmentation, market research, and product portfolios.)

(e) Does marketing adjust to the conditions in each country in which it operates?

(f) What is the role of the marketing manager in the strategic management process?

2. Finance

(a) What are the corporation's current financial objectives, strategies, policies, and programs?

    (i) Are they clearly stated or merely implied from performance and/or budgets?

    (ii) Are they consistent with the corporation's mission, objectives, strategies, policies, and with internal and external environments?

(b) How well is the corporation performing in terms of financial analysis? (Consider ratios, common size statements, and capitalization structure.)

    (i) What trends emerge from this analysis?

    (ii) Are there any significant differences when statements are calculated in constant versus reported dollars?

    (iii) What impact have these trends had on past performance, and how might these trends affect future performance?

(iv) Does this analysis support the corporation's past and pending strategic decisions?

(v) Does finance provide the company with a competitive advantage?

(c) How well does this corporation's financial performance compare with that of similar corporations?

(d) Are financial managers using accepted financial concepts and techniques to evaluate and improve current corporate and divisional performance? (Consider financial leverage, capital budgeting, ratio analysis, and managing foreign currencies.)

(e) Does finance adjust to the conditions in each country in which the company operates?

(f) What is the role of the financial manager in the strategic management process?

3. Research and Development (R&D)

(a) What are the corporation's current R&D objectives, strategies, policies, and programs?

(i) Are they clearly stated or merely implied from performance or budgets?

(ii) Are they consistent with the corporation's mission, objectives, strategies, policies, and with internal and external environments?

(iii) What is the role of technology in corporate performance?

(iv) Is the mix of basic, applied, and engineering research appropriate given the corporate mission and strategies?

(v) Does R&D provide the company with a competitive advantage?

(b) What return is the corporation receiving from its investment in R&D?

(c) Is the corporation competent in technology transfer? Does it use concurrent engineering and cross-functional work teams in product and process design?

(d) What role does technological discontinuity play in the company's products?

(e) How well does the corporation's investment in R&D compare with the investments of similar corporations?

(f) Does R&D adjust to the conditions in each country in which the company operates?

(g) What is the role of the R&D manager in the strategic management process?

4. **Operations and Logistics**
   (a) What are the corporation's current manufacturing and service objectives, strategies, policies, and programs?
      (i) Are they clearly stated or merely implied from performance or budgets?
      (ii) Are they consistent with the corporation's mission, objectives, strategies, policies, and with internal and external environments?
   (b) What is the type and extent of operations capabilities of the corporation? How much is done domestically versus internationally? Is the amount of outsourcing appropriate to be competitive? Is purchasing being handled appropriately?
      (i) If the corporation is product-oriented, consider plant facilities, type of manufacturing system (continuous mass production, intermittent job shop, or flexible manufacturing), age and type of equipment, degree and role of automation and robots, plant capacities and utilization, productivity ratings, and availability and type of transportation.
      (ii) If the corporation is service-oriented, consider service facilities (hospital, theater, or school buildings), type of operations systems (continuous service over time to same clientele or intermittent service over time to varied clientele), age and type of supporting equipment, degree and role of automation and use of mass communication devices (diagnostic machinery, videotape machines), facility capacities and utilization rates, efficiency ratings of professional and service personnel, and availability and type of transportation to bring service staff and clientele together.
   (c) Are manufacturing or service facilities vulnerable to natural disasters, local or national strikes, reduction or limitation of resources from suppliers, substantial cost increases of materials, or nationalization by governments?
   (d) Is there an appropriate mix of people and machines (in manufacturing firms) or of support staff to professionals (in service firms)?
   (e) How well does the corporation perform relative to the competition? Is it balancing inventory costs (warehousing) with logistical costs (just-in-time)? Consider costs per unit of labor, material, and overhead; downtime; inventory control management and scheduling of service staff; production ratings; facility utilization percentages; and number of clients successfully treated by category (if service firm) or percentage of orders shipped on time (if product firm).
      (i) What trends emerge from this analysis?

    (ii) What impact have these trends had on past performance and how might they affect future performance?

    (iii) Does this analysis support the corporation's past and pending strategic decisions?

    (iv) Does operations provide the company with a competitive advantage?

(f) Are operations managers using appropriate concepts and techniques to evaluate and improve current performance? Consider cost systems, quality control and reliability systems, inventory control management, personnel scheduling, TQM, learning curves, safety programs, and engineering programs that can improve efficiency of manufacturing or of service.

(g) Does operations adjust to the conditions in each country in which it has facilities?

(h) What is the role of the operations manager in the strategic management process?

5. **Human Resources Management (HRM)**

(a) What are the corporation's current HRM objectives, strategies, policies, and programs?

    (i) Are they clearly stated, or merely implied from performance and/or budgets?

    (ii) Are they consistent with the corporation's mission, objectives, strategies, policies, and with internal and external environments?

(b) How well is the corporation's HRM performing in terms of improving the fit between the individual employee and the job? Consider turnover, grievances, strikes, layoffs, employee training, and quality of work life.

    (i) What trends emerge from this analysis?

    (ii) What impact have these trends had on past performance and how might they affect future performance?

    (iii) Does this analysis support the corporation's past and pending strategic decisions?

    (iv) Does HRM provide the company with a competitive advantage?

(c) How does this corporation's HRM performance compare with that of similar corporations?

(d) Are HRM managers using appropriate concepts and techniques to evaluate and improve corporate performance? Consider the job analysis program, performance appraisal system, up-to-date job descriptions, training and development programs, attitude surveys, job design programs, quality of relationship with unions, and use of autonomous work teams.

(e) How well is the company managing the diversity of its workforce?

(f) Does HRM adjust to the conditions in each country in which the company operates? Does the company have a code of conduct for HRM in developing nations? Are employees receiving international assignments to prepare them for managerial positions?

(g) What is the role of the HRM manager in the strategic management process?

6. **Information Systems (IS)**

(a) What are the corporation's current IS objectives, strategies, policies, and programs?

    (i) Are they clearly stated or merely implied from performance and/or budgets?

    (ii) Are they consistent with the corporation's mission, objectives, strategies, policies, and with internal and external environments?

(b) How well is the corporation's IS performing in terms of providing a useful database, automating routine clerical operations, assisting managers in making routine decisions, and providing information necessary for strategic decisions?

    (i) What trends emerge from this analysis?

    (ii) What impact have these trends had on past performance and how might they affect future performance?

    (iii) Does this analysis support the corporation's past and pending strategic decisions?

    (iv) Does IS provide the company with a competitive advantage?

(c) How does this corporation's IS performance and stage of development compare with that of similar corporations?

(d) Are IS managers using appropriate concepts and techniques to evaluate and improve corporate performance? Do they know how to build and manage a complex database, conduct system analyses, and implement interactive decision-support systems?

(e) Does the company have a global IS? Does it have difficulty with getting data across national boundaries?

(f) What is the role of the IS manager in the strategic management process?

D. Summary of Internal Factors (IFAS Table)

Which of these factors are the most important to the corporation and to the industries in which it competes at the present time? Which will be important in the future?

V. Analysis of Strategic Factors (SWOT)

A. Situational Analysis (SFAS Table)

What are the most important internal and external factors (*Strengths, Weaknesses, Opportunities, Threats*) that strongly affect the corporation's present and future performance? List 5 to 10 strategic factors.

B. Review of Mission and Objectives

1. Are the current mission and objectives appropriate in light of the key strategic factors and problems?
2. Should the mission and objectives be changed? If so, how?
3. If changed, what will be the effects on the firm?

VI. Strategic Alternatives and Recommended Strategy

A. Strategic Alternatives (See TOWS Matrix)

1. Can the current or revised objectives be met by the simple, more careful implementing of those strategies presently in use (for example, fine-tuning the strategies)?
2. What are the major feasible alternative strategies available to this corporation? What are the pros and cons of each? Can corporate scenarios be developed and agreed upon?
   (a) Consider cost leadership and differentiation as business strategies.
   (b) Consider stability, growth, and retrenchment as corporate strategies.
   (c) Consider any functional strategic alternatives that might be needed for reinforcement of an important corporate or business strategic alternative.

B. Recommended Strategy

1. Specify which of the strategic alternatives you are recommending for the corporate, business, and functional levels of the corporation. Do you recommend different business or functional strategies for different units of the corporation?
2. Justify your recommendation in terms of its ability to resolve both long- and short-term problems and effectively deal with the strategic factors.
3. What *policies* should be developed or revised to guide effective implementation?

VII. Implementation

   A. What kinds of *programs* (for example, restructuring the corporation or instituting TQM) should be developed to implement the recommended strategy?

   1. Who should develop these programs?

   2. Who should be in charge of these programs?

   B. Are the programs financially feasible? Can pro forma *budgets* be developed and agreed upon? Are priorities and timetables appropriate to individual programs?

   C. Will new standard operating *procedures* need to be developed?

VIII. Evaluation and Control

   A. Is the current information system capable of providing sufficient feedback on implementation activities and performance? Can it measure *critical success factors*?

   1. Can performance results be pinpointed by area, unit, project, or function?

   2. Is the information timely?

   B. Are adequate control measures in place to ensure conformance with the recommended strategic plan?

   1. Are appropriate standards and measures being used?

   2. Are reward systems capable of recognizing and rewarding good performance?

INDEX